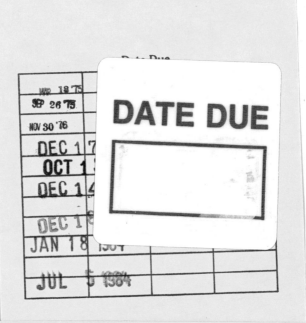

Historical Problems:
Studies and Documents

Edited by
PROFESSOR G. R. ELTON
University of Cambridge

18
THE LAW COURTS OF MEDIEVAL ENGLAND

In the same series

THE LAW COURTS OF MEDIEVAL ENGLAND

Alan Harding
University of Edinburgh

LONDON: GEORGE ALLEN & UNWIN LTD
NEW YORK: BARNES AND NOBLE INC

First published 1973

Published in the USA 1973 by
Harper & Rowe Publishers Inc.
Barnes & Noble Import Division

ISBN 0 04 942106 9 hardback
     0 04 942107 7 paper

Printed in Great Britain
in 10 on 11 point Plantin type
by Alden & Mowbray Ltd
at the Alden Press, Oxford

CONTENTS

AUTHOR'S NOTE

In the footnotes to the introduction, the following abbreviations have been used:

EHD   *English Historical Documents*
BIHR *Bulletin of the Institute of Historical Research*
EHR   *English Historical Review*
TRHS *Transactions of the Royal Historical Society.*

Documents. As far as possible, these have been ordered chronologically. Where the original language is not specified, a document has been translated from Latin; and if the translator is not named (in capitals) at the head of the document, the translation is my own. Square brackets indicate words supplied, usually by the original editor but sometimes by myself, in order to make damaged, illegible or elliptical passages in the document intelligible. For the same purpose, I have taken the liberty of modernizing the spelling and occasionally the language of the few late medieval documents in English, and of supplying a necessary minimum of punctuation.

I wish to thank the following for permission to use their translations: Associated Book Publishers Ltd. for Documents 2, 6 and 8, from *English Historical Documents*, I, ed. Dorothy Whitelock, and *English Historical Documents*, II, ed. David Douglas and G. W. Greenaway; Cambridge University Press for Document 3, from A. J. Robertson: *Anglo-Saxon Charters*, 2nd edition © 1956 Cambridge University Press; Manchester University Press for Documents 4 and 5, from F. E. Harmer, *Anglo-Saxon Writs*; Mr G. D. G. Hall for Document 9, from his edition of *Glanvill*; Dr Antonia Gransden for Document 16, from her edition of *The Chronicle of Bury St Edmunds*; and the Selden Society for Documents 13, 15, 24 and 29, from *Select Cases of Procedure without Writ under Henry III*, ed. H. G. Richardson and G. O. Sayles, *Placita Corone*, ed. J. M. Kaye, *Select Cases in the Court of King's Bench*, VI, ed. G. O. Sayles, and *Select Cases in Exchequer Chamber*, ed. Mary Hemmant.

I should also like to thank Mrs Sheila Somerville and Mrs Jennifer Newman for their assistance in the typing of both introduction and documents.

INTRODUCTION

The Courts of the Anglo-Saxons

THE BEGINNINGS OF LEGAL PROCEDURE

IN origin, courts may be said to have had two functions: first, the maintenance of social peace by the settlement of disputes between individuals, and second, the maintenance of the social dominance of the king or noble who held the court. Practically the two are inseparable, but logically the maintenance of social peace must come first, for society can hardly be said to exist without a means of settling disputes peacefully, while kings and princes are products of society. Kings, princes, and also priests, come onto the scene as the chosen arbiters of society and the enforcers of society's sanctions against disruptive elements.

There were procedures for settling conflicts before there were courts in any formal sense. Until there were legal ways of obtaining compensation for the minor damage which men inevitably do to one another in the various transactions of a reasonably developed society, disputes must often have led to killing and blood-feud. The feud was certainly accepted as a normal thing up to the Norman Conquest and beyond,[1] yet a state of feuding without limit or escape is unbearable, and the pressures were all towards the devising of procedures for buying off vengeance and (seen from the side of the injured man) for getting compensation in money. Even in its pure form, there was 'peace in the feud'. In early times we find kings and clergy emphasizing the moral obligation of vengeance, incumbent on all the kindred and colleagues of a murdered man (the clergy could point to the example of the avenging God), precisely because the threat of vengeance was the only deterrent to violence. But at the same time that vengeance was made the first legal duty, the form vengeance took was softened by royal edict, and it is therefore with the feud that our picture of the growth of a legal system must begin.[2]

The settlement of feuds by arbitration at which Njal was so expert in

[1] See King Edmund's laws on feuding (939–46) and the early eleventh-century regulations of the Cambridge Thegns' guild, *English Historical Documents*, vol. i, ed. Dorothy Whitelock (London, 1955), pp. 391–2 and 557–8.

[2] On the social importance of the feud, see J. M. Wallace-Hadrill, 'The bloodfeud of the Franks', *The Bulletin of the John Rylands Library* (1959).

Iceland took place in regular assemblies of the people, but evidence that the Anglo-Saxons likewise came together in 'folk-moots' for judicial purposes is very scanty.[3] Indeed, the Icelandic type of gathering to fix up a settlement would have been made redundant by the laws made by English kings from as early as *c.* 600, for these set out tariffs of compensation to be paid for all sorts of specific injuries. Because the compulsion to feud was not easily broken, it was still necessary for some authority to force or persuade disputants to stop fighting and come to terms, as Archbishop Theodore stopped a feud between two English kings in the seventh century, but what the terms should be was well known. The wergild is laid down.[4]

So the Old English laws are concerned not with the procedure of trial in court, but with how pressure is put on a man to submit to a peaceful settlement – a matter of formalized threat and siege and riding to and fro.[5] This was the beginning of legal procedure, and a considerable part of it has always remained this pressure before the court hearing – which may make that hearing unnecessary.

THE OWNERS OF THE COURTS

The injured man, out for revenge, provided one of the two necessary elements of this procedure: the unremitting pressure. The other element – control, restraint, delay while tempers cooled – had to be provided by the man with political or moral power, the lord or the cleric, the person whose function it was to 'keep the peace'. The function soon became a right, a possession, almost an object or substance: the peace or *mund* belonging to the man of authority (Doc. 4).[6] Every *ceorl* or yeoman had his peace, and so did the king's cook; within his family and in the area around his house or his kitchen.[7] When the king or a lord sent a messenger off on a journey, he sent his peace along with him as 'protection', and from very early times travellers on 'the king's highway' were regarded as being especially under the king's peace.[8] If a misdeed was committed within a peace, compensation had to be paid to the owner of

[3] *Njal's Saga*, tr. M. Magnusson and H. Palsson (Harmondsworth, 1960), pp. 159, 175 and 208–9; F. M. Stenton, *Anglo-Saxon England*, 2nd edn (Oxford, 1947), pp. 294–5.

[4] Bede, *A History of the English Church and People*, tr. L. Sherley-Price (Harmondsworth, 1955), p. 238; *English Historical Documents*, vol. i, pp. 433 and 557–8.

[5] See also *English Historical Documents* (henceforth *EHD*), i, pp. 379–80, 396–7.

[6] See also *EHD*, i, 392.

[7] J. G. Edwards, 'The Royal Household and the Welsh lawbooks', *Transactions of the Royal Historical Society* (1963).

[8] F. Liebermann, *Die Gesetze der Angelsachsen* (Halle, 1903–16) vol. i, pp. 637–8.

the peace as well as to the person who was directly injured. Here is the fine payable for 'crime', the penalty due to the 'public' authority, along-side the 'civil' damages payable to the private plaintiff: the difference from modern law is that both were payable for the same wrongs.[9]

The strength of a peace was basically a matter of its owner's political power, and as the king's political power increased, the king's peace, which was always there above the other peaces,[10] slowly crushed the others out of existence, but this process was not completed till well after the Norman Conquest. In any case, law enforcement always comes from the man 'on the spot', and in the early Middle Ages kings had virtually no professional servants in the localities, relying instead on the natural rulers of the countryside, the great landowners. For the secure posses-sion of the land which was the foundation of their power, these men were dependent on the king; and the king was dependent on them, as the backbone of his army and as economical deputies in matters of government. So it is not surprising that the Anglo-Saxon kings allowed the great landowners comprehensive powers of peace-keeping.

Strictly speaking all we know is that kings sometimes granted to lords that no fines should be paid from their estates for wrongs committed by the inhabitants: these fines for breaches of the king's nationwide peace, the profits of the king's justice, were in this way diverted to the lords of the wrongdoers.[11] But were the fines to be taken in 'public' courts or in 'private' courts held by the beneficiaries of the grants? This much-debated problem has been shown to be unreal.[12] Fines and compensation are the result of diligent policing, and no early English king had the resources to police anything more than his own immediate household. By his grant of these payments the king was simply pro-viding one more incentive to the local lord to enforce the law in his peace and amongst his own men as only he could do. There cannot have been much need of courts at any level to stand between the wrong-doing and retribution: the peace-keeper compelled the payment of the set compensation or cut down the outlaw and the thief caught in the act.

No doubt, though, the lords did have their 'moots'; meetings of their chief advisers and armed followers, and of the peasantry in each of their manors. In King Ine's seventh-century laws there is evidence that the system of agriculture by which each village tilled two or three open fields as a community was already requiring communal regulations and,

[9] See the laws of Ethelbert and of Hlothere and Eadric, in *EHD*, i, 357–9 and 360–1; on the whole concept of breach of the peace, see J. Goebel, *Felony and Misdemeanor* (New York, 1937).

[10] So that, after a crime, there might be two peaces to satisfy, that of 'him who owns the house' and the king's: see laws of Hlothere and Eadric.

[11] For examples see *EHD*, i, 373 and 474–5.

[12] By Helen M. Cam in 'The evolution of the medieval English franchise', *Speculum* (1957); cf. Stenton, *Anglo-Saxon England*, pp. 485–7.

to enforce these regulations, very likely a 'hall-moot', the 'manorial court' of later times.[13] The court of the manor was the most typical of all courts. It remained active for well over a thousand years, because the rural community of which it was the organ so long remained the foundation of English society. Its law comprised the customary ways of the community, yet it was quickly accepted that the manor court belonged to the dominant landowner in the village, the lord whose dependants and then tenants the rest of the villagers came to be. After the Conquest every considerable landlord was regarded as entitled to his manor court, in which his steward presided to extract fines for his employer.

At the other extreme from the manorial court, the king had a court for his household and greater subjects. This court – the witenagemot – was just the group of 'wise men' (witan) – bishops, abbots and warriors – who were with the king at a particular time, to advise, guard and drink with him; but since they were there, and since many of the king's land-grants were to themselves, they witnessed these grants and joined with the king in their enforcement. It is important to understand what the king's grants by charter or 'land-book' did. This was not feudalism. There was no concept yet that all land came from the king to be 'held' from him in return for a service. A land-book was primarily a political act, conferring the king's special peace and protection on the lands of the churchman or thegn (nobleman) who obtained it, and on the transmission of that land to the churchman's successors or to the thegn's chosen heirs: the moment of transmission was, of course, the dangerous one when the unprotected property was liable to occupation by an outsider (Doc. I).[14] Because land was, and has been till recent times, the one great source of power, the seizure of other people's land was the perennial vice of the aristocracy. The king worked hard to prevent the resulting dissension within the class upon which he relied, partly by punishing violent seizure as crime against his peace, but more by providing 'civil' procedures to arbitrate between rival claimants.

Naturally, the king and his witan would deal with serious offences by his own men, and in these cases the king had available a penalty beyond the ordinary fine: the forfeiture of the land which the culprits had held under the king's protection (Doc. I).[15] Beneath the king, the great lords

---

[13] T. H. Aston, 'The origins of the manor in England', *Transactions of the Royal Historical Society* (henceforth *TRHS*), (1958); laws of Ine in *EHD*, i, 368–9.

[14] On the land-book, see E. John, *Land Tenure in Early England* (Leicester, 1960); for examples and for the problems of the transmission of property, see also F. E. Harmer, *Select English Historical Documents of the Ninth and Tenth Centuries* (Cambridge, 1914), pp. 56–7, and *EHD*, i, 379 and 474–5.

[15] See also *EHD*, i, 430; T. J. Oleson, *The Witenagemot in the Reign of Edward the Confessor* (London, 1955); A. J. Robertson, *Anglo-Saxon Charters*, no. lxiii.

too, ecclesiastical and lay, protected the lands of their followers and made grants by charter,[16] and also received forfeiture of the lands of these followers if they acted disloyally or criminally.[17] It is reasonable to think, therefore, that these nobles held other courts, less regular but more exalted than the manor courts, where their leading retainers could settle their disputes about land, courts corresponding to the 'honour courts' of the post-Conquest Anglo-Norman aristocracy.

THE KING, THE CHURCH AND THE PUBLIC COURTS

The first signs of the administrative area, which in the tenth century came to be called the hundred, appears much earlier than that in the part of central southern England which was the heartland of Wessex. There, the hundreds of Domesday Book have natural boundaries and are each centred upon some landmark, perhaps an old heathen shrine, the name of which often indicates that it was the 'meeting-place' of the area, the place where its moot gathered, though we know nothing of what these meetings did.[18] When information becomes available in the tenth century, the hundred is a fiscal unit, dependent on a royal manor where the king's taxes are collected,[19] and it was imposed artificially on the rest of England as this was conquered from the Norsemen by the Wessex kings. The appearance of the hundred as an administrative unit must be associated with the new official class of thegns which grew up as reeves in the service of the Wessex dynasty in the ninth century and took its power throughout England in the tenth,[20] and similarly its court is to be thought of as the peace-keeping organ of this new class of local potentate, rather than as an age-old popular assembly which suddenly appears in the light of history.

The 'hundred' was a hundred hides, and the hide was reckoned as the amount of land which supported a family. This amount obviously varied from region to region according to the richness of the soil, so that it is possible to give only a rough indication of the size of a medieval hundred by saying that a dozen or so hundreds made up the average shire. The boundaries of hundreds changed continually, but its court ensured each of them its existence through the centuries as a separate social and administrative entity. The idea that a hide corresponded to

[16] P. H. Sawyer, *Anglo-Saxon Charters, an Annotated list and Bibliography* (London, 1968).

[17] Forfeiture to a lord is implied in Doc. 1 and stated in Cnut's laws, *EHD*, i, 420 and 430.

[18] O. S. Anderson, *The English Hundred Names*, vol. III (Lund, 1939).

[19] F. M. Stenton, *The Early History of the Abbey of Abingdon* (Reading, 1912); Helen M. Cam, 'Manerium cum Hundredo', *English Historical Review* (henceforth *EHR*) (1932).

[20] H. R. Loyn, 'Gesiths and thegns in Anglo-Saxon England', *EHR* (1955).

a family seems to have led to a concept of the hundred as a peace-keeping community of a hundred men, who were then divided into groups of ten, called *tithings*, each of them a sort of artificial kinship group responsible for its individual members before the law. An ordinance of the reign of King Athelstan (927–39) shows the community of London being organized on these lines, and another, from the reign of Athelstan's successor, Edmund (939–46) or soon after, decreed how the hundred was to be held throughout the country: '. . . They are to assemble every four weeks and each man is to do justice to another. If the need is urgent, one is to inform the man in charge of the hundred, and he the men over the tithings; and all are to go forth, where God may guide them, that they may reach [the thief]'.[21]

The hundred reeve and the king's reeves or officials at all levels, who so multiplied and prospered that laws began to be made to curb their malpractices,[22] were, of course, the lords, or the deputies of the lords, of the countryside, who were now given explicit responsibility for their localities. This appearance of a system of 'local government' in the tenth century marked the final replacement of the kin-network by lordship as the cement of society. King Alfred and King Edgar recognized this in their laws when they singled out treachery to a lord as the crime for which no mercy could be shown, and Athelstan prescribed summary execution for lordless men, from whom no justice could be obtained.[23] The hundred jurisdiction seems more likely to have been an expansion and definition of the peace-keeping functions of the lord than the annexation by him of the 'public' jurisdiction of an ancient folk court.[24] The manors of which the king was lord were the centres on which the hundred system crystallized, and to that extent the hundred was a 'public' court. But hundredal manors might come into private hands, taking with them the right to demand attendance or 'suit' from the men of the hundred at the moot and to collect the profits of justice done there, and by the time of the Conquest the king was granting away 'hundreds' (meaning by that simply the hundredal jurisdiction) in considerable numbers.[25] The lord thus received the 'sake and soke' of the hundred, 'sake' denoting the right to hear cases and 'soke' the right to extract suit from the inhabitants of the hundred. The king was here defining the ancient peace-keeping functions of the lords in terms of the

21 *EHD*, i, 393–4.

22 *EHD*, i, 66–7 and 382 (3.2).

23 *EHD*, i, 373, 382 (2, 4) and 396–7.

24 For the opposite view, see J. E. A. Jolliffe, 'The era of the folk in English history', in *Oxford Essays in Medieval History presented to H. E. Salter* (Oxford, 1934).

25 Helen M. Cam, 'The "Private" Hundred in England before the Norman Conquest' in *Studies presented to Sir Hilary Jenkinson*, ed. J. Conway Davies (Oxford, 1957).

new 'public' system of jurisdiction rather than giving away public rights which had ever been exercised by him in reality.

By the reign of Edgar (959–75), therefore, the giving of judgment on the king's behalf was so much part of lordship that the automatic penalty for giving wrong judgment was loss of lordly or 'thegnly' status.[26] Not only at manorial but at hundredal level too, private and public justice were henceforth inextricably entangled, and the court-leet through which the magnate of later centuries exercised his terri-torial domination was a fusion of manor and hundred jurisdictions. This did not necessarily or normally mean that the magnate held the court of the entire hundred but rather that he exercised the jurisdiction of the hundred within his own estates, as other lords of that same hundred might in theirs. On the one hand there was the creation of great sokes like those of Peterborough or Bury St Edmunds by the granting of whole groups of hundreds to abbeys;[27] on the other hand, the granting, buying and selling, or acquisition by force of little parcels of jurisdiction (Doc. 5). The right to demand suit of court was sometimes bartered as a right divorced from the lands within which it was exercised, but more and more this right, and the duty to attend court, were regarded as going with the land: as being territorial rather than personal.[28]

Scattered across the pattern of hundreds, which was essentially a pat-tern of territorial lordships, there appears in the tenth century a sprink-ling of burghs, permanent markets and places of defence, distinct in function from the countryside and each inhabited by the men of several different lords, so that they looked to the king for protection. In his laws the king sought to concentrate commercial dealings in the towns, where all could see and witness them 'in open market', and so there had to be a borough or 'port' moot, where the port-reeve presided at the settlement of trading disputes.[29]

The burghs were the natural centres of areas much larger than the hundreds, and thus became the catalysts of the administrative units called shires, the counties of later times. Again, south of the Thames, the shire may have had older roots in the regions settled by whole Saxon tribes, but it is significant that north-of-the-Thames shires almost invariably took their names from boroughs, often, like Bedford and Hertford, established in the early tenth century to consolidate the ad-vance of the Wessex kings against the Danes. In the region of Scandi-

[26] *EHD*, i, 396–7.
[27] F. E. Harmer, *Anglo-Saxon Writs* (Manchester, 1952), Bury St Edmunds no. 10.
[28] F. W. Maitland, *Domesday Book and Beyond* (Cambridge, 1897, and Fontana Library, 1960), pp. 110ff; *EHD*, ii, ed. D. C. Douglas and G. W. Green-away (London, 1953), p. 878; cf. E. Miller, *The Abbey and Bishopric of Ely* (Cambridge, 1951), p. 213.
[29] *EHD*, i, 360–1 and 396–7.

navian settlement in the east, shires developed from the areas of settlement of invading armies, centred upon burghs,[30] and in the West
Midlands, 'shiring' was carried out in the early years of the eleventh
century, again for military purposes but this time for defence against the
second wave of Scandinavian invasions, which wiped out the original
administrative organization of the old kingdom of Mercia under five
bishops and five ealdormen.[31]

The new shires were put in the charge of the magnates who were the
king's *ealdormen* or regional lieutenants. These were essentially military
leaders (after Cnut became King of England in 1016 they received the
cognate Norse title of 'earls'), and, like the bishops with whom they
worked, they each had authority over a number of shires: they must
very early have required deputies or 'shire-reeves' to carry on the
ordinary shire business and publish and execute the increasing number
of orders coming from the king, though the 'sheriff' is not mentioned by
that name till the reign of Cnut. The laws of King Edgar which distinguished (rather than created) the courts of hundred, borough and
shire – the three courts must often have met in the same borough and
had a similar composition – say that 'the hundred court is to be attended
as it was previously established. And the borough court is to be held
thrice a year and the shire court twice.'[32]

In the shire court 'the bishop of the diocese and the ealdorman are to
be present, and there to expound both the ecclesiastical and the secular
law'. It was the Church which had inherited the administrative geo-
graphy of the Roman Empire, preserved the remnants of it through 'the
Dark Ages' and extended it into Germany and Scandinavia. The dio-
cesan bishop, not the count or ealdorman, was the true descendant of the
Roman provincial governor; and he had his own officials, descended also
from the Roman civil service, in the senior clerks or 'deans' of his household and the archdeacons who executed his regulations in the countryside.[33]

The prime duty of the Christian king was to be the moral leader and
defender of his kingdom or *Christendom*, not only by 'strenuousness' in
war against the heathen but also by issuing just laws. The Church was
therefore concerned with all the laws that were made. Meetings of the
witan were often secular assemblies and church synods combined, and
we know that Bishop Wulfstan composed some of the great laws of

---

[30] F. M. Stenton, 'The Danes in England', *Proceedings of the British Academy*
(1928), pp. 5–6; *Idem. Anglo-Saxon England*, p. 502.

[31] C. S. Taylor, 'The origin of the Mercian shires', *Gloucestershire Studies*,
ed. H. P. R. Finberg (Leicester, 1958).

[32] *EHD*, i, 396–7.

[33] Margaret Deanesley, *Sidelights on the Anglo-Saxon Church* (London, 1962);
F. Barlow, *Durham Jurisdictional Peculiars* (London, 1950) (for the complicated
territorial pattern of church government).

King Cnut,[34] introducing to 'secular judgments' the distinctions between degrees of liability for wrong-doing (according to whether for instance it was intentional or unintentional) which had been discovered in 're-ligious penances'.[35] For its ideas, and also for much of its effectiveness, secular law relied on the Church. The sanction for the king's grants – what the Middle Ages called his 'acts' – was for a long time the wrath of God and the pains of Hell for any who infringed them; until, in the eleventh century, the curse began to be replaced by a threat of what might be called government action, of 'the loss of the king's friendship' (Doc. 5), or that 'I [the king] will know that man's name who shall wish to rob God and St Edmund and me'.[36] The king's authority follows on from God's, though it gradually finds its own sphere of activity.

The bishop was much more than an interpreter of the customs of society like the king: he was the interpreter of God's judgment upon society, and therefore its critic, and criticism merged into regulation and legislation. In one role, Wulfstan was the lawgiver, in another, the 'Augustinian' historian who explained the sufferings of the English at the hands of the Danes in terms of the moral shortcomings of the defeated party, as St Augustine had explained the decline of Rome; for:

'God's dues have dwindled too long in every district within this nation, and the laws of the people have deteriorated all too much, and sanctuaries are violated far and wide, and the houses of God are entirely despoiled of ancient privileges and stripped inside of all that is seemly. And widows are wrongfully forced into marriage, and too many are reduced to poverty and greatly humiliated. And poor men are sorely deceived and cruelly defrauded and sold far and wide out of this country into the power of foreigners, although quite innocent; and children in the cradle are enslaved for petty theft by cruel in-justice widely throughout this people. And the rights of freemen are withdrawn and the rights of slaves are restricted and charitable obligations are curtailed; and, in short, God's laws are hated and his precepts despised. And therefore we all through God's anger are frequently disgraced, let him perceive it who can; and this injury will become common to all this people, though one may not think so, unless God protect us.'[37]

While the king's protection covered land-holding and the status and privileges of the great, God's protection covered the whole of society and all His people. For Wulfstan in c. 1014, the ways of a good society could already be described in detail in terms of actual rights and laws, and in

---

[34] Dorothy Whitelock, 'Wulfstan and the laws of Cnut', *EHR* (1948), lxiii.
[35] *EHD*, i, 428.
[36] Harmer, *Anglo-Saxon Writs*, p. 68.
[37] *EHD*, i, 855–6.

the vicissitudes of law social change and decay, social history of a sort, could be perceived.

There was no sharp division between secular courts and church courts, because people still seem to have thought less in terms of courts than in terms of the persons to whom the law belonged. They talked of God's prohibition or the bishop's or the archdeacon's, of compensation 'half to Christ, half to the king'. It is clear from The Law of the Northumbrian Priests that there was a separate body of law applied by archdeacons and bishops to clerics (but also to laymen in matters concerning attacks on clerics or bad faith or in matrimonial cases); and the evidence is that the bishop sat in the shire court to administer the episcopal law only, separate from the sheriff's law.[38] The important fact is that there was a single hierarchy of meetings or synods from the king's court down through the shire to the hundred in which ecclesiastical and lay judges sat side by side. This co-existence of the secular and the ecclesiastical in the same courts kept before the king's servants the total concern for society which the church ideally possessed. Perhaps more important still, no bishop could be thought of as acting entirely in his own right: at a time when there was very little idea of public authority, the bishop in his exercise of justice kept alive the idea of a public responsibility, for he was clearly appointed to an office in the wider church and did not inherit rights of government along with land.

OLD ENGLISH LITIGATION

By the time of Cnut's laws, there was a set of quite elaborate legal procedures regulating the way in which an injured person brought his opponent to court and 'fought' him in court, and binding together the courts themselves in the beginnings of a system. Society was organized to ride in pursuit of the notorious criminal. Yet in fact it was a man's lord and friends[39] and a priest's colleagues,[40] who saw that he got his rights or answered at law, and it was these individual sureties whom the king had to discipline if the law was to prevail. The story of Helmstan the thief shows an influential patron tenaciously defending his man before the king, although that man had been tracked by a reeve as he drove away stolen oxen and betrayed himself when charged by the scratches the brambles had made on his face (Doc. 1).

The king asserted that certain cases were his alone to adjudicate, and these – breach of the king's peace (*mundbryce*), fighting at the king's court, obstructing the king's officials, corrupting the processes of law and neglecting military service – constituted 'the king's pleas'. If he

[38] *EHD*, i, 855–6; C. Morris, 'William I and the church courts', *EHR* (1967).
[39] *EHD*, i, 393–4, 396–7 and 421–3.
[40] *EHD*, i, 435.

wished to honour someone highly, the king might grant away even this 'jurisdiction' (Doc. 5),[41] but it seems that now it really was only profits and not power that he gave. Reserved to the king absolutely, for trial in the shire courts, were the dreadful 'bootless' crimes such as arson, for which mere 'bot' or monetary compensation would not be accepted. Both these types of offence, the king's pleas and the bootless crimes, called down on offenders the particularly stringent and royal processes of outlawry and forfeiture to the king. Perhaps it would be better to say that these cases were the king's just because he turned his heaviest sanctions on to them, and therefore could alone show mercy to offenders, if he chose, by conferring his protection or *mund* on them.[42]

It must be apparent by now that we have no direct evidence of the business transacted in the hundred, private or public, but the effect of the continued increase in the resourcefulness of royal government was to define and limit the powers of the landlords as privileges cut out of, and carefully controlled by, public authority. The lords obtained written grants of *sac* and *soc* in the tenth and later centuries (Doc. 5) to safeguard their privileges in a world where the king's reeves were ubiquitous and ever more active. Even so, 'private' hundreds were not exempt from entry by shire officials in execution of the king's orders, and the most the king seems usually to have granted was jurisdiction in cases of brawling and wounding, and the right to dispose of thieves caught in the act.[43]

The ordinary freeman with a grievance beyond the scope of the manor court made for the burgh or hundred court, but might very often have to go on to the shire court for effective action. For there was the key figure in the peace-keeping system, the sheriff, the immediate recipient of the king's orders, the man who controlled the process of outlawry and eventually went around the hundreds to 'make view of frankpledge', sitting in the special meetings of the hundreds known as 'the sheriff's tourn' to ensure that everyone was in a tithing.[44] Some of the cases heard in the shire court were doubtless brought from the hundred by the initiative of complainants or the king's order. But the great cases were those sent down from the witan by the king for effective settlement in the shire, and here at last we come to some first-hand accounts of court proceedings. Since the king was the ultimate source of all judicial action, the witan might deal with any type of wrong, and we have a picture of it supervising the execution of a criminal.[45] But cases arising from landholding by the king's book were the witan's staple diet as a court and

[41] See also *EHD*, i, 420.
[42] *EHD*, i, 392.
[43] Cam, *Speculum* (1957); N. D. Hurnard, 'The Anglo-Norman franchises', *EHR* (1949).
[44] W. A. Morris, *The Medieval English Sheriff* (Manchester, 1927), pp. 26 and 57; and the same author's *The Frankpledge System* (New York, 1910).
[45] D. Talbot Rice (ed.), *The Dark Ages* (London, 1965), pp. 254-5.

these matters were frequently sent down to the shire for settlement.

It is not too much to say that the basic 'forms of action' of the common law began from the movement of emphasis from the land-book itself to the declaration of its terms to the shire court. Such declarations from the king were of a solemnity to be carried by named envoys of distinction, and were often recorded in gospel-books on minster altars (Doc. 4).[46] But ecclesiastical landlords controlled the recording and were not above copying in 'grants' of their own invention, so King Cnut or King Edward the Confessor (the first genuine writ-charter is of disputed date) replaced the oral declaration to the shire court by a written one authenticated by the wax impression of his seal, which he seems to have copied from the German imperial seal. These 'writs' or 'writ-charters' (Doc. 5), which could be carried in quantities by more lowly and anonymous messengers, soon ousted the old 'diploma' land-books as actual title-deeds.

But they were more than just title-deeds, for they were ideal vehicles for those new, blunt threats of government action if the grants were infringed; threats which could develop into more detailed 'hand-given' protections on the one hand, and, on the other, into orders to the sheriff to take specific action if the protections were broken.[47] English kings were already accustomed to send orders, written or oral, to shire-meetings, by envoys whose authority might be signified by the possession of a wax imprint (unattached to any document) of the king's seal, requiring the assembled thegns 'to settle the case between Wynflaed and Leofwine as justly as they could' (Doc. 3), or to 'settle the dispute between them justly, weighing both claim and counterclaim'.[48] So, well before the Conquest, we find some of the elements of the legal action begun by a writ obtained from the king, though these elements were still far from being brought together in a set form.

During the tenth century, then, the weight of litigation shifts from the witan to the shire, because parties insist that it is in the shire that the truth can be established most reliably, as well as because the king's protection implies – and sometimes specifically requires – that the thegns of the shire 'pronounce for me a judgment' concerning persons who have infringed protected rights (Doc. 5).

JUDGES, TRIALS AND REMEDIES

In court, two adversaries (or their representatives) face each other, one making a formal claim, the other formally denying it, and somehow the

---

[46] For this paragraph, see P. Chaplais, 'The Anglo-Saxon Chancery: from the diploma to the writ', *Journal of the Society of Archivists* (1966).

[47] Harmer, *Anglo-Saxon Writs*, p. 80.

[48] *Ibid.* p. 541.

court must decide between them. Guilt for a criminal act or liability for an injurious one are, as they already knew, subtle things, depending on the intentions of the men who act, which are difficult to fathom even today.[49] It was just because they had a civilized awareness of the complex origins of men's deeds, and the humility to realize that only God, and not they, could search men's hearts, that they made trial a ritual non-rational combat through which God could give the answer. Quite logically, the Normans let the parties fight an actual physical battle, but the Anglo-Saxons preferred trial by ordeal or by oath-helping, and these were methods which required much regulation in the laws, and supervision by the elders of the community. These elders were the only judges, and their allotment of the burden of proof to one side or the other the only judging: whether the proof was good was not a matter of rational judgment, but of the right number of oaths, or a festering wound.

Usually in a dispute over property one side or the other would have to make good its claim by producing a body of supporters, not to fight, but to swear oaths that the claimant's oath could be relied upon.[50] Wynflaed produced before the king, in the witan, witnesses of the 'booking' of her estates, but Leofwine, who claimed them, insisted that the case be sent to the shire court, where Wynflaed assembled twenty-four named supporters 'and many a good thegn and good woman' unnamed, 'to the full number'. Nevertheless, the leading men of the shire persuaded the parties, with difficulty, to come to terms without an oath being sworn, because once legal battle was finally joined in this way, all friendship would be at an end – and not just between the parties but between their followings as well (Doc. 3). In a Kent case of 964–88 it was the claimant, the Archbishop of Canterbury, not the defendant, who made good his claim 'with his own oath' and allegedly the oaths of 'a good thousand men'. The defendant, Leofsunu, would not admit defeat, so the sheriff accepted the oath and awarded victory in the judicial combat.[51]

To tell the truth, oath-helping did not possess the irrational impartiality of the ordeal, for success in it depended on social reasons – the size and respectability of the following a litigant or his patron could call upon (Doc. 1). This is a fact of great significance, because it seems clear that oath-helping lies at the root of the jury system: in Latin the oath-helpers or 'compurgators' were called *juratores*, and were almost always numbered in twelves.[52] It must be admitted that the jury has always

[49] *EHD*, i, 428.

[50] *EHD*, i, 360; Robertson, *Anglo-Saxon Charters*, p. 9.

[51] Robertson, *Anglo-Saxon Charters*, pp. 85–7.

[52] H. C. Lea, *Superstition and Force* (Philadelphia, 1892), pp. 48ff; cf. *EHD*, i, 366, 433 and 437–8.

been a medium for the expression of the distribution of power in society; a thing which was expected to assemble and act in the interests of the dominant people.

There is indirect evidence that in one case, at least, before the Conquest, something like the later jury was made up by agreement from the older tenants of both parties to a dispute, the Abbeys of Ramsey and Thorney, to say, as a group of people who knew the facts, how a certain fen was, and should continue to be, shared between the two abbeys.[53] The group of oath-helpers was changing into the theoretically impartial 'jury of recognition', a number of factors probably contributing to the change. The social status of contending litigants, like these two abbeys, would often be too evenly balanced for oath-helping to produce a decision. Perhaps more important, the case between Ramsey and Thorney concerned the definition of boundaries between two properties which undoubtedly existed, and this was a situation peculiarly suited to adjudication by a sworn group of elders who knew the traditional landmarks – what was later called a jury of perambulation, since it actually walked along the boundary.[54]

A third factor was the unreliability of oath-helping. There was no guarantee against perjury: indeed the logic of the elaborate rules of oath-helping was that some litigants needed to be vouched for by a great number of people for their oaths to be credible at all, and some were of a sort for whom kin or friends 'dare not give that oath'.[55] A better alternative to trial by oath-helping, particularly for criminals who were not likely to stick at perjury, was the ordeal, though that, too, had to be made stiffer for the untrustworthy man; or better still, witnesses and the warranty of an alleged vendor. These were required in commercial transactions, in which 'it did not seem right' to King Cnut 'that any man should make good his claim where there is witness and it can be shown that there has been fraud'.[56]

Evidence and witnessing, of a rather special kind, was intrinsic to every judgment concerning land. The land-book was evidence of the provisions of a land-grant, and if the grant was subsequently disputed and confirmed by legal judgment, this judgment, like the original grant, seems to have been regarded as depending for its effectiveness in the future on the number of great men in court to witness it. The names of the judgment-witnesses – who are distinct both from the judges and

[53] R. C. Van Caenegem (ed.), *Royal Writs in England from the Conquest to Glanville* (Selden Society, London, 1959), pp. 69ff; Harmer, *Anglo-Saxon Writs*, pp. 252–6.

[54] See the case in Harmer, *English Historical Documents*, pp. 56–7; and I. D. Willock, *The Origins and Development of the Jury in Scotland* (Stair Society, Edinburgh, 1966), ch. II.

[55] *EHD*, i, 423; Lea, *Superstition and Force*, pp. 33, 40, 45 and 47.

[56] *EHD*, i, 361 and 422.

from the oath-helpers who may have given their man the verdict – are sometimes recorded after the judgment just as the names of the witnesses are subscribed to the land-book (Doc. 1).[57] Once again we find that a permanent part of English legal practice has Anglo-Saxon beginnings, for the conveyancing of property has been closely linked, through much of the history of English law, with the activities and authority of the courts, to the extent that a large proportion of land-cases were fictitious 'disputes' invented by grantors and grantees in order to get for the grantees the cast-iron title of judgment in court.[58]

Oath-helping was a form of ordeal, since a false oath was reckoned to bring its own supernatural punishment,[59] but it seems to have been a comfortable one and therefore a privilege of the influential: it outlasted the Conquest as clerical compurgation and the merchant's 'wager of law'. The physical ordeals, the technicalities of which must have taken up much of the time and expertise of the judges of the hundred courts, were the lot of the less influential and criminal classes.[60] These ordeals contributed little to the particular development of English law, because they were an unoriginal as well as irrational method of 'identifying' the guilty which is found at a certain stage of social development in all parts of the world and at all periods. Nineteenth-century British missionaries in Africa were horrified to come upon trial by the ordeal of poison, and hastened to establish 'trial by jury instead of these objectionable, and in most cases unjust, proceedings'.[61] The church in 'Dark-Age' Europe could not import such ideal manifestations of a 'superior' culture, and very sensibly took over the pagan ordeal and used it for its own purposes, as it had taken over and used the pagan blood-feud. It was an essential part of the ordeal that God should be invoked to give his judgment through it, as Mithra or Thor had been invoked in earlier times. The priest would pray over the sacred morsel: 'O Lord Jesus Christ . . . grant, we pray thee, by thy Holy name, that he who is guilty of this crime in thought or in deed, when this creature of sanctified bread is presented to him for the proving of the truth, let his throat be narrowed, and in thy name let it be rejected rather than devoured . . .'.[62] This ordeal was at least founded in human experience: such an invocation was calculated to make a guilty man grow dry in the throat and choke, and it was related by many chroniclers how Earl Godwin of Wessex choked to death in this ordeal, voluntarily undergone in 1053, through

---

[57] *EHD*, i, 474–5; Robertson, *Anglo-Saxon Charters*, pp. 9 and 85–7.
[58] See S. J. Bailey, *Cambridge Law Journal* (1961).
[59] Lea, *Superstition and Force*, p. 371.
[60] *EHD*, i, 423.
[61] O. Chadwick, *Mackenzie's Grave* (London, 1959), p. 80; cf. Lea, *Superstition and Force*, p. 375.
[62] Lea, *Superstition and Force*, p. 340; Liebermann, *Die Gesetze der Angelsachsen*, vol. i, p. 408.

guilt at his murder of Prince Alfred.[63] But it is likely that sometimes the innocent too were 'convicted' in this physiological lottery; and more likely still in the most common forms of ordeal, hot iron and boiling water, in which the indication of guilt was the festering of the burn or scald.[64]

The remedy for a wrong followed swiftly upon the trial, if it was a 'bootless' wrong, so dreadful that there could be no compensation. This category, which included treachery to a lord, housebreaking, arson and open murder and theft, represents the beginnings of a concept of crime marked off from civil injury. 'Felonies' such as desertion in war automatically brought death, and all serious crimes put the criminals' lives in the king's mercy.[65] In Cnut's laws, however, there seems a reluctance to execute criminals outright and deprive them of time for repentance, and a preference – outlandish to us – for a sliding scale of mutilation according to whether it is a first or later offence.[66] In monetary terms also, the consequences of infringing the law were very heavy indeed, and it does not seem surprising that many were enslaved in default of payment of a legal penalty, losing their rights before the law as free men with their failure to fulfil a free man's obligations.[67]

Scales of punishment must have provided many problems for the churchmen and reeves who presided in the courts; even more so the tariffs of compensation to the injured persons and fines to king or lord. They were problems not just of deciding on a remedy which was supposed to vary according to the gravity and number of offences and the status of wrong-doer and wronged,[68] but also of getting the remedy carried out. The problems increased as compassion entered into royal justice, alleviating its severity and requiring that 'the weak man must always be judged and prescribed for more leniently that the strong' and distinction made between 'age and youth, wealth and poverty, freedom and slavery, health and sickness'.[69]

The lawmen who allotted proof by oath or ordeal were in some respects nearest to being judges in our sense, and in Domesday Book they appear as a formal institution, limited to twelve in each court, perhaps with a 'doomster' or 'dempster' to pronounce their judgments.[70] But the

[63] Lea, *Superstition and Force*, p. 342.

[64] *Ibid.* pp. 287 and 298.

[65] *EHD*, i, 392, 427 and 430.

[67] *EHD*, i, 423.

[67] *EHD*, i, 423 and 433; H. R. Loyn, *Anglo-Saxon England and the Norman Conquest* (London, 1962), pp. 87 and 132; F. Pollock and F. W. Maitland, *The History of English Law before the Time of Edward I*, 2nd edn (Cambridge, 1898), vol. ii, p. 457.

[68] *EHD*, i, 366–9 and 423.

[69] *EHD*, i, 428.

[70] *EHD*, i, 360–1, 392; Helen M. Cam, 'Suitors and Scabini', *Speculum* (1935).

judges in the sense of the presidents of the courts were the royal officials and churchmen who, from very early times, kept legal proceedings moving, received the judicial oaths, saw that remedies were carried out and took the money due to the king (Doc. 2). Probably it was their control of proceedings which brought to the fore more rational methods such as the admission of blatant evidence (like the bramble-scratches which gave away the Fonthill thief: Doc. 1) and the use of witnesses to land-books, business transactions and judgments. From the witnesses on the one hand and the oath-helpers on the other emerged the jurors who swore to facts they knew personally, and it seems probable that it was the reeve who created this new group in court. The jury of three twelves used in the eleventh century may have included a group of 'independent witnesses', and we know that the jurymen were sometimes chosen by the reeve (Doc. 2).[71]

THE COURTS IN OLD ENGLISH SOCIETY

A great deal of the formation of the basic structure of English legal procedure in fact took place before the Conquest.[72] Already the shire court had crystallized around the crucial royal official, the sheriff, as the centre of the network of legal procedure; and already the principle of the detection of crime by local notoriety and the discovery of the truth of a matter through local knowledge was finding expression in the jury. What has been called the 'adversary method' of trial, in which the hearing is a formalized contest between the two sides, with the judges simply as umpires, was already established as a main feature of English law.

It has sometimes been remarked that Anglo-Norman and Angevin government grew 'jurisprudentially', by the deciding of particular cases or problems of administration as they arose in sessions or 'assizes' of the king's court, rather than 'legislatively', by the enactment of comprehensive schemes of government, as happened in the precocious Norman-Sicilian state.[73] The activities of the courts, under the direction of the king or his reeves, were already so much the vital part of English law before 1066, that one must believe that this basic principle of the growth of English government began in Anglo-Saxon times.

The system of courts which appeared in the tenth century, itself represents the emergence of definably English government and law from the forms of social organization found all over the Germanic world. In Carolingian France, a system of counties and courts under the control of the king had emerged early and was ripe to fragment into the hands of

---

[71] Cf. *EHD*, i, 437–8; Lea, *Superstition and Force*, pp. 48 and 51.
[72] Doris M. Stenton, *English Justice between the Norman Conquest and the Great Charter* (London, 1965), ch. 1.
[73] C. Cahen, *Le Regime Feodal de l'Italie Normande* (Paris, 1940).

the local magnates when royal government crumbled under the attacks of the Vikings: in France, very full judicial and governmental powers thenceforth accompanied the possession of great estates, and 'public' authority and 'private' status were fused to produce one of the main characteristics of 'feudalism'. In ninth-century England, however, there was not a great deal of government to destroy, and instead the Vikings gave the Wessex kings the opportunity to establish strong government throughout England as they reconquered it. So the courts, which in France fell piecemeal to the magnates, in England were to be the backbone of royal government. But the Old English courts can be said to have constituted a system only because they were the organs of a hierarchy of officials acting on the commission of the king: if the courts were the backbone of government, the king's reeves were the spinal cord. The sheriff, going around twice a year to sit in the hundred courts and inspect the frankpledge system, exhibits at the beginning another basic aspect of the English judicial system, the visitation and spurring-on of lower courts by itinerant justices from a higher level, which can also be seen as the inspection of local government by royal commissioners. One last area of interaction between justice and government was the use of written messages and records. These began to be used only to preserve or publicize oral processes of law which had their own solemnity and validity. The written instrument then took over the solemn force, and bureaucratic government began its career.

Of course, it cannot be denied that the legal processes of pre-Conquest England were used by the powerful to their own advantage, no less than they were under a feudal regime,[74] but this had to be by the manipulation and corruption of parts of a system which as a whole was beyond the magnates' control, and which was developed further by the king in reaction to such abuses.[75] Yet the king could not prevent litigation from becoming an increasingly sophisticated game between the gentry, a game in which few victories could be final: 'And . . . when will any suit be settled, if it cannot be settled either with money or with an oath? And if every decision is to be set aside, when shall we be done with negotiating?' (Doc. I).

The two social forces expressed in the judicial system, which the king could to some extent balance against each other, were communal solidarity and lordship. We are back once more at the two functions of courts with which we started, the maintenance of social peace and community and the maintenance of the social status of the court-holders. The pattern of Anglo-Saxon communities was expressed in the courts of shire, hundred and borough, but the factor of communal soli-

---

[74] E. John, 'English feudalism and the structure of Anglo-Saxon Society', *Bulletin of the John Rylands Library* (1963–4).

[75] *EHD*, i, 396–7 and 421.

darity declined before the landlords' proprietorial attitude to the courts and the king's bureaucratic use of them. Juries arose from the communities of neighbours but achieved such permanence because they were perfectly adapted to a society dominated more and more by the followings of great men. The community narrowed to the group having the obligation to do suit of court, defined in the end as the holders of specific pieces of land, and the court became a court of freeholders rather than free men; though at least the emphasis on the duty of the more substantial people to attend court preserved the idea of collective judgment.[76] By the Conquest the courts are already feudal, in the sense that they are primarily places for the conveying of land amongst the freeholders, under the lord's sanction. It was lordship which brought into the law the notion, without which proper courts would never have existed, of an authority, a peace or *mund*, which sanctioned lawful procedures and provided facilities for the hearing of complaints against unlawful acts – provided them because such acts seemed to attack the lord's political power, expressed as protection over people and property. Though the law started from the voluntary settlement of feuds within the community, the emergence of formal jurisdictions depended on the sense that all wrongs are crimes against some authority. The hundred courts, often held at some rural landmark, fell in large numbers to the landlords: the towns, lying across the pattern of estates, preserved in the courts of shire and borough the authority of their lord, the king.

[76] Miller, *Ely*, p. 225; Maitland, *Domesday Book and Beyond*, pp. 378–9; Cam, *Speculum* (1935).

2

The Age of the Travelling Justices, 1066–c. 1300

It would have been surprising if the Conquest of England by Duke William of Normandy in 1066 had produced any sudden change in English law. The Norman dukes had been struggling to bring order into Norman society much as the Wessex kings had been working in England, and the pleas reserved for the duke – breaking into a homestead and the rest – were almost identical with 'the king's pleas' of Cnut. In Normandy, Duke William had established a single peace – 'the Peace of God', but enforced by ducal agents – and serious criminals put themselves 'in the mercy of the Duke' as in England they were in the mercy of the king, for him to do with them as he chose. In the *vicomte* (Latin, *vicecomes*) the Duke possessed a regional official roughly equivalent to the sheriff, and after 1066 *vicecomes* was the term used of the sheriff in English governmental records. In Normandy, however, the *vicomtes* had often been difficult to control. They were not the presiding officers of developed courts like those of the English shire and hundred and therefore had not become accustomed to receive writs from the duke for publication in court. The Conqueror was well satisfied to take over the tighter English administrative system.[1]

HONOUR COURT AND *CURIA REGIS*

The one new thing which stemmed from the Conquest was a pyramidal system of land-tenure culminating in the king. This was not brought from Normandy but rather created by the circumstances of the Conquest. The new king shared out the conquered country between his principal followers in return for the service of fixed numbers of knights, since William's first requirement in a hostile land was an army supported by incomes from land. The amount of land each tenant-in-chief

---

[1] D. C. Douglas, *William the Conqueror* (London, 1964); J.-F. Lemarignier, *Recherches sur l'hommage en marche* (Lille, 1945), pp. 28–9; M. Fauroux (ed.), *Recueil des actes des ducs de Normandie (911–1066)*, (Caen, 1961), no. 121.

held from the king and the amount of service he owed for it were the result of the confused events of the Conquest. The service of sixty knights owed by some great abbey might begin with the arrival of a Norman cleric at the head of sixty Norman horsemen to establish himself as the new abbot of the hostile English community. To provide the service due to the king from his holding or *tenure*, the abbot or lay baron might maintain warriors in his household, but more often he did what the king had done to him and gave lands ('knights' fees') to his followers in return for knight-service. The process of subinfeudation could be carried many stages further down, and tenure became a legal concept of universal application, every occupant of land being presumed to have a tenure, defined by some form of service.

From tenures and the services attached to them were built up the wealth and power and *honour* of the Anglo-Norman baron, and so, in whatever way his English predecessor had settled the disputes of the men whose lands he 'protected', the king's baron after the Conquest needed to have a court for his 'honour' – thought of territorially – where he could make land-grants and decide disputes between, and with the help of, his own tenants-in-chief or barons (Doc. 11).[2]

The great baron might, like the Abbot of Ramsey, hold a number of separate courts corresponding to his different types of jurisdiction, an honour court at Broughton, manor courts at Hemingford and elsewhere on his estates, a special court for the traders coming to the internationally famous fair of St Ives, and private hundred courts such as the one possessed by the Abbess of Romsey at Whorwelsdown in Wiltshire (Doc. 11). But most lords required the suit of their barons at a hundred or manor court, rather than maintain a separate honour court. Some of the matters handled in a lesser gentleman's manor court were purely manorial: the customary tenants had shirked their boon-works or done their ploughing badly; peasant tenements changed hands ceaselessly, the conveyances taking place by surrender to the lord, who reconveyed the property to the purchaser; and male villeins paid for licences to marry and females the 'leyerwite' fine for illicit associations. But often petty misdemeanours against the general law of the realm were also dealt with in the manor court: a jury said this man had committed an assault, that man was not in a tithing, these women had broken the assize of beer. There were even 'inquests' in disputes about leasehold and pleading of descent from ancestors. In the honour court of the greater lord, the knight-service of the feudal tenants was enforced, but there were also pleas of trespass 'against the peace of the lord Abbot'

[2] W. E. Wightman, *The Lacy Family in England and Normandy, 1066–1194* (Oxford, 1966), pp. 106ff; see the agreement made in the honour court of Roger de Lacy at Pontefract in 1201, which is printed in W. Farrer (ed.), *Early Yorkshire Charters* (Edinburgh, 1916), vol. iii. no. 1526.

according to the form of the action of trespass as it developed in the king's common-law courts (Doc. 11).[3]

In fact, during the century after the Conquest, men did not distinguish at all clearly between franchise jurisdiction – the public sake and soke of the hundred, fallen into private hands – and the seignorial jurisdiction exercised by every landlord over his tenants, whether in 'honour court', 'hundred court' or 'manor'.[4] The distinction which was made was between the *libera curia* composed of free tenants and the 'hall-moot' of the manor where there happened to be only unfree tenants or *villeins*. Even this distinction was blurred. The villein was a 'tenant-at-will', reckoned to occupy his allotment on sufferance, in return for any labour or money services which the lord cared to exact: he had no rights in the land, and no access to the common-law courts where the landed property of freemen was protected. This was the theory: but the fact that the lord handled the disputes of all his tenants, often in a single court, meant that there were attributed to villeins rights 'by custom of the manor' which were parallel to the free tenants' rights by law. 'Ancient demesne villeins', who lived on royal manors, or manors they could argue had once belonged to the king, made use of the special facilities which this most powerful of landlords could supply, to the extent of obtaining their own writ, 'the little writ of right close', to protect their holdings (Doc. 11).

The 'civil' jurisdiction of the lord, though it increasingly imitated the forms developed in the king's courts, followed from simply being a land-lord. His 'criminal' jurisdiction, on the other hand, grew as the king's administrative and judicial resources grew, because the king had progressively more powers to give away or for the lords to usurp. In the first half of the twelfth century, a great baron would have *infangenetheof*, the right to hang thieves caught in possession of the stolen goods within his estates, and perhaps *utfangenetheof*, the right to hang his own men wherever they were caught thieving; in exceptional cases – one of the archbishops, a marcher-baron like de Lacy – he might also have been granted some of the king's pleas, the right to dispatch homicides or arsonists.[5] It was still just a matter of the lord keeping his peace by disposing of criminals caught red-handed in the disturbing of it. But then there occurred the enormous expansion of the machinery for enforcing the king's peace. Already at the beginning of the twelfth century, in the so-called 'Laws of Henry I', the sheriff is described holding his twice-yearly tourn of the hundred courts to make 'view of frankpledge', that is

---

[3] F. W. Maitland (ed.), *Select Pleas in Manorial Courts* (Selden Society, London, 1888); W. O. Ault, *Private Jurisdiction in England* (New Haven, 1923).

[4] Wightman, *Lacy Family*, p. 107.

[5] F. W. Maitland, *Domesday Book and Beyond* (Cambridge, 1897 and Fontana Library, 1960), p. 118; Wightman, *Lacy Family*, p. 140.

to ensure that everyone was in a tithing which would provide him with pledges in a court of law; and upon this was superimposed in 1166 the procedure of the Assize of Clarendon which required the presentation of criminals by a jury in each hundred and the chief men of the townships (Doc. 8). At this new procedure 'the feudal lords grasped wholesale'.[6] View of frankpledge became the commonest of franchises; and the lord's 'court-leet', the standard form of seignorial jurisdiction for centuries to come, was based on the private version of the sheriff's tourn. In 1066 there were six private hundreds in Wiltshire, in 1275 there were twenty-seven. The rolls of a number of private hundred courts survive, whereas there are none for 'public' ones, because they constituted title-deeds to a very important form of property (Doc. 11).[7]

A few thirteenth-century lords, such as the Abbots of Ramsey and Battle, had the right to act as the king's sole justices of *oyer and terminer* for criminal pleas within the *banlieux* of their abbeys, or, as in the case of the Prior of Dunstable, to preside over the king's justices in eyre when they arrived at their domains (cf. Doc. 16). 'Feeding upon the new processes of government', the 'liberties' of Durham and Chester grew by the later thirteenth century into 'palatinates' in which the Bishop of Durham and the Earl of Chester had their own shire courts, appointed their own justices in eyre and issued their own writs, and within which they appeared like kings.[8]

The appearance was false: the king's government had really been feeding upon the local power of the barons. A franchise was not the gift of power by the king so much as the delegation of administrative functions to those who already possessed the power locally, power which was in this way harnessed by the king and carefully limited in its operation. In the thirteenth century, the position was made absolutely plain to the barons by the *quo warranto* proceedings. Henry III and Edward I made everyone who claimed to exercise powers of government produce a warrant for his claim, in the form of the royal charter which had granted the franchise or proof that it had been enjoyed over a long period of time. In the latter case a lost royal grant was presumed, for a lord could wield powers of government (the king maintained) only by royal commission.[9]

[6] *EHD* ii. 460; Maitland, *Select Pleas in Manorial Courts*.
[7] Helen M. Cam, 'The evolution of the medieval English franchise', *Speculum* (1957).
[8] G. Barraclough, *The Earldom and County Palatine of Chester* (Oxford, 1953); J. W. Alexander, 'New evidence on the Palatinate of Chester', *EHR* (1971). The Bishop of Ely received the profits from the Eyre when it was in his territory and his bailiffs executed the orders of the justices; E. Miller, *The Abbey and Bishopric of Ely* (Cambridge, 1951), pp. 201ff.
[9] D. W. Sutherland, *Quo Warranto Proceedings in the Reign of Edward I* (Oxford, 1963).

Quo warranto did no more than register the subordination of the barons' courts; a subordination which had been established right from the Conquest by the ceaseless activity of the king's honour court, the *curia regis*. The king had his own feudal dues to extract from his tenants-in-chief – dues which were eventually to be transformed into national taxation. Domesday Book was the product of a survey of the king's feudal resources, made in 1086, when the Conqueror at last had time to draw breath and look around him; and it was compiled by means of the three devices which gave the king's honour court its advantage, the writ, the travelling commission of justices, and the jury.[10] These were at the king's sole disposal because of his inheritance of the Anglo-Saxon public courts: the sheriff received royal writs and saw to their execution, and it was in the shire court that the itinerant justices sat to take the findings (verdicts, *veredicta*, 'true sayings') of juries representing shire and hundreds and townships. Even before Domesday, William I was putting the Anglo-Saxon machinery to this new use: inquiry into the rights accompanying the land which had come to him or his magnates from their English predecessors.[11] Information was obtained from juries of Englishmen assembled under the instructions of writs which, operating now at an earlier stage in proceedings than the writ-charters when they confirmed disputed land-rights, thus acquired a truly judicial function.

But, rather than set on foot these large-scale inquiries, which amounted to the creation of a special court for each occasion, the king preferred if possible to instruct an existing court to see that right was done. It seems that an order to a lord to do 'full right' to a plaintiff, or even an order to the lord or the defendant himself to restore his property or redress an injustice in some other specific way,[12] was often intended to lead to a hearing of both sides of the case in the honour court. Men bought such 'writs of right' from the king in growing numbers and the rule was eventually enunciated that no one might sue or 'implead' another for his land unless he got one of these writs to the honour court; probably this was done by Henry II soon after his accession in 1154, when he was faced by the clamour of the gentry 'seeking to recover land which they had lost during the fifteen years of what the Saxons would have called "unpeace" ' under King Stephen.[13]

10 *EHD*, ii, 851 and 853; V. H. Galbraith, *The Making of Domesday Book* (Oxford, 1961).

11 See the writ of 1082 ordering an inquiry concerning the lands of the Abbey of Ely, tr. in C. Stephenson and F. G. Marcham, *Sources of English Constitutional History* (New York, 1937), pp. 39–40.

12 Such writs are examined in detail in R. C. Van Caenegem (ed.), *Royal Writs in England from the Conquest to Glanville* (Selden Society, London, 1959).

13 Doris M. Stenton, *English Justice between the Norman Conquest and the Great Charter* (London, 1965), pp. 29 and 78; G. D. G. Hall (ed.), *The treatise on*

An essential part of the writ of right was the warning that if the recipient did not do justice, the sheriff would. The king was bound to provide justice for those who appealed from the courts of his tenants-in-chief, and in the years after the Conquest he could best do this through the sheriffs. In 1108, an edict, communicated to the shires by writs, asserted that the king's shire and hundred courts were to be held at the same times and places as before the Conquest ('and not otherwise') and attended by all the men of the shires to hear the king's pleas and judgments; and it extended the shire court's jurisdiction in land-cases to cover disputes between the men of two different lords (and not just where these lords were tenants-in-chief), since there were then also two competing honour courts.[14] But normally the sheriff's jurisdiction consisted of doing right where a lord had failed to do it, and probably from the time of the Conquest[15] there was the procedure called *tolt* (at first, before there were procedural writs, set in motion by a simple complaint to the sheriff) for demonstrating to four knights that there had been a default of right which justified the shire court in taking over.[16] It must be this procedure which is threatened in the writ of right: 'and if you do not do it . . .'.

The king also instructed the sheriff directly to deal with particular cases in a hundred court or the shire court or, in at least one case, a special session of three and a half hundreds.[17] Eventually there were a number of varieties of writs of *justicies*, issued as a matter *of course*, ordering the sheriff to institute hearings in the shire court of cases of debt, breach of covenant, nuisance and other things.[18] In the twelfth century, however, many orders went to the sheriff for the remedying of specific injustices which, like the earliest 'writs of right' to private lords, may or may not have been intended to lead to judicial investigation.[19] Very often the litigation kept going by these 'administrative' writs must have been long and frustrating,[20] because the shire court lacked the expertise and authority to decide issues conclusively. This is one of the reasons why another procedure was added to *tolt*, that called *recordari*, for transferring a case from the shire court to *curia regis*;[21] and why the

the laws and customs of the realm of England commonly called Glanvill (London, 1965), pp. 102–3 and 136ff.
[14] *EHD*, ii, 433–4.
[15] G. J. Turner (ed.), *Brevia Placitata* (Selden Society, London, 1947), pp. xliii and lxxxvi.
[16] Hall, *Glanvill*, p. 139.
[17] H. G. Richardson and G. O. Sayles, *Law and Legislation from Aethelberht to Magna Carta* (Edinburgh, 1966), p. 50.
[18] Turner, *Brevia Placitata*, p. lvii; for examples, Van Caenegem, *Royal Writs*, pp. 482–95.
[19] Turner, *Brevia Placitata*, p. xliii.
[20] Stenton, *English Justice*, p. 24.
[21] Turner, *Brevia Placitata*, p. xlv; Hall, *Glanvill*, p. 62.

king assembled a little group of experienced justices to send out from the *curia regis* to sit in the shire courts of England (rather as the sheriffs went round to sit in the hundred courts). The king's court moved about ceaselessly with the king, hearing disputes between the magnates at the manors where the king happened to stop (Doc. 6), and it was natural to detach a judge or two from it, as occasion required, or to send a number of groups of justices itinerant (on an *iter* or journey, or 'in eyre') to do similar jobs at the same time in different parts of the country. The commissioners who compiled Domesday Book were the model for the judicial eyres and they were in fact already in 1086 compelled to decide disputes about land tenure before they could make accurate returns.[22]

The centre and control of the judicial system was the *curia regis*, the king's honour court, and it was feudalism which caused both the great increase in litigation and the centralization of justice. The many different types of feudal land-tenure and all the profits flowing from them meant that a magnate like the Archbishop of Canterbury – however distasteful a St Anselm might find it – was all the time surrounded by a 'crowd of litigants . . . laying their heads together, discussing the crafts and wiles by which they could help their own case and fraudulently injure his'.[23] The local courts, public and private, handled every possible sort of dispute, giving redress of a kind even in cases of slander, long before the king's court did so. Inevitably, and throughout the history of law, the causes of dispute well up from below, coming first into the local courts. But it is the legal experts around the king who work out forms of action specific to new problems, and the power dispensed from above by the king which gives these forms a cutting edge. Systematic communication between the king's court and the local courts was therefore crucial to the growth of a body of law, and this feudalism provided also, by introducing a hierarchical system of land-tenure which involved a hierarchy of courts and the principle of appeal from lord's court to overlord's court to *curia regis*. (The court – the *curia* of the landlord surrounded by his tenants – was itself very much a feudal concept.) As the case of the Bishop of Durham in 1088 shows,[24] the pyramidal shape of English feudalism meant that the *curia regis* was one court the jurisdiction of which none could escape, whether he was earl or prelate.

Nevertheless, the actual scope of royal justice depended, as before 1066, on the king's power, the proved strength of his *protection*. In the

---

[22] Galbraith, *Domesday Book*; the relevant cases are collected together by M. M. Bigelow in *Placita Anglo-Normannica* (London, 1879), pp. 38–60.

[23] *The Life of St Anselm by Eadmer*, ed. and tr. R. W. Southern (London, 1962), p. 45.

[24] *EHD*, ii, 616–18.

customary law of the different parts of the country recorded in Domesday Book and in 'The Laws of Henry I',[25] it is 'the peace given by the king with his own hand, or by his writ, or by his messenger' which appears as the basis of law, not the king's feudal overlordship; and the successful litigant at this period was the man who had secured the king's 'hand-given peace' in the form of a charter of protection for his tenements and retainers, and who went on getting exertions of royal power in his favour, such as writs of right, writs of reseisin ordering the sheriff to restore property before or after a court-judgment, and writs giving the king's political backing to the enforcement of decisions in lower courts (Doc. 7).[26] It could be argued that royal justice, on its civil side, was expanded first of all as a service to those who enjoyed the king's special peace, for grants of land often included protection from being sued for it, except perhaps before the king himself; and, in suing someone else, the assistance of a writ of right may have been the privilege, to start with, of those who had received special protection of their lands.[27] Until the time of Henry II it was not a case of all men enjoying a legal right to forms of action in the king's courts, but only of some men having a moral right to the king's continued political support in their land-transactions, just as an Anglo-Saxon thegn who had once received a land-book could appeal to the king and his court to uphold its provisions. The growth of civil actions, no less than of criminal prosecutions, depended on the widening concept of the king's peace.

The actual trials of the Anglo-Norman period (Doc. 6) do not look very different from those of Anglo-Saxon times (e.g. Doc. 3), except in one respect, that ordeal by battle was now the normal way to decide the issue in both civil and criminal cases.[28] To make the parties fight it out under the supervision of the court was an obvious and easy means of discovering the judgment of God and one which was used all over Europe in early times. The interesting fact is not that the Normans introduced the judicial duel to England, but that the Anglo-Saxons had never felt the need of it.[29] Proof by battle did not have to be awarded to

[25] W. Stubbs, *Charters*, 9th edn (Oxford, 1913), p. 125; *EHD*, ii, 866–9.

[26] See the writs for the execution of judgment printed in Van Caenegem, *Royal Writs*, pp. 508–15; on restoring seisin after trial by battle, Hall, *Glanvill*, p. 26.

[27] A. Harding, 'The medieval brieves of protection and the development of the common law', *Juridical Review* (1966), pp. 126–8; cf. the writs of Naifty printed by Van Caenegem, *Royal Writs*, pp. 467–77 (especially no. 107), in which the order to the sheriff to restore fugitive serfs to a lord again seems to follow from a grant to the latter of the king's peace.

[28] See, e.g. the Domesday cases, Bigelow, *Placita Anglo-Normannica*, pp. 38–60, and *The Anglo-Saxon Chronicle*, ed. and tr. G. N. Garmonsway (London, 1953), p. 232.

[29] But see the interesting though inconclusive article by Morton W. Bloomfield, *Speculum* (1969); William I's ordinance concerning methods of trial is

one side or the other;[30] it was less subtle and required less judicial expertise even than the ordeals of hot iron and cold water. Because it was so much simpler, battle was the enemy of all but the most inescapable of the rational methods of trial. This setback was balanced by the king's increasing use of juries to inquire into his own rights. After the Conquest, the jury or 'inquest' therefore became very much a royal instrument, but it was one which the Domesday survey showed to be ideal for settling doubts and *clamores* about land-tenure under the king,[31] who quickly got the idea of selling the jury-inquest as a 'royal benefit', an alternative to trial by battle, to men whose property was threatened.[32] The Anglo-Saxon technique of mobilizing local knowledge certainly continued to be used in courts at all levels, and for some years after 1066 the people who knew were often men of English blood.[33] In one of the *clamores* of Domesday, the man in possession of the disputed land, Picot, Sheriff of Cambridgeshire, produced 'villeins and mean folk and reeves' to support his case.[34] But once more it was the king who had the resources to develop this old English procedural device, who through his reeves in shire and hundred could compel juries to assemble. Juries carrying up local knowledge met the itinerant justices sent down from the king's court, and so forged the last link in a system of royal justice. The lawmen of the local courts can be glimpsed indicting criminals under oath at the first judicial eyres, in the reign of Henry I (1100–35):[35] this shows the continuity of the old English presenting-jury. But the behaviour of civil trial-juries also required increasing supervision from above, and well before 1100 there is an apparent instance of a twelve-man jury in a land-case in a shire court being attainted (convicted) of perjury by another jury of barons in a special court at London, as a result of which the whole shire was fined £300.[36]

The story of the century between the Conquest and the leap forward in Henry II's reign constituted by the invention of the returnable writ is thus a story of continuity, of the king's progressive tightening of Anglo-Saxon procedures into a coherent system. The lords' courts were incorporated into this royal system, losing their civil jurisdiction to the king's more effective methods and exercising their generally minor criminal jurisdiction on the king's behalf.

translated in Stephenson and Marcham, *English Constitutional History*, p. 35.
[30] Cf. above, p. 25.
[31] Galbraith, *Domesday Book*, pp. 72–3 and 176.
[32] Hall, *Glanvill*, pp. 28 and 30.
[33] Stenton, *English Justice*, pp. 19–21.
[34] Maitland, *Domesday Book and Beyond*, p. 79.
[35] H. G. Richardson and G. O. Sayles, *The Governance of Medieval England* (Edinburgh, 1963), p. 184; but the argument here for criminal jury-*trial* is unconvincing.
[36] Richardson and Sayles, *Law and Legislation*, pp. 37–8.

MERCHANTS' COURTS AND CLERGY'S COURTS

In the twelfth century there was a great revival of Roman legal ideas in western Europe, explicable only in terms of a rapid growth of towns in relatively more peaceful conditions. Commerce flourished, requiring finer legal distinctions between different types of contract and of property less palpable, more 'incorporeal', than land, and better procedures for recovering debts. The bishops who dominated the old *civitates* built up their chanceries and assembled teams of officials whom they trained in the cathedral schools, the seeds of the thirteenth-century universities, where theology and jurisprudence were studied side by side. 'Town air makes free', they said, and it literally did this for the villeins who escaped to live in the towns, which were consolidating their freedoms at the very time, and perhaps because of the fact, that personal freedom in the manorial community was being restricted in the interests of more productive agriculture.[37] The distinctions between town and country were as much legal as social or economic: boroughs were simply rural villages to start with, or even stretches of uninhabited waste with commercial possibilities, to which the king gave, or for which a lord secured, legal privileges in the hope, not always fulfilled, of attracting the artisans and merchants who would make life more civilized and, through tolls and taxes, certainly more profitable. The 'free borough' (*liber burgus*) was founded on charters which gave or confirmed to the community, amongst other privileges, special legal rights and procedures: that the borough will have its own court is assumed. Though this court may have begun as a genuine English folkmoot, its jurisdiction was defined in terms of royal justice, for the towns were part of the king's administrative system. Generally speaking, the early borough court behaved as a separate hundred court, concerned with the king's, not the town's, peace; but the hundred court, where the king's reeve presided but the lawmen or aldermen were the judges, was a good basis for communal government (Doc. 17).[38] When it came in from the open air, the borough court was often called a 'house-thing' or *husting*.

London was unique in privilege, and there the folk-moot which became the husting was the equivalent of a shire court, and the public hundreds were the wards (comparable to the Norwich *leets*: Doc. 17) the private hundreds the 'sokes' of the magnates with town houses. The shire-moot or folk-moot which assembled at St Paul's Cross at the tolling of the cathedral's great bell rapidly became obsolete. The sheriffs

---

[37] M. Beresford, *New Towns of the Middle Ages* (London, 1967), p. 207; Mary Bateson (ed.), *Borough Customs* (Selden Society, London, 1904 and 1906), vol. i, p. 202.

[38] J. Tait, *The Medieval English Borough* (Manchester, 1936), ch. 2, esp. p. 62; *EHD*, ii, 869.

(for London had two at a time) held a court in their own houses to deal with trespasses. But the husting, which seems to have existed from the tenth century to handle commercial disputes, alongside the folk-moot, was the court where Londoners came to transact all their civil litigation.[39] In the twelfth century the husting sat every Monday at the Guildhall, and by 1193 the Mayor dominated its proceedings, though the aldermen were its lawmen.[40] Eventually, two types of husting sessions were distinguished, the Monday 'Husting of Common Pleas', where mayor, sheriffs and aldermen 'did the citizens right' in the king's name and on his writ 'in respect of their lands', and the Mayor's Court, increasingly important, where any day of the week, on mere complaint, the mayor would enforce the public order and commercial regulations of the city, punish fraudulent traders and hear appeals from the Sheriffs' Court. Late thirteenth-century London had an elaborate system of justice, independent of the king's justice except at the apex, where appeals from the husting were taken to royal justices appointed *ad hoc* to sit at St Martin's le Grand.

The normal procedures of English law, devised for a land-holding aristocracy, had to be jettisoned or transformed in the towns where moveable wealth was the important thing. Because the merchant needed to be able to dispose of his capital freely and leave it by will, and might legally deprive his 'next heir' of the inheritance, the Assize of Mort d'Ancestor did not run in the towns.[41] Through their own version of the Assize of Novel Disseisin, called the Assize of Fresh Force, the towns took the lead in transforming a 'remedy devised primarily for an agrarian society' into one which could be used to protect rent-charges and other 'incorporeal things' in an urban society.[42] Amongst business people, pleading and proof were more commonsensical. A perfectly good case should not fail through *miskenning*, some trivial slip in the words of formal pleading to which foreign traders would be particularly liable, 'but such people shall be suffered to state the substance of the case'.[43] 'Excessive usury' was punished in the Norwice leets (Doc. 17); a rudimentary law of agency, the responsibility of a master for the transactions of his servants, is apparent in a London custom of 1285;[44] and in the court of the Fair of St Ives, prices were adjusted and juries of merchants empanelled (Doc. 11). Trade was the basic reason for the

[39] *EHD*, ii, 945 and 959; F. M. Stenton, *Norman London* (Historical Association Pamphlet, London, 1934); Helen M. Cam, 'The law courts of medieval London', in *Lawfinders and Lawmakers in Medieval England* (London, 1962).

[40] A. H. Thomas (ed.), *Calendar of the Early Mayors' Court Rolls of the City of London* (London, 1924), p. xxi.

[41] Bateson, *Borough Customs*, ii, 243.

[42] *Ibid.* 183; Cam, 'Law courts', pp. 96 and 100.

[43] Bateson, *Borough Customs*, i, 233, ii, 88–9.

[44] *Ibid.* ii, 91.

existence of a town court, and the exigencies of trade caused new courts to be improvised, courts of 'Piepowder' which settled the claims of a peripatetic trader 'with dusty feet' (*pieds poudrés*) in time for him to sail on the next tide, or get to tomorrow's market in another town.[45]

The church courts did not, like the town courts, enforce the king's peace. The jurisdiction of the officials of the church in spiritual matters was quite independent in origin of the king's authority in the secular sphere: yet, just because there were these two universal communities of equal authority, the temporal community which was the state and the spiritual community of the church, both claiming the individual man's allegiance, the jurisdiction of the church was much harder to demarcate than that of a particular community of townsmen. Judges no less than the judged moved backwards and forwards across the invisible dividing line between the two worlds. In the secular courts, in *curia regis* and in county, the king's judges were churchmen.[46] When William of St Calais, in 1088, appealed to the Pope from the judgment of Lanfranc and others of the king's barons, he was forcefully reminded that he was not being tried by canon law, but as a contumacious vassal in the feudal *curia regis*: the fact that he was a bishop and Lanfranc an archbishop was irrelevant there.[47]

All churchmen were thus subject to the feudal courts,[48] and the greater ones had their own. A bishop would hold honour courts and hundred courts for the 'private' estates of his bishopric, which might be scattered through several dioceses.[49] Such secular courts should in theory be distinguished from the 'court-christian' held by the bishop for spiritual cases within his own diocese, but it is not clear that the bishop himself always made the distinction: was it a synod or an honour court, that company of bishops, archdeacons and laymen assembled by the Bishop of Bath at 'the apostolic feast' in 1121, which received the king's writ of right (attested, incidentally, by the Bishop of Salisbury as Justiciar of England) and decided the case between a layman and the cathedral monastery of Bath (of which the bishop was the ecclesiastical head, not the overlord)?[50]

In the pre-Conquest situation, where churchmen sat alongside the king's lay officials in shire and hundred to administer the church's law,

---

[45] *Ibid.* 1 and 184.
[46] Stenton, *English Justice*, p. 65.
[47] *EHD*, ii, 609–24.
[48] See ch. 11 of the Constitutions of Clarendon, *EHD*, ii, 719–21.
[49] F. R. H. Du Boulay, *The Lordship of Canterbury* (London, 1966), pp. 297ff; N. R. Holt (ed.), *The Pipe Roll of the Bishopric of Winchester* (Manchester, 1964), pp. xxixff.
[50] This interesting case is printed in Bigelow, *Placita Anglo-Normannica*, pp. 114–17; cf. Van Caenegem, *Royal Writs*, p. 210, n2.

competition between lay and ecclesiastical courts was avoided. But it
seems that the financial penalties imposed at the hundred court for
moral crimes or failure in the ordeal, the judgment of God, which
should have gone to the bishop, were often appropriated by the lay
owners of hundreds.[51] For this reason, and since by then there were
generally archdeacons to act as the bishops' judicial agents, the Conqueror decreed, probably in 1072, that 'no bishop or archdeacon should
henceforth hold pleas relating to the episcopal laws in the hundred
court' but at 'the place which the bishop shall choose and name'.[52] Yet
real ecclesiastical courts were a creation only of the twelfth century,
when the great code of church law, based on papal legislation, was compiled, and a European-wide system of ecclesiastical justice was con-
structed under the pope's direction.[53]

Not until Henry II was king and Thomas Becket, once the king's
Chancellor, Archbishop of Canterbury, were there church courts distinct enough for the possibility to exist of conflict between them and the
king's courts. In the Constitutions of Clarendon of 1164, the king produced, and asked the bishops to accept, his definition of the relationship
of the king's justice and the church's justice, one which was of course
favourable to the king's power and profit.[54]

On one of the two main issues between King Henry and Archbishop
Thomas, the punishment of clergy who had committed crimes, the
archbishop was neither wrong in canon law nor arguing a trivial point
when he maintained that a criminous clerk should not be punished
twice for the same offence (that is, both by deprivation of his orders in
the church court and by the secular penalty in the king's court). The
whole intention of clause (3) of the Constitutions, which seems to have
envisaged that a clerk would first be accused in the king's court, transferred – when he was found to be a clerk – to the ecclesiastical court and
tried there under the eye of a royal official, finally to be returned to the
king's court shorn of his orders, was to make the Church a subordinate
cog in the king's judicial machine: the Church was to be intimidated
into doing the mechanical thing, the deprivation of orders, which would
bring the accused within the scope of secular penalties.[55]

Becket's resistance forced the king to come to terms on the issue
of criminous clerks. Thenceforward, it was agreed, a clerk would
claim benefit of clergy on being accused in the king's court and be
handed over to the bishop's officer for the church court to deal with
him finally: he would not be returned to the secular authority. But the

[51] Colin Morris, 'William I and the Church courts', *EHR* (1967), lxxxii.
[52] *EHD*, ii, 604.
[53] G. le Bras, *Histoire du droit de l'Eglise: L'Age Classique* (Paris, 1965).
[54] *EHD*, ii, 719–21.
[55] C. Duggan, 'The Becket Dispute and the criminous clerks', *Bulletin of the
Institute of Historical Research* (henceforth *BIHR*) (1961).

king's officials – clerks themselves, be it noted – went on fighting for the interests of the state, within the limits set by canonical principles. As jury-trial came to be applied to criminals at the beginning of the thirteenth century, the royal officials insisted that before a criminous clerk was surrendered to the Church, a verdict on his guilt should be taken in the lay court (Doc. 12 (28*d*)). If the clerk was convicted then, he forfeited his goods to the king like any layman, and even if he purged himself in the church court would get them back only by the king's grace. A clerk suspected of crime who fled before being brought to court was outlawed in the normal way. Towards the end of the thirteenth century, the church courts, partly under royal pressure, replaced the easy test of compurgation by jury-trial. Clerks convicted by the ecclesiastical trial were sometimes compelled to abjure the realm after degradation. Or they might be made to undergo limited or perpetual imprisonment as an alternative to degradation, so that the bishops' prisons bulked large in medieval England, containing as they did both clerks who had been sentenced and those intentionally kept waiting by the secular authorities for the preliminary trial without which they could not purge themselves in Court Christian and gain release.[56]

More serious still than the issue of the criminous clerks was the claim of the first clause of the Constitutions that the king's courts must have jurisdiction in disputes concerning advowsons. The right to present to a living was a valuable piece of property to its owner, whether he was a layman or an ecclesiastical corporation like a monastery, but to the Church as a whole the presentation of clerks fit for their task was essentially a spiritual matter. The papacy could not, and never did, give up the right to decide whether a particular clerk was acceptable or not, while the King of England was bound to insist that the right to present was subject to his developing law of property.[57] In the days before the two types of court had separated, the *curia regis*, filled with high ecclesiastics, had decided disputes about the profits arising from such apparently spiritual functions as burying the dead (Doc. 6). Two of Henry II's four 'petty assizes', applying jury-trial to specific property issues, were concerned with ecclesiastical property. The writ in the assize of *darrein presentment* asked who had presented to a vacant living when it was last vacant: he should have the presentation again. The assize called *utrum* decided the preliminary issue, whether the disputed tenement of a priest was held in free alms or for some real feudal ser-

[56] Leona Gabel, *Benefit of clergy in England in the later Middle Ages* (Smith College Studies in History, 1929); A. L. Poole in *Historical Essays in Honour of James Tait* (Manchester, 1933); R. B. Pugh, *Imprisonment in Medieval England* (Cambridge, 1968), pp. 237–9.
[57] C. R. Cheney, *From Becket to Langton* (Manchester, 1956), pp. 109ff; J. W. Gray, 'The *Ius Praesentandi* in England from the Constitutions of Clarendon to Bracton', *EHR* (1952), lxvii.

vice: if feudally, the dispute should be heard in the lord's feudal court, or, if the tenant and claimant were the vassals of different lords, then in the court of the king (Doc. 9). In fact, no priest would want to take a land case through the church courts and perhaps all the way to Rome. He preferred to use *utrum* in the king's court to protect the land he lived from, proving that it was held in free alms and therefore his glebe-land. The writ initiating *utrum* became 'the parson's writ of right'.[58]

The king's courts could be 'a good thing' for the lower clergy; and better still, once the two types of court had separated, was the opportunity to play one off against the other. If a church court heard a case arising from an advowson and inhabiting the debatable land between the temporal and the spiritual, or a plea which could be construed as concerning a lay fee or a debt, the defendant could obtain a royal writ of *prohibition* to halt the case and take it into the king's court. The plaintiff might not think it worth while, however, to start his case over again, and so this writ (perhaps invented towards 1170, at the height of Henry II's struggle with Becket) was another of those procedural manoeuvres by which the clever defendant could put off judgment to kingdom come. To the fury of the prelates, whose jurisdiction was diminished, it was a manoeuvre at which their own clergy were particularly adept.[59]

The writ of prohibition shows once again the formidable nature of the king's procedural armoury, which subordinated the prelate's courts to the interests of the king's justice in the same way as it subordinated the courts of the lay barons. Justice was a matter of effective procedures, which belonged to the supreme political power in the country; and there could only be one such power. Yet the co-operation and inter-dependence of the jurisdictions of Church and king should be emphasized quite as much as conflict. There were some issues, marital issues like that on which Richard of Anstey's case turned,[60] which no one disputed that the Church alone could decide: when they arose in a case before the king's judges, they would be referred thankfully to the bishop by the king's writ. The Church was essential to the workings of the secular courts themselves, for no case could be settled by oath or ordeal without the participation of a priest. Certain major churches, it seems, had the right to 'stage' ordeals, and royal and seignorial justices had to send criminals to them for trial. Consequently the bishops preserved an important rôle in the king's justice after 1072, and are found granting the right to hold ordeals to other churches and to laymen. The possession of this right may have been the basis for the later privilege of cer-

[58] For *utrum* see the Constitutions of Clarendon, ch. 9, and S. E. Thorne, *Columbia Law Review* (1933).

[59] Cheney, *Becket to Langton*, p. 110; G. B. Flahiff on the writ of prohibition in *Medieval Studies* (1941).

[60] For the celebrated Anstey case, see *EHD*, ii, 456–7.

tain bishops and abbots to have separate sessions of the justices of the eyre on their territory.[61]

Conversely, the sheriff's executive power was essential to the functioning of the church's jurisdiction. The lay power was needed to burn the convicted apostate from the Christian religion and, later on, the heretic.[62] As indictment by 'the witness of the neighbourhood' and trial by jury, were adopted in the Church courts, it was the sheriff who assembled the jurors.[63] And it was for the execution of the judgment, as much as for the judgment itself, that cases like Richard of Anstey's went back to the king's court.[64]

Ecclesiastical justice and lay justice needed each other, but the balance of need moved steadily towards the Church. Churchmen could not be directly involved in punishment involving the shedding of blood, and so were at a disadvantage as royal judges. The Old English ordeal, which required the participation of the Church, gave way before trial by battle, which excluded it,[65] and before trial by juries which were summoned by the sheriff for the Church courts as well as the king's. Excommunication was the only resource the Church had against those who defied its courts – this was the ecclesiastical equivalent of outlawry. It would have carried little weight if there had not been developed, by the early thirteenth century, a procedure by which the bishop could apply to the king's chancery for a writ (of *Significavit*) ordering the sheriff to imprison the excommunicate who remained defiant. The procedure was in constant use till the early seventeenth century and was a testimony to the co-operation and interdependence of Church and State in England.[66] The reason for this relationship, unique in Western Europe, was surely the procedural resourcefulness of the king's government rather than any special characteristic of the English Church.

Some of the English king's authority and executive power rubbed off on to the primate, and helped him to acquire judicial rights in England not known elsewhere in the Catholic Church. In the teeth of the protests of his bishops, the archbishop entertained direct complaints from the subjects of his diocesans and enforced a claim to testamentary jurisdiction throughout his province where the testators' property was distributed over more than one diocese.[67]

[61] Naomi Hurnard, 'The Anglo-Norman franchises', *EHR* (1949), lxiv.

[62] F. W. Maitland, *Roman Canon Law in the Church of England* (London, 1898), pp. 158ff.

[63] Richardson and Sayles, *Law and Legislation*, p. 88; cf. ch. 6 of the Constitutions of Clarendon.

[64] Richardson and Sayles, *Law and Legislation*, p. 61.

[65] Hurnard, *EHR* (1949), p. 457.

[66] F. D. Logan, *Excommunication and the secular arm in Medieval England* (Toronto, 1968).

[67] F. M. Powicke and C. R. Cheney (eds.), *Councils and Synods of the English*

It is likely nevertheless that in the middle years of the twelfth century, when the church courts and the king's courts had still not broken completely apart, the Church contributed a good deal to the growth of the common law. The Church may have made the crucial distinction between possessory and proprietary questions first, and used juries of rural deans and local priests to decide questions of rightful possession of incumbencies before the king did;[68] and it had its books of procedure (the *ordines judiciarii*) to carry forward cases in the church courts, and formal missives which read rather like (for instance) writs of praecipe.[69] Further, the written complaint of trespass is, in form, quite like the *libellus* or 'bill' of Roman-Canon law, and was presented to a royal justice who was a churchman. Finally, one should note that all the 'original writs' which initiated the forms of action invented in the later twelfth century were framed, in answer to the bills of plaintiffs, by clerics in the king's chancery who must have been familiar with papal *rescripts*, multiplying in the mid-twelfth century. By rescript, the pope gave instructions to his judges-delegate on the handling of a case, referring to the plaintiff's *libellus* by the very phrase (*Conquerente nobis R.*) which began the writ of novel disseisin (*Questus est mihi N.*).[70]

The greater complication of the relationship between the various church courts and the distances involved in appeals to Rome meant a greater reliance on documents to maintain communications.[71] Bishops' registers are largely made up of copies of such legal documents. This kind of resourcefulness in the Church's judicial system was transferred to the king's new 'conciliar' courts of the later Middle Ages,[72] Chancery, Star Chamber and the rest, which were designed to make up for defects in common-law procedures, and relied extensively (like the church courts) on written instructions to local commissioners to take evidence,

Church (Oxford, 1964) (for the diocesans' protests against the archbishop's claims to jurisdiction in 1281); I. J. Churchill, *Canterbury Administration* (London, 1933), vol. i, pp. 380ff and 460ff; Priscilla J. Wood, 'Tuitorial appeal to the Archbishops of Canterbury and York in the thirteenth century' (Edinburgh M.Litt. thesis, 1970).

[68] Gray, *EHR* (1962); A. Harding, *Scottish Historical Review* (1967), p. 153.

[69] Jane E. Sayers, 'A judge delegate formulary from Canterbury', *BIHR* (1962), p. 202, no. 2: '. . . tibi mandamus quatinus admoneatis prefatum H . . .'; cf. F. Schulz, 'The writ "praecipe quod reddat" and its continental models', *Juridical Review* (1942), liv.

[70] William J. La Due, *Papal Rescripts of Justice and English Royal Procedural Writs 1150–1250* (Rome, 1960); for examples of rescripts, see Sayers, *loc. cit.* and Robert Brentano, *York Metropolitan Jurisdiction and Papal Judges Delegate (1279–1296)* (Berkeley and Los Angeles, 1959), pp. 226ff. The authoritative work on canon-law procedure in England is now Jane E. Sayers, *Papal Judges Delegate in the Province of Canterbury* (Oxford, 1971).

[71] Sayers, *BIHR* (1962), p. 202 no. 2; Maitland, *Roman Canon Law*, ch. III, 'The Universal Ordinary'.

[72] See below, ch. 3, for the conciliar courts.

written 'interrogatories' listing the questions to be asked,[73] and injunctions (comparable to ecclesiastical inhibitions) ordering or prohibiting specific actions by the parties.

Cases in the church courts were divided into those *ex officio promoto*, in which the judges exercised their disciplinary authority on behalf of the Church (roughly equivalent to a criminal indictment in the king's courts); those brought at the instance (*ad instantiam*) of private individuals, which we might call 'civil' cases; and those *ex officio promoto ad instantiam*, which, like the later 'informations' in the king's courts,[74] were initiated by private individuals but taken up officially by the judges. Ecclesiastical judges normally worked without juries and therefore had a much more positive rôle than their secular colleagues in weighing evidence and testing the reliability of witnesses.[75] Knowing, like Abbot Samson of Bury St Edmunds, that 'the merits of causes are revealed by the statements of the parties', the judge in a church court disbelieved what he heard on principle, and used a glance which was 'sharp and penetrating' and a brow 'worthy of Cato'.[76]

THE ANGEVIN REVOLUTION IN JUSTICE

Henry, son of Geoffrey, Count of Anjou, and Matilda, daughter of Henry I, succeeded to the English throne in 1154, beginning a reign which lasted thirty-five years. This event merely added England to enormous territorial possessions in France which already comprised Anjou, Normandy (wrested from King Stephen by Count Geoffrey) and Aquitaine. The coming of the Angevin dynasty had a double significance for English law. Firstly, it represented the triumph of hereditary succession to the realm of England, regarded simply as a piece of land, and Henry II registered this fact by changing his title from 'king of the English' to 'King of England'. Because recognition of hereditary succession to the realm entailed recognition on the king's part of his barons' right to inherit their lordships within the realm,[77] Henry was concerned from the start with devising legal processes for settling disputes about land-titles, which had been left over in quantities from the civil war of Stephen's reign. Secondly, Henry was not only *rex Angliae* but *dux Normanniae et Aquitaniae et comes Andegaviae*: Poitiers, not London, was the centre of 'the Angevin empire', of which England was only a

---

[73] Churchill, *Canterbury Administration*, i, 427ff, 486–7 and 495–7 for the commissioners; Brentano, *York Metropolitan Jurisdiction*, pp. 235ff for interrogatories.

[74] See below, ch. 3.

[75] Brentano, *York Metropolitan Jurisdiction*, pp. 235ff.

[76] *The Chronicle of Jocelin of Brakelond*, ed. and tr. by H. E. Butler (London, 1949), pp. 33–4.

[77] R. H. C. Davis, 'What happened in Stephen's reign', *History* (1964).

province. The king was almost always somewhere else than in *this* part of his territories, and either plaintiffs had, like Richard of Anstey, to pursue the king abroad for justice, or (as Anstey's case also shows) the government and law of each particular territory had to become 'self-propelled', capable of working automatically in the absence of their master.[78]

The office of the Justiciar of England provided the basis for such judicial machinery. It seems to have been Henry I who created this office, back in the first decade of the twelfth century, when he reunited England with the Duchy of Normandy, separated from the kingdom since the death of the Conqueror, and was thereafter compelled to devote a good deal of time to his possessions across the Channel.[79] The main responsibility of the first justiciar, Roger, Bishop of Salisbury, was to supervise the king's fast-growing fiscal organization, the Exchequer; but the *curia regis* was not divided up into departments, and Roger was also, as his title suggests,[80] the chief of the 'justices of all England' (*justiciarii totius Anglie*) who could be sent out from the *curia* to hear pleas anywhere in the country, and so-called in contrast to the justiciars of the individual counties (*justiciarii comitatuum*). Roger of Salisbury made the office of justiciar and made it very much his own, until his family's control of the government became so threatening that King Stephen precipitately removed him in 1139. Henry II, unlike Stephen but like his grandfather, kept his servants within bounds. After the Anarchy, his choice of ministers was limited – he had to go begging to Archbishop Theobald of Canterbury for a chancellor, and was given Becket – but eventually he found two men to share the functions of justiciar. Robert, Earl of Leicester, Henry chose because he was the richest of the barons, whose loyalty needed securing; Richard de Lucy, because, though a layman, he was able and willing to do the work. Richard may have drafted the Constitutions of Clarendon. From the Earl of Leicester's death in 1168 until he himself retired into a monastery of his own foundation in 1178, he was Henry's sole justiciar.[81]

Richard's great work was the organization of the Exchequer, which he presided over as an increasingly specialized court, sitting

> 'to interpret the law and to decide disputed points which frequently arise from incidental questions. For the superior science of the Exchequer consists not in its methods of reckoning but in the multiplicity of its judgments. . . . When one begins to make a detailed

[78] *EHD*, ii, 456–7.

[79] The best account of the origins of the justiciarship is in Richardson and Sayles, *Governance*.

[80] In fact, Roger of Salisbury was usually called *procurator*.

[81] F. J. West, *The Justiciarship in England, 1066–1232* (Cambridge, 1966), for the careers of the justiciars.

investigation of the moneys which come into the Treasury in various ways, and are due for different accounts and are not collected by the sheriffs in the same manner, to be able to discover if the latter have acted in any wise other than they should, this is in many ways a serious business. . . .'[82]

The *memoranda rolls* of the Exchequer, which probably started during Richard de Lucy's justiciarship though they survive only from a later date, record this multiplicity of judgments and may be regarded as the earliest series of plea-rolls from any court.[83] Similarly, the sign of Richard's greatness to the outside world, the writs issued on his own authority to summon sheriffs and others to the Exchequer, some running in the king's name, some in his own, may be regarded as the first writs emanating from a regular office, rather than from the personal will of the king; and the purpose of these writs, sealed with a copy of the Great Seal kept in the treasury, was to originate judicial processes.

But there was no sense yet that the justiciar was the director and organizer of English justice as a whole. Finance, not justice, made the justiciarship into an office of government which had to continue even when Henry II appointed his wife or son to act as his viceroys in England. Certainly, Richard de Lucy headed the eyres which enforced the Assize of Clarendon[84] – but then the eyre always had a general administrative function. Gradually, however, administration broadened out to justice for all in all matters. First the Exchequer brought the sheriff under a strong central control by calling him up twice yearly to account for the shire revenues, and then the shire court was subordinated to a centralized system of justice. The *Dialogue of the Exchequer* was Richard de Lucy's memorial: the memorial of his successor as justiciar, Rannulf Glanvill, was the great *Treatise on the laws and customs of the realm of England commonly called Glanvill*, composed just a decade after the *Dialogue*.[85]

Whether Glanvill did write the book has been argued for a long time.[86] What is clear is that his justiciarship was the period when a methodical organization of justice was undertaken; though the tentative air of *Glanvill* as compared with the *Dialogue* shows that legal change and innovation continued unabated. For Glanvill there are laws and customs of the realm 'which had their origin in reason' and which the king follows, though they are unwritten and though there is a 'confused

[82] *EHD*, ii, 499.

[83] On the origins of plea-rolls, see H. G. Richardson's introduction to *The Memoranda Roll for the Michaelmas Term of the First Year of the Reign of King John* (Pipe Roll Society, London, 1943).

[84] For the Assize of Clarendon, see below, p. 55.

[85] *Dialogus de Scaccario*, ed. and tr. by C. Johnson (London, 1950); also printed in translation in *EHD*, ii; Hall, *Glanvill*.

[86] Hall, *Glanvill*, pp. xxx–xxxiii.

multiplicity of these same laws and rules'.[87] Moreover, the legal machinery is now 'self-propelled' too: writs come from the king 'or the chief justice', and examples given in the book are witnessed by Glanvill himself.[88] The answer to Professor Holt's question 'why a vice-regent should be necessary when the king journeyed to Normandy but not when he journeyed to Northumberland'[89] is surely that there was now a judicial system recognized as specific to, and co-terminous with, the kingdom of England, and needing constant direction. In fact, after the two years interval between de Lucy's retirement and Glanvill's appointment, there is a justiciar whether the king is at home or abroad. *Glanvill* was a new sort of law-book, made necessary by a new common law, which was a working collection of procedures continually supplemented by a new sort of legislation, the working judgments of *assizes* or sessions of the king's court. It is interesting to contrast the procedural rules of the English judicial system as *Glanvill* presents them at the end of Henry II's reign (Doc. 9), and the Old English laws prescribing the worth and duties of the various ranks of society which really end with the 'Laws of Henry I': clearly there is a watershed in the mid-twelfth century. The continued elaboration of this new legal machinery was guaranteed by the presence in Rannulf Glanvill's household of two great justices of the next generation, Hubert Walter and the future King John.

The basis of Henry II's new judicial structure was the general eyre. Despite the *justiciarii totius Anglie*, Henry I's reign must be described as a time when the local public courts reigned supreme (Doc. 7), and even the most powerful abbey made enormous annual payments to the sheriff for his judicial favours.[90] Henry I was intent on strengthening shire justice, rather than on replacing it by royal eyres. He fostered the office of the county justiciar, with his own court and quite independent of the sheriff, to handle the pleas (either criminal or based on a royal grant of land or peace) which were reserved to the crown.[91] In fact, it seems more and more probable that Henry I only confirmed an office the beginnings of which lay in the reign of William II or even that of the Conqueror himself. It was in the 1070s that a special shire justice with

[87] *Ibid.* pp. 2–3.

[88] *Ibid.* pp. 9, 105, 112 and 148.

[89] Professor J. C. Holt in a review of West, *The Justiciarship*, in *EHR* (1969), p. 606.

[90] J. Stevenson (ed.), *Chronicon monasterii de Abingdon* (Rolls Series, London, 1858), vol. ii, p. 230. For the debate on the judicial arrangements of Henry I's reign, see Richardson and Sayles, *Governance* and *Law and Legislation*; Stenton, *English Justice*; West, *The Justiciarship*, and W. T. Reedy, *Speculum* (1966).

[91] Stenton, *English Justice*, pp. 65–6; H. A. Cronne in *University of Birmingham Historical Journal* (1937); H. A. Cronne and R. H. C. Davis (eds.), *Regesta Regum Anglo-Normannorum* (Oxford, 1967), vol. III, nos. 84 and 490.

more judicial expertise than the sheriff became necessary, for the ordinance of *c.* 1072 reduced the participation of churchmen in shire and hundred courts.[92] At any rate, by Stephen's reign, the office of county justiciar had become an object of ambition for the greatest barons. In Lincolnshire it was granted in 1154 to the third Bishop of Lincoln in succession.[93]

Brilliant innovation, rather than continuity with earlier judicial patterns, is therefore the mark of Henry II's actions in 1166, when he sent out the second Geoffrey de Mandeville and Richard de Lucy on an eyre which was intended to cover all England (though, in the event, counties in the north and west escaped 'the pleas of Earl Geoffrey and Richard de Lucy').[94] The aftermath of civil war was the classic situation, many times repeated in the history of medieval England, for judicial experiment. The *Dialogus* tells us that 'from the very beginning of his reign' Henry II 'applied his whole mind to this, that by manifold victories he might destroy rebels and malcontents, and altogether seal the hearts of men with the blessings of peace and confidence'.[95] The situation was repeated more than once in Henry's own reign. In 1173 a great baronial revolt led by his own sons broke around Henry's head.

> 'When, therefore peace had been restored, after the shipwrecked state of the kingdom, the king strove to renew the times of his grandfather, and choosing discreet men he divided the realm into six parts in order that the justices selected, whom we call itinerant, might pass through it on circuit, and re-establish the laws which had been abandoned. So, giving the king abundant opportunity of seeking advice in the several counties, and exhibiting full justice to those who considered themselves wronged, they spared the poor both labour and expense.'

The general eyre was forged in repeated crises.[96]

By 1168 the justiciars of counties had disappeared from sight, for it was the justice of the local public courts, rather than seignorial justice, which the eyre immediately displaced. Henry II built up a new corps of judges based on the *curia regis*.[97] They are classified by the Pipe Roll of 1176–7 as justices *errantes* (in eyre), *in curia regis* and *ad scaccarium* (at

---

[92] See above, p. 44.

[93] Stenton, *English Justice*, p. 66; Cronne and Davis, *Regesta Regum* vol. III, nos. 274–6; for a general view of 'Law and the Administration of Justice under Stephen' see H. A. Cronne, *The Reign of Stephen* (London, 1970), ch. 9.

[94] Stenton, *English Justice*, pp. 71–2; and now J. C. Holt, 'The assizes of Henry II: the texts' in *The Study of Medieval Records: Essays in Honour of Kathleen Major*, ed. D. A. Bullough and R. L. Storey (Oxford, 1971).

[95] *EHD*, ii, 535.

[96] *EHD*, ii, 537.

[97] Stenton, *English Justice*, pp. 73ff.

the Exchequer), but these were not distinct groups of specialists. Difficult cases would be adjourned from the shire courts, where the eyre
happened to be, for the king's decision as he himself moved about the
country, and in 1178 Henry told off five justices to remain always in his
court to deal with such cases and remit only those which even they
could not decide to the actual presence of the king in the wider *curia
regis*.[98] In this way a new law court *coram rege* (later known as 'King's
Bench') was created within the *curia regis*, which of course had heard
land-cases amongst the feudal magnates since the time of the Conquest.[99]
Other cases which could not be settled before the eyre in a particular
shire, on account, perhaps, of the absence of parties or juries, might be
adjourned to the exchequer, which had the great advantage of a fixed
and known location in Westminster Hall.

In his council at Windsor at Easter 1179, Henry set on foot his most
extensive eyre of all, at the same time as he introduced the Grand
Assize.[100] Twenty-one judges were to tour the country on four circuits,
the six on the northern circuit also holding themselves ready, like the
five judges of 1178, to hear appeals to the king. A chronicler writes that
'at one time the king made use of the abbots, at another of the earls, at
another of the tenants-in-chief, at other times of the servants of his
household and his most intimate counsellors to hear and judge cases'.
But for the chief justices of the circuits in 1179 Henry could find no
uncorruptible men till 'he raised his eyes to heaven and borrowed help
from the spiritual order'. He chose, in fact, three prelates known for their
services in the world, Richard of Ilchester, formerly Archdeacon of
Poitiers, royal ambassador and reformer of the administration of Normandy, then bishop of the immensely wealthy see of Winchester (he
may have introduced the post of the bishop's official to England);[101]
Geoffrey Ridel, Bishop of Ely, formerly Archdeacon of Canterbury and
the king's agent against Becket; and John of Oxford, then Bishop of
Norwich. And as the leader of the northern group who were also the
justices *coram rege*, he appointed Rannulf Glanvill, one of the sheriffs
removed for corruption in 1170 who had redeemed himself as Sheriff
of Lancashire and captor of the invading Scottish king, William the
Lion, in 1174.

The scale of Henry II's venture can be measured in the fines taken.
The Pipe Roll for 1176–7 records 1215 debts to the king arising from
this eyre, amounting to £2794 and 7625 marks: the comparable figures
for fines taken by the king's justices in the roll of 1129–30 are a mere 162

[98] *EHD*, ii, 482; Stenton, *English Justice*, p. 75.
[99] Miller, *Ely*, p. 173; Richardson and Sayles, *Governance*, p. 192.
[100] For the grand assize see below, p. 60; for the eyre of 1179, Stenton,
English Justice, p. 76; and *EHD*, ii, 481.
[101] C. Duggan, *TRHS* (1966).

debts amounting to £438 and 2722 marks.[102] The parties in a civil case
had to pay the king for each step in the procedure, and the defeated party
in a civil case was also fined (fine meaning the payment or *amercement*
'finally' agreed upon by the king and the man who had put himself in
the king's mercy by his legal defeat); but the impression the *Dialogue*
gives of the eyre as essentially a criminal court is correct, at least for its
early days. The Assize of Clarendon of 1166, from which Henry II's
eyres stem, decreed that twelve free and lawful men from each hundred
and four men from each township should 'present' lists of people suspected of 'murder or theft or robbery or of harbouring men who do such
things', and that these people should be imprisoned to await trial
before the justices when they came to the shire (cf. Doc. 8).[103] The
method of presentment, which, in the grand jury, survived till this
century in England and survives still in the United States, was not new
even in 1166. Mentioned in Ethelred's laws (Doc. 2), it was fostered by
the events of the eleventh century. William I tried to stop the murder of
his followers by the natives 'in woods and remote places', as Cnut may
have done before him, by the law that whenever a corpse was found the
hundred should 'make presentment of Englishry' (swear that the corpse
was that of an Englishman) or pay a crippling fine for *murdrum*.[104] The
presentment of offenders was probably well-developed at the tourn of
the sheriff in the hundred courts, before it was required at the visitations
of the justices in eyre to the shire courts. Nevertheless, the record in the
Pipe Rolls of fines for harbouring outlaws, the confiscation of outlaws'
chattels, the building of county jails (required by the Assize of Clarendon) and the digging and blessing of ordeal pits, and the lists of 'those
who perished in the ordeal of water', testify to the quite new intensity
and thoroughness of the campaign against crime in 1166.[105]

Machinery which was effective in catching criminals was easily con-
vertible to the demands of administration in general.

The parties of itinerant justices inevitably attracted the sort of functions the Domesday commissioners had performed. The Assize of
Northampton of 1176 which remedied the defects of the Assize of
Clarendon[106] instructed the justices to inquire into the king's feudal
profits – the 'escheats, churches, lands and women, who are in the gift

[102] Reedy, *Speculum* (1966).

[103] *EHD*, ii, 407–10; Holt, 'Assizes of Henry II'. Professor Holt argues that
the sheriffs not only imprisoned, but also tried, the criminals presented in the
counties which the justices did not reach.

[104] *EHD*, ii, 523; Naomi Hurnard, 'The jury of presentment and the Assize of
Clarendon', *EHR* (1941), lvi; Richardson and Sayles, *Law and Legislation*, p. 52.

[105] Stenton, *English Justice*, p. 71; cf. G. Neilson, *Trial by Combat* (Glasgow,
1890), p. 82, for the Scottish 'Assize of Clarendon', issued by King William in
1175 when he was released from Henry II's prison.

[106] Richardson and Sayles, *Law and Legislation*, pp. 96–9.

of the lord king'. The scope of the inquiry was widened further still to include the custody of castles and the names of fugitives from the king-dom; and the justices were told to receive oaths of fealty to the king from everyone, from the earls downwards, who 'wished to remain in the kingdom', and to see (under pain of judgment in the *curia* for contempt) to the razing of the castles of the rebels of 1173 (Doc. 8). This was an exceptionally troubled time: yet administration grew by making un-usual expedients into routine techniques. Articles of inquiry like those of 1176 and of the Inquest of Sheriffs, a systematic inquiry in 1170 into the malpractices of sheriffs and other local officials, chiefly in the execu-tion of the Assize of Clarendon, and of ecclesiastical and baronial officials as well,[107] were the basis of the 'chapters of the Eyre', first codified in 1194.[108] In the last ten years of Henry II's reign eyres be-came still more frequent, they were given the Assize of Arms of 1181 and the Assize of the Forests of 1184 to enforce, and they steadily grew in importance 'as a means of communication between the King and his subjects'.[109]

Henry II's innovations on the criminal side all concerned the initial prosecution of criminals: trial mostly remained as it had been from the earliest times of English law. Even as a way of indicting criminals the Assize of Clarendon was not an unmitigated success, for its immediate result was the mass flight of men threatened with arrest, and accusations 'for reward or promise or from hatred or other unjust cause'.[110] The Assize of Northampton, which reinforced and to some extent revised the earlier measure, shows the criminal law still resting on ancient practices like the banishment from the kingdom of men of ill-fame, even if they have come safely through the ordeal of water (Doc. 8). And the personal accusation or 'Appeal' of the wronged person or (in the case of homicide) his next-of-kin remained the normal way of securing redress for individual injuries, presentment being too crude an instrument to do more than indict or 'point out' notorious criminals with long records of serious felonies (Doc. 10).

After the Conquest, battle between accuser and accused became an alternative method of trial in these cases of private accusation of crime, just as it did in land disputes; it is doubtful indeed whether accusations of crime and civil suits were distinguished at all clearly even in the twelfth century. For a time after 1066, Englishmen were allowed to choose the old familiar ordeals in preference to battle, but eventually appellants and the men they accused were made to fight it out, and they

---

[107] Stenton, *English Justice*, p. 74; *EHD*, ii, 437ff.
[108] See below, p. 65.
[109] Stenton, *English Justice*, pp. 76–7; cf. Richardson and Sayles, *Law and Legislation*, pp. 99 and 102.
[110] *EHD*, ii, 440.

did so with a ferocity lacking in the duels of champions in land-cases.[111] Particularly savage were the duels in which a criminal, turned 'approver', tried to save his own life by convicting his accomplices 'on their bodies'. Bracton appears to recommend the teeth as weapons in the judicial duel;[112] and at Fordwich an approver who accused a freeman of the town had to fight up to his navel in the waters of the Stour.[113] God and His saints passed judgment on the accused man if he lost, and the king's judges saw to his speedy execution, while the defeated accuser was a convicted perjurer. For crimes brought to court other than by Appeal, the ordeals of water or hot iron provided the mode of trial. The jury was used by Henry II to answer every conceivable question except that of guilt, for 'only God knows the heart of a man'.

A great change took place in the course of the twelfth century in the penalties for crime, one which reflected the growth of kingship as a public office, responsible for maintaining order in society. The elaborate Old English tariffs of compensation 'disappeared with marvellous suddenness'.[114] The felonies, from homicide down to theft of more than a certain value, placed the felons' lives and limbs in the king's mercy, and for lesser offences the criminal was 'amerced' in money. In practice, the fate of the convicted felon was left to the judges' discretion, so long as the king got all his property. (Land which the felon held in fee was returned to the felon's lord after being wasted for the king's profit for a year and a day.) At one time it was fashionable to remove a felon's hand and foot, at another, eyes and testicles: the popularity of stories in which a St Wulfstan of Worcester or St Thomas of Canterbury makes whole again the mutilated felon is some indication of the frequency of these horrible punishments.[115] In the thirteenth century, however, hanging, already normal for homicide, was gradually extended to all felonies. The idea of the felony, the peculiarly nasty offence which somehow poisoned the felon's blood and his family's, and the blood-punishment which it was regarded as meriting, at last gave rise to the crucial distinction between criminal and civil law. In the thirteenth century, the Appeal became a specifically criminal action by which the appellant could get no compensation for the injuries to himself as a private person. It was seen to be wrong to encourage people, by hope of monetary gain, to send others to the executioner's rope or knife.

[111] The most detailed account of a criminal duel is to be found in R. R. Darlington (ed.), *The Vita Wulfstani of William of Malmesbury* (Camden Society, London, 1928), pp. 170–5.
[112] *Bracton on the Laws and Customs of England*, vol. ii, tr. S. E. Thorne (Cambridge, Mass., 1968), p. 410.
[113] Bateson, *Borough Customs*, i, 33.
[114] F. Pollock and F. M. Maitland, *The History of English Law before the Time of Edward I*, 2nd edn (Cambridge, 1898), vol. ii, pp. 458ff.
[115] Richardson, *Vita Wulfstani*, pp. 170–5.

The other great innovation of Henry II, alongside the systematic eyre, was the writ ordering the sheriff to summon the defendant in a land dispute (usually the sitting tenant) to appear before the justices and concluding with the words: 'And have there the summoners and this writ' (Doc. 9). In this last clause is the heart of the matter. The earlier 'executive' writs of right were writs-patent (left open for all to see), which relied on the majesty of the king's Great Seal to secure compliance from those to whom they were exhibited.[116] The new 'returnable' writs were folded over and sealed 'close', since they contained instructions for the sheriff alone; instructions to summon parties and juries, view the land in dispute, and above all return the writs themselves to the justices endorsed with notes of the action taken. From the nature of the writ the justices would know what the dispute was about, what 'form of action' they were dealing with. This type of writ was thus an 'original writ', intended to originate a quite specific judicial process before royal justices. It is difficult to see in it Professor Van Caenegem's gradual evolution from the earlier writs of right, or anything but a stroke of genius on the part of Henry II's government.

Naturally enough the clause 'And have . . .' was probably first attached to the executive writ which ordered a lord or the defendant himself to do right. Called *Precipe* ('Command . . .'), this writ now goes to the sheriff and instructs him to pass on the order to the defendant. It is the first writ in Glanvill's *Treatise*:

'When anyone complains to the lord king or his justices concerning his fee or free tenement, and the case is such that it ought to be, or the lord king is willing that it should be, tried in the king's court, then the complainant shall have the following writ of summons: the king to the sheriff greeting. Command N. to render to R., justly and without delay, one hide of land in such-and-such a vill, which the said R. complains that the aforesaid N. is withholding from him. If he does not do so, summon him by good summoners to be before me or my justices on the day after the Octave of Easter, to show why he has not done so. And have there the summoners and this writ. Witness Rannulf Glanvill, at Clarendon.'[117]

It is clear that the command by the sheriff is a formality, not expected to be obeyed: the intention is normally that there shall be a hearing about the title to the land before the king's justices.

The technique of 'the writ of right *Precipe*' opened the way for a further stroke of genius – though, if we are to believe Bracton, sleepless nights were necessary also for the devising of the Assize of Novel Dis-

---

[116] Hall, *Glanvill*, pp. 17ff; Stenton, *English Justice*, pp. 32–4; for executive writs, see above, p. 36.
[117] Hall, *Glanvill*, p. 5.

seisin, the most important of the petty or 'possessory' assizes. (Since 'assize' simply means 'a session', it was used of a meeting of the *curia regis*, an edict made there, the new form of action the edict announced and each session of a jury summoned by the form of action: finally, it came to mean the sessions of judges to hear these 'assizes'.) The sheriff's instructions in the Writ of Novel Disseisin included the summoning of a jury of recognition (in the tradition of the Domesday inquest) to answer quite specific and narrow questions about the recent history of the land in dispute. 'Has R. unjustly and without a judgment disseised N. of his free tenement in such-and-such a vill since my [the king's] last voyage to Normandy?'[118] If the jury says that there has been such a disseisin, the justices will amerce the disseisor, order the restoration to the plaintiff of the disputed property and award him damages (Doc. 12 (1)). The genius was in the isolation of the simple question of recent fact which a jury of neighbours could reasonably be expected to answer and the redressing of the immediate wrong, leaving over the much more complicated issue of ultimate right to the land till tempers had simmered down.

One can see this device suggesting itself when Henry was trying to bring England under control in the early years of his reign: the first task was to reverse the novel disseisins which had occurred since his accession and so remove the necessity for violent 'self-help' by the disseised. But the exact dating of these momentous inventions still eludes us. Behind novel disseisin lies the old Roman and Canon law principle that the balance must be restored and a man put back into the property from which he has been ejected before the question of legal right is tried, and this principle was reaffirmed in many executive writs of reseisin back at least to 1077.[119] But none of these writs were returnable writs, originating a legal action. Nor is there any suggestion of a returnable writ in connection with the possessory Assize of *Utrum*[120] when that is first mentioned in the Constitutions of Clarendon in 1164 though the other great step of using a jury to decide a specific question of fact has by then been taken, perhaps by the church courts. The punishment of recent disseisins was one of the jobs of the eyre of 1166, as it was of the eyre of 1176 (Doc. 8), but the first indication of the existence of returnable writs to institute possessory assizes on behalf of individual plaintiffs is in payments in the pipe rolls from 1168 onwards 'for having an assize of land', 'for having the recognition of the county', and at length 'for an assize of novel disseisin'.[121]

---

[118] *Ibid.* pp. 167ff.
[119] Van Caenegem, *Royal Writs*, pp. 281–2; Stenton, *English Justice*, pp. 23 and 34–5.
[120] See above, p. 45.
[121] Stenton, *English Justice*, p. 36; Van Caenegem, *Royal Writs*, p. 294.

One possessory assize we can date exactly. The Assize of Mort d'Ancestor (Doc. 9) was instituted in 1176 by the Assize of Northampton (Doc. 8) as a matter of feudal administration, to protect the heir whose lord denied him his feudal inheritance. In this assize there were several questions to be answered by the jury (did the ancestor die seized of a fee, was it since the king's coronation, is the claimant the 'next' or nearest heir?), and the issue came closer to the ultimate one of right. In most cases the possessory assize would in fact settle the dispute and the defeated party would not go on to challenge the tenant's right.

If he did, or if he started with a writ of right, he had to be prepared for trial by battle.[122] The use of hired champions, still disapproved of in Henry II's reign when battle was even waged (i.e. agreed upon and pledged) though not necessarily fought between churchmen over advowsons, was obligatory by the mid-thirteenth century; and after 1275 these champions no longer had to be witnesses to the facts of the matter. The great religious houses kept champions in permanent training (Doc. 16), but men who fought for pay were unwilling to push the contest to extremes: a compromise was almost always reached, even after the duel had started, and the worst that usually happened was that one of the champions had to cry craven, so losing the case for his principal.[123] Though the idea died hard that only God could judge the right, the ordeal of battle was recognized to be unsatisfactory in land cases before it was in criminal cases. Henry II's Assize of Windsor of 1179 accordingly allowed a tenant whose title was challenged to make use of the sworn inquest which the Crown had been employing for its own purposes since Domesday: a 'royal benefit' indeed, since the tenant's application to chancery for a 'writ of peace' prohibiting battle and setting in train the assembly of a jury of twelve knights instantly brought the case under the control of the royal justices.[124] Henceforth tenants in cases of right always preferred the Grand Assize (so called in distinction from the 'petty' or possessory assizes), unless they had some reason to mistrust their neighbours who would make up the jury (Doc. 16), and the Assize drained business from the lords' to the king's courts more effectively than *tolt* and *pone*.[125]

By the end of Henry II's reign, the writ *Precipe* and the Grand Assize had been extended to cover cases where the claim concerned an

[122] Hall, *Glanvill*, pp. 22–5.

[123] Richardson and Sayles, *Law and Legislation*, p. 113n: V. H. Galbraith, 'The Death of a Champion', in *Studies in Medieval History presented to F. M. Powicke*, ed. R. W. Hunt *et al.* (Oxford, 1948); F. W. Maitland and W. P. Baildon (eds.), *The Court Baron* (Selden Society, London, 1890), pp. 77–8, for the champion's oath before battle; C. H. Williams (ed.), *Year Book 1, Henry VI* (Selden Society, London, 1933), for the ritual of the civil duel.

[124] Hall, *Glanvill*, pp. 26ff.

[125] Cf. above, p. 37.

advowson, a widow's dower (the third of her husband's land which she kept during her lifetime), the repayment of a debt or the fulfilment of a covenant, and also where a lord wished to call his bailiff to account. 'It is easy', says *Glanvill*, 'to formulate writs to fit the different circumstances.'[126] Likewise, *utrum* had been extended to questions such as whether the land a man held at his death was freehold or leasehold, whether it was held in fee or in wardship and whether an heir is under age or of full age. 'And if similar questions arise as they frequently do when both parties are present in court, then recognitions [jury-verdicts] are used to settle the dispute, whether by consent of the parties or by award of the court.'[127] Novel disseisin was extended to cases of nuisance, the making of a pond to another's harm and interference with common rights.[128]

The new forms of action which were framed to remedy newly recognized grievances used the same few procedural elements with increasing resourcefulness. One of these elements was the date of limitation. As is still the case, the wrong complained of must have occurred within a recent and defined period of years; or to put it another way, the plaintiff in a petty assize need not go into the long history which alone could prove his right to the land but simply had to prove a seisin lost since the prescribed date. The emphasis on seisin at a particular date first appears in Stephen's troubled reign as a way of stabilizing the land-holding pattern, and Henry II seized on the idea and developed it.[129] The Assize of Northampton (Doc. 8) moved the date of limitation for alleged disseisin on from Henry's 'first coronation' to his return to England after the rebellion of 1173, thereby stabilizing the tenurial situation as it emerged from that upheaval.

Another procedural device was the *essoin*, a formal excuse by the tenant for non-appearance, to which *Glanvill* devotes eighteen of the thirty-three chapters of his first book.[130] A man can send an essoiner to the court at three successive return-days (which were at least a fortnight apart),[131] on the grounds that he is too ill to travel (*de malo veniendi*). But at the fourth return-day he must appear himself, or send an attorney to win or lose the case for him, or lose the case by default; and when he does appear he must support the essoin on oath, or the essoiner will suffer arrest as a 'false essoiner'. After excusing himself *de malo veniendi*

---

[126] Hall, *Glanvill*, pp. 33, 45, 66, 97, 116, 118, 122 and 125.

[127] *Ibid.* p. 149.

[128] Richardson and Sayles, *Law and Legislation*, p. 109; Hall, *Glanvill*, pp. 168–9.

[129] Cronne and Davis, *Regesta Regum*, vol. III, p. xxvi; Hall, *Glanvill*, pp. 167 and 180; Hall, *EHR* (1968), p. 783.

[130] Hall, *Glanvill*, pp. 7–17; D. M. Stenton (ed.), *Pleas Before the King or his Justices, 1198–1202*, vol. i (Selden Society, London, 1952), pp. 150–70.

[131] On return days, see Hall, *Glanvill*, pp. 5–21.

the tenant in a case in Common Pleas or King's Bench (but not in eyre) might send two essoiners to say that his illness had worsened and he had taken to his bed (*de malo lecti*). In this situation four knights were sent to visit the tenant and (if they could swear that he was too ill to put on his clothes) assign him a day a year later at which to appear at the Tower of London (Doc. 10). From the time of Geoffrey fitz Peter, who was both Justiciar (1198–1213) and Keeper of the Tower, there seems to have been a permanent office in the Tower, open even when the courts were not, which could arrange for the resumption of the plea. There were also essoins for the king's service overseas and for pilgrimages to Jerusalem and elsewhere. Furthermore, attorneys and jurors and essoiners themselves could put in essoins, and joint defendants could put in essoins alternately, doubling the delay. Yet essoining should not be seen as a fantastic system for avoiding any conclusion to litigation. Men always must be and always had been able to send reasonable excuses: the judges were now regulating these ancient practices and they pressed tenants as much as they could to appear by attorney rather than essoin.

Essoins and the other procedural moves were at the heart of English law. The bulk of law-making was concerned with such things, and the makers were the judges.[132] The real difference between the Assize of Battle and the Grand Assize was that in the latter fewer essoins were allowed, 'and so people generally are saved trouble and the poor are saved money';[133] and between Grand Assize and Novel Disseisin that in the possessory assize no essoin was allowed at all (Doc. 9).

Of the procedural devices used in many different ways, the jury was the most important. Here a crucial if unconscious choice was made, affecting the whole future course of English law. Instead of the multiplicity of judges of continental law, themselves sifting evidence and deciding the facts of cases according to Roman law methods, English kings made do with a very few powerful justices drawn from the inner ranks of his ministers, who got through the business by peremptorily demanding simple answers from juries: yes or no?[134] The forms of action were designed to isolate relatively simple issues for the jury, thus compelled to take on the job of judging the facts and, in so far as these can never be entirely divorced from issues of law, those as well. Even the Grand Assize was not made to decide the metaphysical question of right – merely that of the greater right.[135] The dates of limitation – and there was one for the Grand Assize, too, though it was more remote than

132 Richardson and Sayles, *Law and Legislation*, p. 104.
133 Hall, *Glanvill* pp 28 and 169.
134 This is the thesis of J. P. Dawson, *A History of Lay Judges* (Cambridge, Mass., 1960).
135 Hall, *Glanvill*, pp. 30, 33 *etc.*

those for the petty assizes – limited the knowledge required of juries. The question of the greater right was difficult enough, but in the 1180s the judges hit on the technique of bringing the pleading, even in a suitable case of right, to some issue of seisin vital to the plaintiff's claim, and putting this to jury-trial 'by consent of the parties' (Doc. 9).[136]

The various procedural elements were drawn together into specific forms of action by the invention, basic to all the others, of the 'original writ'. But when that has been said, it is time to play down a little the pre-eminence which has been given to the writ by modern scholarship. Every writ presupposed something more basic still, an oral complaint to chancery which issued the writ, indicated by the phrase at the beginning of the Writ of Novel Disseisin; 'Questus est mihi N' (N. has complained to me). Both 'civil' and 'criminal' cases began with an oral complaint or *querela*, which was always the natural and sufficient way of bringing most cases in the local courts.[137] Prosecution of criminals by way of presentment did not destroy the complaint or 'appeal' of the individual victims of crime, and presentment itself must usually have originated in the complaints of individuals: the Grand Jury of later times simply found that the individual's complaint was 'a true bill'.[138] But at this stage of oral complaint, the litigant can rarely have known whether he was complaining of a crime or a civil injury. In 1166, even the justices in eyre may not have made this distinction, but accepted jurisdiction over all wrongs, even disseisins, as offences against the king's peace.

Only gradually did the king and his justices create writs and forms, and sort the heterogeneous mass of grievances which was the life of the countryside into the artificial categories of the courts, 'crown pleas' (crimes) and 'common pleas' (land cases and torts). Even when writs had become plentiful, however, the courts were still bound to listen to direct complaints (written down as *bills*) from those too poor or ignorant or for some reason unable to go to chancery first.[139] The bills which flowed inexhaustibly from the local reservoir of grievances went on to inspire new forms and institutions at the centre – the action of trespass, to some extent parliament. The returnable writ was not the culmination it has sometimes been made to appear.

THE THIRTEENTH CENTURY

The thirteenth century was the heyday of the eyre, the operation of which may be examined in the seventh General Eyre of the reign of Henry III (1216–72). This took from 1252 till 1258 to cover the whole

[136] Stneton, *English Justice*, pp. 49–50.
[137] Miller, *Ely*, p. 227; Turner, *Brevia Placitata*, pp. xliv and lix.
[138] See below, p. 89.
[139] See below, p. 86.

country, despite the fact that it was carried out by two parties of justices, and the session of the eyre for Shropshire lasted from Friday 14 January, 1256 till about Wednesday 16 February.[140] The justices, moving through the country under the direction of a stream of royal writs, came to Shrewsbury from Hereford and went on afterwards to Northumberland, Cumberland, Westmorland and Lancaster. John de Vaux, Abbot of Peterborough and later Treasurer of England, was the nominal head of the party of four justices, but his presence was perhaps intended to lend awe to the occasion, for the real leader was Simon of Walton, one of the class of professional justices which was well-established by the middle of the century. Simon had first acted as a justice in eyre in 1246, rose to the court of Common Pleas at Michaelmas term 1251, and returned to that court as the senior effective justice after the Shrewsbury session in 1256: he eventually became Bishop of Norwich. Simon was a Warwickshire man, the other two active justices both Kentishmen. Robert of Shottenden, a royal clerk who had been rewarded by the Deanery of Chester, had been a justice in eyre since 1254 and died on eyre in 1257 after some service in the court of Common Pleas. Nicholas of Hadlow, the only layman amongst the justices, probably specialized in the hearing of Crown Pleas (criminal cases) since clerks were not supposed to be involved in blood-punishments. Nicholas had made his reputation in Kent as one of the most trusted of the king's sheriffs, and he went on to be a leading justice of the court of King's Bench.

When the session of the eyre begins, says Bracton,[141]

'First let the writs be read which authorize and empower them to proceed on eyre, that their authority may be known. When these have been heard, and if the justices so wish, let one of the senior and more distinguished among them publicly declare in the presence of all the reason for their coming, the purpose of the eyre and the advantage to be derived from keeping the peace. . . . And that the king orders all his lieges, in the faith whereby they are bound to him and as they wish to save their possessions, to lend effective and diligent counsel and aid for the preservation of his peace and justice and the suppression and extirpation of wrongdoing. . . . These remarks having been made, the justices ought to betake themselves to some private place and call before them four or six or more of the greater men of the county, who are called the "buzones"[142] of the county and on whose nod the views of the others depend, and let them consult with those men in turn. . . .'

---

[140] The following description of the Shropshire Eyre of 1256 is based on my own edition of the roll of the session (unpublished B.Litt. thesis, Oxford, 1957).
[141] *Bracton*, tr. Thorne, vol. ii, pp. 327ff.
[142] On buzones, see G. Lapsley in *EHR* (1932).

The justices remind the leaders of the shire of the oath which all have taken not to harbour felons, of their duty to organize the hue and cry after wrongdoers and not to give lodging to suspicious strangers. Then the justices call together the bailiffs of the hundreds to arrange for the empanelling of a presenting jury from each hundred, and the jurymen swear individually 'that I will speak the truth as to that on which you shall question me on the lord king's behalf'. When the oath has been taken,

'let the chapters, as to which they shall answer before the justices, be read to them in order. Having heard them, let them be told to answer in their *veredictum* fully, clearly and openly to each chapter, separately and by itself, and to have that veredictum ready at an appointed day. And let them be told in private that if anyone in their hundred or wapentake is suspected of some crime they are to arrest him at once if they can. If they cannot, let them give his name, and the names of all those who are under suspicion, privately to the justices in a schedule and the sheriff will be ordered to arrest them at once and bring them under arrest before the justices, that the latter may do justice upon them. . . .'

The prototype of the instructions issued to the thirteenth-century eyres was the set of articles or 'chapters' (*capitula*) of inquiry of the Eyre of 1194. Confronted by King Richard's enormous demands from abroad for money, first for his crusade and then to ransom himself from the Emperor's prison, and at home by the revolt of Count John the king's brother, the Justiciar and Archbishop of Canterbury, Hubert Walter, turned the eyre into a highly organized political and financial as well as judicial instrument.[143] Justice was *magnum emolumentum*, a great source of profit to the king, and a chronicler described the Eyre of 1194 as reducing all England to poverty. The chapters were concerned with such things as the condition of the king's demesne lands and the affairs of the Jews on whose wealth the king depended even more than on the profits of justice, and constituted a new and important form of legislation – the only form open to Hubert Walter in the absence and inaccessibility of the king. In the thirteenth century, the addition from time to time of new chapters of inquiry reflects the deeper workings of English society and administration, as much as the vicissitudes of politics. In the period from 1246 to 1254, about twenty new chapters were introduced,[144] most of them concerned with the malpractices of

[143] Stenton, *English Justice*, p. 83; West, *The Justiciarship*, pp. 78ff; Richardson and Sayles, *Law and Legislation*, pp. 132–3.
[144] Helen M. Cam, 'Studies in the hundred rolls', *Oxford Studies in Legal and Social History* (1921); C. A. F. Meekings, *The Crown Pleas of the Wiltshire Eyre* (Wiltshire Archaeological Society, Devizes, 1961), pp. 27ff.

sheriffs and other officials in the enforcement of the multiplying legal processes. Has the sheriff fomented lawsuits to gain lands, wardships and debts; has a bailiff taken the same amercement twice over or more than the assessed amercement; have the king's officials imprisoned men wrongfully and extorted money for their release?[145] The presentments at the Shropshire Eyre of 1256 show that new chapters were speedy and accurate correctives for the real faults of the administration (Doc. 12 (21d, 22d, 24d)).

The great majority of presentments in the jurors' *veredictum* (which was still recited in one session of the 1194 Eyre but already written down in a session of 1203) came under chapters 1 and 2 and were criminal or Crown Pleas in a narrow sense of the term (Doc. 12 (22, 22d, 24d)). There were no less than 183 presentments of homicide which had occurred in Shropshire since the last visit of the eyre in 1248. Three suicides were recorded; and twelve people had been found dead (sometimes *occupati frigore*: 'frozen stiff'). Sixty-one people had died by misadventure, twenty-eight having been drowned, fourteen killed by falling from trees, horses, rocks and ladders, eight buried in marl-pits, seven crushed by carts or animals, one caught up in a mill-wheel and one (a small child) bitten by a pig. It seems odd, after the long tale of homicides, to find only two presentments of robbery or theft. The reason is that the juries could not possibly cope with the huge numbers of specific crimes in these categories. All they could do was to indicate or 'indict' those who were notorious for their repeated thieving. One person is presented as 'a robber of fishponds', but it was not in their public presentments but in the *privata*, the jurors' secret communication to the justices of the names of suspects, that notorious thieves were marked down for arrest. Sixty-two people are listed as suspected of thieving and consorting with thieves, twenty-three in one batch. Many other thieves must have been included in the lists of those who have run away and (simply for that reason?) are suspected (*malecreduntur*) of unspecified misdeeds.

The specific killings listed in the *veredicta* are almost always said to have been the work of 'unknown malefactors' or of people who have absconded. On the other hand, the sixty-two reputed thieves and ten reputed killers, secretly delated to the justices and given less warning of arrest, were brought to court and tried by jury (Doc. 12 (30d)). From the beginning of the century, the justices had been encouraging the use of juries to decide whether indictments or appeals were inspired by hatred and spite (*de odio et athia*) and brought just to pay off old scores (Doc. 12 (27d, 30d)), but there was a natural reluctance to use the

---

[145] The chapters of the eyre of 1254 are to be found in W. H. Hart (ed.), *Historia et Cartularium Monasterii Gloucestriae* (Rolls Series, London, 1865), pp. 276–80.

presenting jury to give a verdict on the guilt or innocence of those it had already reported as suspect.[146] The Fourth Lateran Council of 1215, at which Pope Innocent III forbade the clergy to take any part in trial by ordeal, forced the justices' hands. The eyre which went out in 1219, at the end of the civil war which followed Magna Carta, was confronted by large numbers of criminals whom it could not try. Sometimes the justices solved the problem by taking the presenting jury's suspicion as conviction, though they could hardly impose heavy penalties in such circumstances; and sometimes they compelled the accused to submit to the verdict of the presenting jury supplemented by twenty-four knights, forcing him to abjure the realm if this jury's opinion was divided. In fact accused people were usually eager to clear themselves by the verdict of their 'country', and the ultimate solution was to allow them special ('petty') trial-juries, formally distinct from the presenting juries though no doubt often composed of the same people. The accused's confidence was justified: only five of our sixty-two reputed thieves were found guilty and hanged. Hardened criminals were of course unwilling to trust their necks to their neighbours' opinion, and the doctrine remained that they could not be compelled to submit to purely human judgment. If they would not plead, they were kept in prison, and in later times *prison forte et dure* was somehow changed into the horrible *peine forte et dure*, pressing to death as the prisoners lay stretched naked on the dungeon floor. The man who was prepared to undergo this at least avoided for himself the ignominy of the convicted felon and for his children the forfeiture of the family property. Of more significance for the growth of court-practice were the verbal trickeries of the judges to persuade suspects to 'put themselves upon the country' (Doc. 15).

For a time around 1215 to 1220, the appeal of felony and trial by battle was the only procedure, apart from the summary execution of 'hand-having' thieves and red-handed killers caught by the hue and cry, which would secure adequate punishment for serious crimes. The rise of trial by jury meant the decline of the appeal, but the process was a slow one. Thirty of the crown pleas on the Shropshire Roll of 1256 are appeals of felony, five alleging homicide, four rape, four false imprisonment, six robbery and eight assault (Doc. 12 (28d)). In ten cases appellants withdrew or, more often, failed to appear, and in ten others the appellants were 'non-suited' for losing their way in the bewildering technicalities of appeal procedure. Benefit of clergy was pleaded in five cases. Whether or not the appeal was prosecuted in due form (and in none of these thirty cases was the stage of wager of battle ever reached)

---

[146] D. M. Stenton, *Rolls of the Justices in Eyre for Lincolnshire and Worcestershire* (Selden Society, London, 1934), p. lxviii, *Rolls of the Justices in Eyre in Yorkshire (1218–19)* (1937), pp. xli and xlvii, *Rolls of the Justices in Eyre for Gloucestershire, Warwickshire, and Shropshire (1221–22)* (1940), p. lx.

the accused man was forced to clear himself of the alleged trespass against the king's peace. Ten accused were found not guilty and four were guilty and imprisoned for the breach of the peace.

Altogether, only nineteen of the hundreds of felons accused at the Shropshire Eyre and not acquitted were hanged; of the rest some had abjured the realm but most had absconded and were outlawed. A few of the better-off outlaws will later have bought pardons from the king: others had got them in anticipation of accusation. Almost all killing, even accidental killing by children, was treated as crime, and the inflexibility of the law was mitigated only by the kindly instincts of juries who concealed such incidents at the risk of amercement, or by the judges' remission of the cases for discussion with the king and perhaps pardon. Homicide by accident or in self-defence was still somehow culpable and required pardon. Those who fled in panic from the scene of accidental or even natural death, fearing accusations of homicide, were regarded as committing an offence and were amerced at the same time that they were found guiltless of the death and encouraged to return.[147]

At the end of the eyre roll there is the list of the amercements and other profits for the king assessed by the juries at the concluding fiscal session (the imposition of amercement having been noted in the margin of the roll against the relevant cases as they were heard). For a start, the whole county was subjected to a customary 'common fine', unrelated to actual offences, which amounted to sixty marks for averagely rich Shropshire. Then there are listed on the Shropshire Roll between 600 and 700 separate amercements arising from the crown pleas, mostly of half-a-mark (6s 8d) or one mark in amount, and mostly for such routine offences as the burying of (stinking) bodies by townships before the coroners arrived to view them, the failure of townships and individuals to pursue criminals, and the manifold shortcomings of officials (failure of coroners to attend inquests in person or the negligence of the sheriff in allowing prisoners to escape). The Shropshire peasantry, whether the honest members of townships or felons like Richard Bugge, filled the king's coffers with a mass of small contributions. The rich and powerful ran no danger of the penalties of felons, however much they deserved them, but they appear quite frequently amongst the two or three hundred persons amerced in the civil pleas for harming neighbouring landowners of their own sort. Altogether, the Shropshire session was worth more than £700 to the king (in theory at least, for much was never collected), and a year's journeying of the justices more than £4000, perhaps an eighth of the king's total yearly income.

There are 482 items in the civil pleas section of the Shropshire Roll

[147] Naomi Hurnard, *The King's Pardon for Homicide* (Oxford, 1969), pp. 311ff.

(the *juratae et assisae*), and eighty-nine of them concern assizes of novel disseisin (twenty-one, disseisin of common rights), most of them brief and to the point, as the assize was intended to be (Doc. 12 (4d)). They do, nonetheless, reflect the political conflicts of the localities, in which the lords directed against each other's lands gangs of their peasantry, the alleged disseisors, who sometimes plead that they acted only at their lords' will. A famous romance tells how 'Fulk FitzWarin', a Shropshire knight, fought for the patrimony of which he had been disseised by King John, whose disregard for other people's property is obvious in Magna Carta. It is possible that the romance was written to sustain the FitzWarin family in fighting the action of novel disseisin brought against Thomas Corbet at the eyre of 1256 by Fulk FitzWarin's son, another Fulk.[148] The story was that the lords of the Welsh marches had assembled at a 'love-day' to settle a dispute between Thomas Corbet and his nephew, Griffith, the prince of Powis; and there Corbet quarrelled violently with Fulk, who was his vassal, and taunted him with the treachery of his father against King John. In a fury, Fulk renounced his homage to Corbet and said he would be his tenant no longer. Corbet therefore took possession of Fulk's manor of Alberbury, and Fulk brought the assize. The record of the case gives us a rare glimpse of the judges in action. In reply to their questions, the jury declares that Fulk had not renounced his homage in person and that he had continued to cultivate his land till he was ejected. On the strength of these answers, Fulk won his case: land-tenure is now too serious a thing to be affected by feudal histrionics, and the romance of 'Fulk FitzWarin' is common-law rather than feudal mythology.

Fifty-one cases at Shrewsbury were assizes of mort d'ancestor (Doc. 12 (5)), three of which failed because the juries found that the plaintiff's ancestors had not been seized of the disputed land when they had died or gone on pilgrimage, and five because they had not had the fee simple (only, for instance, a life-lease). Two plaintiffs were found to be bastards, incapable of inheriting, and one plaintiff had an older brother who ought to succeed before him. Only two assizes of *utrum* are recorded, but there are nineteen instances of the assize of nuisance, an off-shoot of the assize of novel disseisin[149] which alleged some incidental damage to the plaintiff's tenement: eight complain of the breaking down of the banks of the plaintiffs' fishponds, five of the making of banks and ditches which obstruct access to their lands, and four of the setting-up of markets by the defendants which attract trade from the plaintiffs' markets. The Abbot of Pershore has a clever answer to the complaint that his new market at Hawkesbury deprives Matthew de Bezil of trade

[148] E. A. Francis, 'The background to Fulk FitzWarin' in *Studies in Medieval French presented to Alfred Ewert* (Oxford, 1961).
[149] Hall, *Glanvill*, pp. 168–9.

and consequent tolls and stall-dues at his market at Sherston: the abbot says that his Monday market has increased the overall volume of trade, merchants buying there to sell at Matthew's market on Tuesday.

Forty-two pleas concern right to land, only one of which succeeds, though ten get as far as the summoning of the Grand Assize. Many of the forty-two cases progress no further at Shrewsbury than the appointment of attorneys. In one case the evidence of witnesses to a charter is taken. In another, the defendant, Hugh of Stratford, produces a charter of enfeoffment and vouches to warranty a certain Peter, whose seal it bears. Peter is forced to compensate Hugh for the land he loses to the claimant, although he protests that he gave his seal to Hugh to append to a quite different document, a five-year lease: the evidence of a seal is incontrovertible, and Hugh successfully resists an attempt to call the witnesses listed in the charter. Three writs of right to advowsons were pleaded at Shrewsbury, seven to varieties of feudal service, eleven to debts and thirty-six to dower. Clearly doweresses had good cause for complaint: in seven instances the defendants admitted the claims and surrendered the land. Two defendants pleaded that the claimants' husbands had held in villeinage, another defendant that the claimant had never been married, and one claim failed because the husband was found to have died a felon, all of whose property was forfeit. The readiness of widows to remarry adds to the complications, and we find a woman and her new husband claiming the third part of a third part – dower from lands which her first husband's mother held in dower. There were eight claims for breach of covenant, one of which was answered by the plea that no weight could be attached to the plaintiff's mere word (*simplex dictum*) that there was an agreement. As yet the law knew how to enforce only those contracts enshrined in charters.

The remaining two actions represented in fair numbers on the Shropshire Roll were those of *quod permittat* and *entry*. The first (appearing fourteen times) was an action for the recovery of common rights, most often the right to take wood (*estovers*) from someone else's copse for one's own fires, though it could also be used to recover offices such as a forest-bailiffry with all its perquisites. The writs of entry took their name from the allegation of the claimants that the tenants had *entry* to the disputed property, though peacefully, yet under a title which had never been or was no longer valid. Thus, six demandants at Shrewsbury claimed that the tenants had entry to the property under leases which had now expired (*ad terminum qui preteriit*); four, that the tenants had entry through illegal grants by husbands of their wives' lands, or by guardians of their wards'; and four that the tenants had entry by purchase from the tenants of guardians or doweresses. Both *quod permittat* and *entry* show the old demarcation between actions of right and actions for seisin breaking down, as more complex situations had to be sorted out. In some instances the parties counted (as in actions by writ of right) on the descent of the property through a line of ancestors, and the general issue of title was tried by a grand assize of twelve knights; in others, they counted on the facts of entry or seisin, and trial was by an ordinary *jurata*. Writs of entry, which multiplied in the early thirteenth century and had become by the end of it 'the most popular of all writs for the recovery of land', show the increasing flexibility and subtlety of civil procedure.[150]

Greater elaboration and flexibility of procedure were accompanied, however, by increasing delay. Sixty-nine of the civil cases on the Shropshire Roll are 'foreign pleas' adjourned to Shropshire from the ten counties which this group of justices had already visited; and eleven of these pleas were adjourned to the next stopping-place of the eyre at Newcastle-upon-Tyne, and twenty-nine to Westminster. Only eighteen foreign pleas were settled at Shrewsbury – some by default or a final concord (a sign of the parties' exhaustion), only one by the appearance of a defendant who had previously been recalcitrant and the straight-forward hearing of the case. The record at Newcastle was even worse: not one of the twenty-one cases sent there seems to have been settled, the majority being adjourned to Lancaster.

It was to keep track of all the adjournments and procedural steps that the plea-rolls of the various courts became indispensable: without them, running on for Common Pleas and King's Bench, a great wadge of parchment for each of the three terms of each court in each year, right down to the nineteenth century, English law would have had to develop quite differently. The rolls become an intrinsic part of the legal process. In Glanvill's time, a 'record' was not something written down, but the testimony of a court to its own proceedings – oral testimony which would be carried from the shire court to the king's court by four knights.[151] Such solemn record was authoritative in subsequent pro-ceedings, and it was natural that the authority should be transferred to the writing-down of the proceedings, when the keeping of registers and rolls suddenly took hold throughout Western Europe in the late twelfth century.[152] Thereafter, for example, a defendant was instantly quit if he could invoke a roll which recorded the plaintiff's earlier failure in the same case. In fact, however, the rolls of the shire and hundred courts were not accorded this authoritative status; and in a world of Westminster-centred bureaucracy, the local courts were pushed even further into a subordinate role, as not 'courts of record'.

[150] Hall, *Glanvill*, pp. 190–1; Stenton, *English Justice*, p. 50; Turner, *Brevia Placitata*, pp. lxxviiff.

[151] Hall, *Glanvill*, pp. 99ff.

[152] C. R. Cheney, 'The study of the medieval Papal Chancery', *Edwards Lecture* (Glasgow University, 1966).

The mass of ink and parchment the courts were generating, significant enough in itself, should not be allowed to screen the people: the clerks who kept the rolls, just occasionally permitting themselves a doodled face in the margin or a personal comment like 'it's my little love affairs that keep me gay and given me fun' (under a cancelled entry),[153] and the parties, essoiners, attorneys and jurors, trailing across England between the dryly noted adjournments. The different handwritings on eyre-rolls and final concords show that each judge had his own clerk or clerks, necessarily so when the justices sat separately, as they often did, to deal with crown pleas and common pleas concurrently. Some of the clerks may have been local men hired for the occasion, but there was a core of professionals who would themselves be judges in the near future. They were maintained largely from the damages (one mark or half a mark a time) awarded to successful plaintiffs, which were diverted automatically to the clerks in whole or in part. Already at the beginning of the thirteenth century, 'professional attorneys are appearing alongside the personal representatives, kinsmen or servants of the parties . . . Even the lowly essoiner is ceasing to be a mere unnamed messenger, relative, or fellow villager of the party, his cook, his forester or some chance merchant who has passed through his house. He is showing signs of becoming a professional man.'[154] But this professionalism had developed more at Westminster than in the eyre: many of the hundred-odd attorneys appointed at Shrewsbury were husbands or sons of the parties (Doc. 12 (9)).

The actual session of the eyre was only the hub of a system which involved the efforts of many officials and other courts throughout the year. The activities of the sheriff and the hundred and shire courts as the agents of the higher courts now outweighed their other work in importance. The shire court supervised proceedings in the hundred courts, and in a great liberty like that of Ely the hundred court in turn supervised the lesser courts of halimote. At the now three-weekly ordinary meetings of the hundred court, attended by perhaps forty or fifty people, summary justice might be done on the thief caught in the act, the opening formalities of an appeal of homicide be recorded, and minor brawls punished and small debts collected. But the hundred was really important as the 'country' (*patria*) the opinion of which was invoked by accused criminal and civil defendant, and as the instrument of the sheriff in carrying out his 'immense amount of police work connected with criminal and civil justice, serving writs, distraining beasts, taking charge of the goods and chattels of felons, arresting accused persons, and either bailing them or providing for their custody'. The sheriff's twice-yearly tourn in the hundred courts, attended by many more people than an

---

153 Meekings, *Crown Pleas of the Wiltshire Eyre*, p. 25.
154 Stenton, *English Justice*, pp. 86–7.

ordinary hundred court including the reeve and four men as the representatives of each village community, was the occasion for the presentment of those numerous robberies, thefts and serious assaults which the
eyre had no time for, the accused being arrested and held over for trial
by the justices of gaol delivery.[155]

The sheriff was debarred by chapter 24 of Magna Carta from trying
these crown pleas himself at the four-weekly shire court in castle or
shire-hall as he was certainly still doing in 1170. But before going to the
royal justices every appeal of felony had to be brought to four successive
meetings of the shire court, which was also essential to legal proceedings
in every other court as the location of the process of outlawry (again
stretching over four meetings): though, once more, it proclaimed outlaws at the bidding of higher authorities (Doc. 10). The bulk of civil
litigation still took place in the shire court. Indeed, the court's civil
business increased with the activities of the royal justices: but the cases
which were multiplying in the ordinary shire court were not those in
which the sheriff acted as the president of an independent moot, rather
ones in which he acted as a subordinate royal judge under writ of
justicies. The matters in which the sheriff was ordered to 'do justice'
included cases of account, covenant, customs and services due to lords,
debt, nuisance, naifty (an action for the recovery of fugitive villeins) and
replevin (complaints of the unjust seizure of farm-animals and chattels under pretext of distraint: Doc. 19). Distraint or 'distress', in particular, went to the heart of local society, and the sheriff's responsibility
for curbing this 'beginning of all wars' was further developed by the
great statutes of Edward I. For matters like this, and as the place where
solemn proclamations were made and land-transactions published and
witnessed (Doc. 18 (34, 36)), the shire court remained of immense
importance for centuries to come; as the court, too, through which the
sheriff controlled civil procedures, such as essoining and the provision
of juries.[156]

The coroners, even more than the sheriffs, show the subordination of

---

[155] W. S. Holdsworth, *A History of English Law*, 7th edn, vol. i (London,
1956), introductory essay by S. B. Chrimes, pp. 11*–12*; W. A. Morris, *The
Medieval English Sheriff* (Manchester, 1927), pp. 202–4; Helen M. Cam,
The Hundred and the Hundred Rolls (London, 1930), pp. 118–28; *Idem*,
'Cambridgeshire sheriffs in the thirteenth century' in *Liberties and Communities
in Medieval England* (Cambridge, 1944); Miller, *Ely*, pp. 228–9; C. A. F.
Meekings, *The Crown Pleas of the Wiltshire Eyre*; and 'The *Veredictum* of
Chippenham Hundred' in *Collectanea* (Wiltshire Archaeological Society,
Devizes, 1956).

[156] Chrimes in Holdsworth, *History of English Law*, vol. i, pp. 1*–7*; Morris,
Medieval English Sheriff, pp. 192–9; Stenton, *English Justice*, pp. 81–2; Turner,
Brevia Placitata, p. lvii; for a land-transaction witnessed in the shire court, see
R. R. Darlington (ed.), *The Cartulary of Worcester Cathedral Priory* (Pipe Roll
Society, London, 1968), no. 100.

the local courts to the needs of a centralized judicial system. They were to some extent the heirs of the county justiciars, who disappeared from view early in Henry II's reign, but they were much more cogs in a machine – the machine perfected by Hubert Walter in the 1190s. Chapter 20 of the instructions for the Eyre of 1194 commanded that 'in each county three knights and a clerk shall be elected as keepers of the crown pleas'. This meant that the coroners were to keep a record of the initial proceedings in cases of felony: the finding of a body, the felon's confession or abjuration of the realm or outlawry, the appellant's exhibition of his wounds and formal commencement of his appeal in the shire court (Doc. 10). At his inquests on dead bodies, the coroner received indictments of the suspected killers from the juries of the neighbouring townships. He was sometimes described as 'the principal guardian of the king's peace', but he was rather the guardian of the king's profit. His rolls, which also helped the juries of the county in making their presentments to the eyre, told the king's justices of such things as the value of the chattels of outlawed or exiled felons. The justices dealt strictly with coroners who were slow to the scene of killings or whose rolls were deficient.[157]

As well as the officials who worked in subordination to the eyre, there were limited commissions of itinerant justices working in parallel with it, to deal with particularly numerous or urgent types of cases at more frequent visitations than was possible for the 'general' eyre. Already in the 1190s, the eyre had begun to clog up from sheer weight of business. At the same time, the records of the coroners permitted longer intervals between eyres without profitable jurisdiction being lost to the crown, intervals which could be filled by the lesser commissions if an intolerable backlog of cases built up. In 1195–6 and again in 1206, justices were commissioned to clear off petty assizes in the counties and to 'deliver' the gaols, bulging with prisoners indicted at the sheriffs' tourns or coroners' inquests. In 1206 the justices were the sheriffs themselves and other local men. Magna Carta, though condemning the sheriffs' involvement in the trial of crown pleas, required the petty assizes to be heard only in the counties from which they originated and decreed that two royal justices should be sent out four times a year to hold assizes along with four knights elected in each county, 'on the day and at the place of the county court'. Quarterly assizes constituted an impossibly heavy programme, but assize justices continued to be commissioned as they were required, and in the 1270s the same parties of two judges and four knights were increasingly often instructed to deliver the gaols as well. It was at gaol delivery rather than in the eyre that the majority of

[157] R. F. Hunnisett, *The Medieval Coroner* (Cambridge, 1961); *Select Cases from the Coroners' Rolls* (Selden Society, London, 1896); Meekings, '*Veredictum* of Chippenham Hundred'.

felons were tried and executed, though gaol delivery became entirely separate from the eyre only in 1271–2, when gaol-delivery membranes disappeared from the eyre rolls and the distinct series of gaol-delivery rolls got under way. A separate series of assize rolls had begun in 1248.[158]

Throughout the thirteenth century, the small band of judges from the 'central' royal courts were commissioned with great frequency, singly or in pairs, to try particular petty assizes (the 'grace' of a special assize always being available to the plaintiff who could pay for it), deliver particular gaols, 'hear and determine' (oyer and terminer) a group of offences in a particular area, or investigate an individual murder (Doc. 21). Such commissions appear in huge numbers in the patent rolls. Once a great mass of special jurisdiction of this sort spilled over from the eyre, there was bound to be an attempt by the local gentry to regain it: sheriffs and gaolers sometimes got themselves on to commissions of oyer and terminer in order to provide themselves with the prisoners whom they could then bail – at a handsome profit. It was always a hard struggle for the small corps of royal judges to maintain an efficient system of justice which would serve the needs of the localities without falling into the hands of local interests.

For the moment, the opposite happened: in the mid-thirteenth century the bulk of litigation moved further towards the centre, where the royal justices became more and more sedentary in the Courts of King's Bench and Common Pleas. About the year 1196, during the justiciarship of Hubert Walter which began so much (coroners, chapters of the eyre, the depositing of the feet of fines), a regular bench of professional justices had appeared at the Exchequer, men of lesser social status than Henry II's all-purpose baronial courtiers, who thus released other ministers to specialize in financial work. The pipe rolls are full of payments by litigants to have their suits heard by Archbishop Walter, Simon of Patishall and their colleagues, and from Richard I's accession royal charters regularly included the right of beneficiaries not to be sued except before the king or his chief justiciar: two palfreys was a common offering. The eyres could not have gone on without the continued use of magnates as justices, but at Westminster a new class of professional judges perpetuated itself as (to take just one line of succession) Simon of Patishall's clerk, Martin of Patishall, rose to the bench in his turn, to be followed by *his* clerk, Henry de Bracton, whose great treatise *The Laws and Customs of England* was built on the decisions of Simon and Martin, examined diligently, says Bracton, 'long into the night watches'. These judges were 'generally the first of their families to rise from rustic obscurity. Sometimes they are the younger

[158] Stenton, *English Justice*, pp. 83 and 92; *Magna Carta*, chs. 18–19; Pugh, *Imprisonment in Medieval England*, chs. xii–xiii.

sons of modestly landed families, like Geoffrey fitz Peter son of Peter the forester of Ludgershall', King John's Justiciar.[159]

Despite his reputation, John was a great dispenser of justice, and he removed important cases from the bench in the exchequer to his own feverishly mobile court. Because of its movement, John's court constituted an eyre of enormous authority, bringing the poorer litigant the highest justice in his own locality – eventually. But the greater barons who framed Magna Carta wanted a high court in a fixed place where they (who could afford it) knew they could go and get a decision at any time during the law terms. 'Common pleas', said chapter 17 of Magna Carta, 'shall not follow our court, but shall be held in some definite place'. The establishment of the Court of Common Pleas, and of Westminster as the headquarters of the English legal profession, answered the interests of the class of greater barons. It was advanced by the minority of John's successor, Henry III, during which the court *coram rege* was necessarily in eclipse. Then from 1234, after Henry III assumed control, there is a continuous series of plea-rolls for both 'King's Bench' and 'Common Pleas', stretching down to the second half of the nineteenth century, in place of the single series of *curia regis* rolls which go back to the beginning of Richard I's reign. The dominance of the eyre, working with shire and hundred, lasted a few years longer, but after 1249 the Bench ceased to be suspended when an eyre was in progress, and it was in this decade that there was a sudden increase in business at Westminster. This was apparently because the chancery (under the more immediate control of the king, since he had temporarily dispensed with a chancellor) began to make writs which had previously instituted cases in the shire court (often to be transferred to the eyre by *pone*) returnable in the Bench.[160]

The evolution of the writ continued to be the central strand in the growth of the legal system. The most fruitful new writ of the time, the Writ of Trespass, came into existence stealthily, about a quarter of the way through the thirteenth century. Really a whole constellation of writs, Trespass brought before the royal judges the enormous residue of civil injuries (claims for damages from personal assault, trespass on another's land, defamation, fraud, negligence and breach of contract) by the simple expedient of labelling these acts as trespasses against the king's peace (Doc. 12 (20)). Since at the beginning the allegation of trespass against the peace was given colour by talk of violence (*vi et armis* in the Latin writs and rolls, *tort et force* in the 'law-French' plead-

[159] West, *The Justiciarship*, pp. 83ff; *Bracton*, tr. Thorne, vol. ii, p. 19; Stenton, *Rolls of Eyre for Lincolnshire*, pp. xvi–xx; *Idem, English Justice*, pp. 84–7.

[160] Stenton, *English Justice*, ch. iv: 'King John and the Courts of Justice'; West, *The Justiciarship*, pp. 151ff; C. T. Flower (ed.), *Curia Regis Rolls* (14 vols., London, 1923–); Turner, *Brevia Placitata*, p. lvi.

ings), this category of civil pleas acquired – and retains – the name of 'tort'. It is arguable that the formulation of the Writ of Trespass in Henry III's reign was as great a breakthrough as Henry II's invention of the assizes.[161]

The 'registers of writs' which were compiled for the use of litigious monasteries or working attorneys, giving the 'styles' of all the writs – and therefore remedies – available, grew from ten or twelve pages and fifty or sixty writs each in the early years of Henry III's reign to 120 writs by the end of the reign, and 890 writs by 1320. There are approaching 650 pages and 2500 writs in *The Register of Writs Original and Judicial*, printed at London by William Rastell in 1531. The printed *Register* was so much the structure of English law itself that in Maitland's words 'to ask for its date would be like asking for the date of one of our great cathedrals'. Roughly eighty of its pages are taken up by Trespass and closely related writs. There are some separate registers of judicial (as opposed to original) writs, giving the 'styles' of writs issued by judges themselves in the course of hearings to 'attach' recalcitrant defendants, summon juries for the grand assize or witnesses to charters, or order views of the property in dispute. Many judicial writs might be needed to keep an important case in motion over the years.[162]

There was no clear division of business between King's Bench and Common Pleas. The existence of two courts where there should have been only one was 'an accident of politics'; and it was simply the special interest of a case to the king which brought it into the court before him. By 'common pleas' Magna Carta meant no more than ordinary pleas between commoners. Convenience produced a rough sharing of business after the legal reorganization of 1234. Indictment and trial of crown pleas were left for the itinerant justices to carry on locally; 'pleas that touched property rights and needed formal and unhurried procedure' were channelled to the Common Bench, sedentary at Westminster; appeals of felony and actions of trespass were shared between the two central courts; and King's Bench got any cases which the king took special steps to bring before it, and reviewed cases from any other court (including the Common Bench) on 'writ of error'. A case was brought to the peripatetic King's Bench by making the writ returnable 'wheresoever we may then be in England' (*ubicumque fuerimus in Anglia*). By the manipulation of the writ-system all great business could be directed to the central courts: though it must be said that much business was also

[161] On the authorization of new writs, see B. Wilkinson, *Studies in the Constitutional History of the Thirteenth and Fourteenth Centuries*; on trespass, S. F. C. Milsom in *Law Quarterly Review* (1958).

[162] F. W. Maitland, 'the History of the register of original writs', *Harvard Law Review* (1889) (reprinted in Maitland, *Collected Papers*, ed. Fisher, vol. ii); Elsa de Haas and G. D. G. Hall (eds.), *Early Registers of Writs* (Selden Society, London, 1970).

sent the other way, by the adjournment of cases to future days in King's Bench or Common Pleas 'unless before that time' (*nisi prius*) the justices in eyre or of assize should visit the counties from which the cases arose – in which event these justices would deal with them. The Exchequer, no longer a court of general resort, continued as a special court for enforcing the king's 'prerogative' or financial rights, but also for providing private citizens with remedies against extortionate royal officials and even (through the remarkable statutory action of 'account') against their own dishonest bailiffs or commercial agents.[163]

In the central courts the legal profession and its curious arts grew quickly. Professional attorneys assumed responsibility for the procedural moves in litigation, and professional pleaders took over the job of actually speaking for the parties in court. By 1235 there were several 'advocates or counters' in Common Pleas, and in 1275 there is reference to a 'serjeant-counter'. The victory of the term *serjeant* (or 'servant') for the pleader suggests that he had become an essential and permanent servant for each of the great men of the realm, who were also great litigants. The twenty or so serjeants-at-law in the 1270s were the *counsel* of particular employers on every legal question – sometimes actually members of their permanent councils – but they were also available to be 'retained' by anyone with a case to argue in Common Pleas.[164]

Cases were often decided by the pleading-contest rather than by jury or the other methods of trial.[165] *Placita Corone* (Doc. 15), a mid-thirteenth-century handbook for accused felons, telling them how to resist the verbal trickery of judges, asserts that 'a man will never be hanged so long as he does not admit his guilt by his own mouth'. In a civil case, the tongue of a clever serjeant could literally drive the other party out of court, so that when he was called the next day 'he came not' (Doc. 20). This was not a game of mere rhetoric, however, but of strict rules and formidable technique, refereed by judges who were not easily satisfied. The plaintiff or appellant must not depart in the least detail from what was contained in the writ or he had pleaded at an earlier stage of his appeal. He must not stumble in uttering the almost ritual words of his 'count', nor must the defendant fail to deny the charge 'word for word' (*de verbo in verbum*). In trying to prove his 'better right' to a piece of land by tracing its descent he must not miss out a single ancestor. Large treatises such as *Brevia Placitata* (how to plead on writs) and *Novae Narrationes* (new forms of plea) were written in

[163] G. O. Sayles, *The Court of King's Bench in Law and History* (Selden Society Lecture, London, 1959), p. 10; Holdsworth, *History of English Law*, vol. i, pp. 278–9; H. Jenkinson and Beryl Fermoy (eds.), *Select Cases in the Exchequer of Pleas* (Selden Society, London, 1931).

[164] Pollock and Maitland, *History of English Law*, vol. i, 211ff.

[165] Stenton, *Rolls of the Eyre in Yorkshire*, p. xlix.

the thirteenth century, giving the plaintiffs' 'counts', the answering 'defences', the plaintiffs' 'replications' to the defences and so on, in all the quickly diversifying forms of action.[166] *Placita Corone* is not a law-report, but it does illustrate its advice by extracts from real cases – before Laurence de Brok, for instance. From 1283 to *c*. 1600 runs the first great series of reports proper, the Year Books, which record in French – the language of pleading – all the big cases as they passed before the legal apprentices sitting in the part of the court jocularly known as 'the crib'. This was the day-to-day journalism of the heroic age of pleading, uninhibited and exciting argument amongst the judges and serjeants, which began in the last decade of the thirteenth century (Doc. 20).

In the twelfth century, the Anglo-Saxon lawmen–judges, familiar figures in the local community, had been replaced by the remote and awesome justices-in-eyre, descending on the shire with the whole weight of royal administration, from before whose faces the men of Cornwall fled to the shelter of the woods. Such men were great public figures and could not avoid the vicissitudes of public life. Particularly vulnerable to charges of corruption, the royal justices were apt for sacrifice as political scapegoats.[167] When Edward I returned, in August 1289, from a three-year visit to France, to find England seething with resentment against the royal government, the entire corps of judges suffered. The king appointed a small body of men whom he still trusted, Chancellor Robert Burnell, the Earl of Lincoln and a few others, to receive complaints 'of trespasses done by the King's ministers, while the King was absent from the kingdom', and report to him at the next parliament. For three years *auditores querelarum* were sitting at Westminster (Doc. 16). As a result of their hearings, Thomas de Weyland, Chief Justice of Common Pleas since 1278, fled the country; Ralph de Hengham, Chief Justice of King's Bench since 1274, retired into private life for almost ten years, burdened by the enormous fine of 8000 marks; and Solomon of Rochester, an experienced justice in eyre whose eventual fate was to be poisoned by a village priest in 1293, was fined 4000 marks.

Even as their public position was reaffirmed in this dramatic way, the judges were becoming an increasingly professional group. The chief justiciarship itself was made redundant as a political office by the French king's conquest of Normandy in 1204 – a king with nowhere else to be but England did not want a viceroy – though it was only in 1234, after Henry III's minority was over, that the justiciar was dispensed with. That was also the year when the court *coram rege* began its unbroken

[166] Turner, *Brevia Placitata*; Elsie Shanks (ed.), *Novae Narrationes*, completed by S. F. C. Milsom (Selden Society, London, 1963).
[167] C. A. F. Meekings, 'Robert of Nottingham, justice of the Bench', *BIHR* (1968).

existence as an institution no longer dependent on the king's person, and the Chief Justice of King's Bench inherited some of the justiciar's pre-eminence in the judicial system. In Henry III's reign and for most of Edward I's the judges were still clerks in both senses of the word, men in clerical orders and rewarded by ecclesiastical benefices who had risen through arduous years of work amongst the clerks of the king or of the previous generation of judges; still required, moreover, to do all kinds of non-judicial work for the king, such as to collect taxes, array troops and inspect rivers 'as well as attend Parliament, administer Scotland, or go abroad' on diplomatic missions. By the end of the thirteenth century, however, they were often neither clerks nor clerics, since expert referees in the game of pleading had themselves to be drawn from the ranks of the professional pleaders.[168]

THE COURTS IN GOVERNMENT AND POLITICS

In 1236, Adam, Sub-Dean of Salisbury, excused himself from appearance in the court *coram rege* at Woodstock, and the case was adjourned 'to Parliament at Westminster on the octave of St Hilary'.[169] A new court, known to *Fleta* later in the century as the king's 'court in his council in his parliaments', had appeared upon the scene. The court of King's Bench was the normal place for the correction of errors of justice in other courts, including the errors of the justices of Common Pleas, who might be called into King's Bench to account for processes in their court. But what of cases which could not be settled by King's Bench (no longer, after 1234, the immediate expression of the king's judicial supremacy), or of state trials of 'justices and king's ministers', like those of 1290, where 'specially appointed auditors' investigated but the king reserved to himself the allotment of penalties? In these cases it must be the king himself, along with the intimate advisors of his sworn council, who 'determines doubts regarding judgments', devises 'new remedies . . . for wrongs newly brought to light' and dispenses 'justice . . . to everyone according to his deserts'. In the proceedings of the council, solemn judgments concerning the rights of the baronage were naturally distinguished from ordinary administrative decisions, and it was expedient to pronounce them in a wider, more political assembly. The occasions were provided by the great festivals of the liturgical year, when men flocked to court and the king wore his crown. Once again 1234 was a landmark, for a political crisis in that year began a period when Henry III consciously strove to emphasize the unity of

---

[168] Meekings, *BIHR* (1968); F. M. Powicke, *The Thirteenth Century* (Oxford, 1953), p. 341; W. C. Bolland, *Chief Justice William Bereford* (Cambridge, 1924).

[169] H. G. Richardson and G. O. Sayles, 'The earliest-known official use of the term "parliament" ', *EHR* (1967).

himself and his barons by ceremonial gatherings, parleys, 'parliaments'.[170]

Parliament was an occasion, not an institution, but an occasion which recurred with predictable regularity: if it had not, cases could not have been adjourned to it in the way that, in 1258, we find the case between John de Verdon and the Abbot of Mellifont being adjourned by the royal justices at Dublin to 'the King's great Parliament' at Oxford, where the abbot produced his charters for the disputed property, John de Verdon withdrew his suit, and the case was remitted to Ireland.[171] It was as part of a comprehensive judicial scheme for the redress of the abuses of officials that the king and baronage at that same momentous Oxford parliament of 1258 ordained the holding of three *parlemenz* a year, at Candlemas, in June and at Michaelmas, a provision observed with some exactness until the 'baronial reform movement' broke up in 1261.[172]

There is no doubt, then, that the English parliament began as the place of justice which its great French equivalent, the Parlement of Paris, always was[173] – but not mere justice. The Middle Ages thought of public life in judicial categories, and there was no sharp demarcation between legal pleas and political petitions, the judgment of a law court in *this* case and the statute of the high court of parliament intended to be applicable to all cases. In some ways, parliaments did the job which eyres had done, acting as the ultimate guardians of justice and order in the kingdom. Petitions or 'bills' to parliament were anticipated by 'bills in eyre', the growing mass of written *querelae* to the justices, alleging injuries which no existing writ would remedy, or remedy in time (Docs. 14 and 22). Edward I appointed 'receivers' and 'auditors' to deal with petitions from anyone (not just 'members of parliament') at parliament time, and often such bills were referred back to the common-law courts. But it is true that the majority of 'parliamentary petitions' were asking for political favours or reforms, not for justice in a strict sense, and if this had not been so bill-procedure could hardly have given rise to general legislation by statute.[174]

[170] *Fleta*, vol. ii, ed. and tr. H. G. Richardson and G. O. Sayles (Selden Society, London, 1955), pp. 109–10; Powicke, *Thirteenth Century*, pp. 327–8.

[171] H. S. Sweetman (ed.), *Calendar of Documents relating to Ireland, 1252–1284* (London, 1877), p. 95.

[172] Richardson and Sayles on the Provisions of Oxford in *Bulletin of the John Rylands Library* (1933).

[173] On *Parlement*, in which the King of England sometimes had to plead, see H. G. Richardson, *TRHS* (1927); J. H. Shennan, *The Parlement of Paris* (London, 1968).

[174] For the debate over the judicial origins of Parliament, see Richardson and Sayles, *BIHR* (1929), and *Law Quarterly Review* (1961); J. G. Edwards, *BIHR* (1954). The best account of what an early parliament did is contained in an article by E. F. Jacob, *TRHS* (1928).

At this time, no representatives were needed for there to be a parliament, yet Edward I (1272–1307) found it so useful to set out his requirements to a body which included representatives of the knights and townsmen, and the support of these classes was so valuable a prize in the political struggles of Edward II's reign, that by 1327 parliament could no longer be thought of without the representative element and its petitions to the king for the remedying of defects in government and law. (These petitions were still, however, mostly the bills of private citizens, taken up or 'avowed' by parliament as matters of common concern.) In this way parliament seized from the small group of royal judges at least a share in the development of the law in its technical aspect. The law embodied in *Glanvill* and *Bracton* was judge-made law, and Bracton represents the culmination of the pre-statutory period of English law, which was also the period during which the eyre dominated the judicial system. The great statutes of Edward I's reign, which defined the legal rights and remedies of the main groups in society, were promulgated in parliaments, though the judges still had a dominating voice in their formulation: at least, if we are to believe Chief Justice Hengham, who once chided a party for telling him what a statute meant, for 'we know it better than you . . . we made it'. In the fourteenth century, however, when the statutory definition of crimes, and even of torts like conspiracy (Doc. 20), became normal, the scope of political crimes such as treason was an issue between king and parliament, and the judges were reduced to the position and exposed to the dangers of political tools of the king.[175]

Still, it was as a court as much as a legislature that parliament achieved political power. According to the great Treasons Act of 1352, parliament was to judge whether particular cases which were still doubtful after the statute's definitions were treason or felony, though the decision was probably to be left to the judges, who were always called to sit in parliament. In 1283, Edward I had set a precedent by calling a 'general parliament' which included elected representatives of shires and boroughs to Shrewsbury, to decide on the punishment of the rebellious Prince David of Wales: the novel penalties decreed were drawing, hanging and quartering. This was a momentous beginning, for again and again in the fourteenth and fifteenth centuries parliament was used by king or barons for the trial and condemnation of their political enemies on charges of high treason.[176]

[175] On parliamentary petitions, see A. R. Myers, G. L. Haskins and Doris Rayner, *EHR* (1937, 1938 and 1941); on judge-made law, Richardson and Sayles, *Law and Legislation*, pp. 114 and 117; on treason and the political hazards of being a judge, J. G. Bellamy, *The Law of Treason in England in the Later Middle Ages* (Cambridge, 1970).

[176] Bellamy, *Law of Treason*, esp. pp. 26 and 88.

Because it combined the functions of high court and representative assembly, parliament survived and flourished in England, while in France Parlement and Estates General, in their separation, were vulnerable to royal despotism. The really interesting question in the history of the English parliament is not whether it began as a high court – there can be no doubt about that – but how this court came to have political functions grafted on to it. Probably what was different in England was the existence already of strong 'central courts', so that another pure law court was not required; and the fact that the king had long been accustomed to make political use of the small corps of royal justices, contrasting so markedly with the mass of judges in France. In England, justice was always an important dimension of politics. The whole range of courts was enlisted in the service of the new national assembly. Members of parliament ('knights of the shire' and 'burgesses') were elected in shire and borough courts, and without these close-knit associations it is difficult to see how a system of representation could have arisen: apart from the shire court, the gathering of *buzones*, there was certainly no shire community which could be represented. If, as a high court, parliament took on some of the characteristics of the eyre in its openness to bills, it also acquired some of the characteristics of the shire court as a place where public business was transacted in the eye of the community. Men talked of royal writs being read out in open county court (*in pleno comitatu*) long before they could speak of national ordinances being promulgated *in pleno parliamento*. England was governed through the shire courts, because it was there that statutes and administrative orders were published (Doc. 18 (37, 38)); but in a small way, the shire courts also legislated themselves, their doomsmen sometimes anticipating the rules imposed by statute years later. The election there of members of parliament meant above all that the grass-roots of English politics were in the shire court, where the county gentry arranged amongst themselves who should fill many of the public positions of the land, both political and administrative.[177]

Local procedures remained one of the twin poles of English law and government, and many remedies besides that against the slanderer must have been worked out in the local courts, for the common law grew up first of all to preserve from disruption the local communities, on which was built up in the thirteenth century 'the community of the realm'. In the seignorial court, the lord might provide the sanctioning force, but there as in the king's court, custom was always being opposed

[177] Morris, *Medieval English Sheriff*, pp. 199ff; Helen M. Cam, 'From witness of the shire to Full Parliament', in *Law-finders and Law-makers*; Holdsworth, *History of English Law*, vol. i, p. 6*; T. F. T. Plucknett in *Harvard Law Journal* (1928–9).

to the arbitrary use of power. The law could be regarded as in a real sense the heritage of the people, this attitude showing itself at the national level in the barons' demand that John should appoint as justices, constables, sheriffs and bailiffs men who knew 'the law of the land', and their refusal at Merton in 1236 to 'change the laws of England' to conform with canon law in the matter of bastardy.[178]

Nevertheless, for the whole of the period from c. 1160 to c. 1290, legal business was flowing strongly to the other pole, the king's 'central' courts. In England as in France, litigants, rather than the king, provided the impetus for the portentous growth of royal jurisdiction.[179] The aristocracy wanted their conflicts over landownership settled in the speediest way by the final authority. Most of all, perhaps, they wanted their land transactions sealed by 'final concords' in the witness of the most solemn of tribunals, just as Anglo-Saxon landbooks were made in the witan. About the year 1170, final concords (previously arranged in the honour court or, if in the king's court, then taking the form of an ordinary charter) began to be made in the form of a chirograph before the justices itinerant. In 1195 came the important decision that all fines in the king's court should be made in triplicate and the third copy (the 'foot of the fine') be filed in the Treasury where the parties' copies could be tested against it in case of dispute. In the 1198 eyre, 'over 200 final concords were made by Norfolk litigants alone'.[180]

The enormous growth of legal business which was clear to observers all over western Europe was not so universally welcomed. In Henry I's reign there were already complaints of 'the avarice and sinister and odious activity of legal experts' whose 'new way of pleading' obscured 'the certain truth of the law' and involved legal process 'in so many and great anxieties and deceits, that men avoid these actions and the uncertain dice of pleas'.[181] The major beneficiary of the increase in litigation was in fact the state, and royal power was 'adorned with laws' quite as much as 'furnished with arms'. Royal government did not grow continuously but in a series of leaps, which occurred when kings

[178] Powicke, *Thirteenth Century*, esp. pp. 142–3; R. H. Hilton, *A Medieval Society* (London, 1966), p. 158; Articles of the Barons, ch. 42, and Magna Carta, ch. 46.

[179] Cf. B. Guenée, *Tribunaux et gens de justice dans le bailliage de Senlis* (Paris, 1963).

[180] S. J. Bailey, *Cambridge Law Journal* (1961); Richardson and Sayles, *Law and Legislation*, pp. 114–15; Stenton, *English Justice*, pp. 52 and 107; Hall, *Glanvill*, pp. 94 and 96–7; J. H. Round, *Feudal England* (London, 1895), pp. 385ff. Even Scottish magnates might trek to Westminster to make final concords concerning lands in Scotland: see G. W. S. Barrow in *Juridical Review* (1971), pp. 125–6.

[181] Antonia Gransden (ed.), *The Chronicle of Bury St Edmunds* (London, 1964), p. 47; Cronne and Davis, *Regesta Regum* vol. III, pp. xxvi–xxvii, and cf. *Leges Henrici Primi*, ed. and tr. L. J. Downer (Oxford, 1972), p. 99.

turned their courts to the settling of the private wars left over by periods of rebellion. This process can be seen in the reign of Henry II, following 'the Anarchy', and in the years after Simon de Montfort's defeat at Evesham in 1265. It can be seen in Scotland, too, in the legislation of King Robert Bruce at the end of the Scottish War of Independence. Yet medieval Scottish government never enjoyed the power of its English counterpart because its structure was different in one major respect: the judicial system continued to hinge on the sheriff court and central law courts were relatively undeveloped. In England, on the other hand, the shire court was pulled apart by the enormous strains set up by the growth of central institutions. The people of the county struggled against the process which transformed the sheriff from the president of their moot into a royal judge and tax-collector. The ambiguity of the sheriff's office drained it of power, for the king transferred many of the sheriff's functions to new officials who were unequivocally his agents, such as the escheators created in Henry III's reign to look after the royal lands. The eyre was left in the last quarter of the thirteenth century as the one strong link between the king and the local community, and that too was under strain.[182]

[182] For the king 'adorned with laws', see Hall, *Glanvill*, p. 1, and E. H. Kantorowicz, 'Kingship under the impact of scientific jurisprudence', in *Twelfth Century Europe*, ed. M. Clagett *et al.* (Madison, 1966); on the Scottish legislation, A. A. M. Duncan, 'Regiam Maiestatem', *Juridical Review* (1961); on Scottish justice, see now G. W. S. Barrow, 'The Scottish justiciar in the twelfth and thirteenth centuries', *Juridical Review* (1971); on the 'ambiguity' of the sheriff's office, Morris, *Medieval English Sheriff*, pp. 192–5, and F. W. Maitland (ed.), *Bracton's Note Book* (London, 1887), no. 1730.

3

English Law Courts in the Later Middle Ages

THE breakdown of the eyre system in the last decade of the thirteenth century was caused by the burden placed upon it by the poorer class of litigants. Wherever the justices went, complaints of trespass crowded in upon them. The action of trespass seems likely to have grown out of the Appeal of Felony. 'For the sake of the king's peace', a verdict was taken on the guilt of the accused, even though the appellant failed to appear when the case moved from the shire court to the eyre or though he was 'non-suited' for a procedural mistake; and if the verdict was 'guilty', the convicted man was punished for his 'trespass against the king's peace' (Doc. 12 (24)). It is difficult to understand why appeals were begun in such large numbers in the shires and then not prosecuted before the eyre, unless ordinary people, too poor to buy writs, were adapting this criminal procedure to getting redress for 'civil' injuries without incurring the risks of battle.[1] Whatever the stages in the development, by the mid-thirteenth century oral complaints of 'trespass' quite unconnected with appeals were being accepted by the justices and from time to time were solicited by the king against unpopular officials. On the one hand, this was the beginning of the prosecution of 'misdemeanours', the class of crimes less than felony. On the other hand, this mass of complaints had been answered by the provision of a writ to give damages in a civil action of trespass – the writ which brought into the king's court every type of injury to a man's person, crops or pocket by means of the label 'against the king's peace'.[2]

The oral complaints to the justices and their written equivalents, 'bills in eyre' (Doc. 14), represent a flooding into the royal courts of litigation from the shire courts, where the oral complaint was the normal

[1] C. A. F. Meekings, *The Crown Pleas of the Wiltshire Eyre*; though it is difficult to accept Mr Meekings's concept of a 'civil appeal', recognized by the judges.

[2] Above, p. 76.

way of bringing a suit.[3] The royal judges were compelled to take cognisance of all kinds of debt and contract cases.[4]

Queritur, 'he complains', is the word which provides the key to both
the transformation of the legal system at the end of the thirteenth
century and the development of the English constitution. Charges of
maladministration by the king's servants were at the heart of the political crises of Henry III's reign and were answered by instructions to the
eyre to receive *querelae* from individuals as well as jury-presentments of
official abuses. By 'the law and custom of the realm', all justices were
obliged to listen to bills of complaint presented corporately by village
communities, even against their own lords.[5] The eyres were the *parlemenz* of the real commons of England. Central to the reforming programme of the baronial regime in 1258 was the eyre headed by the
justiciar, Hugh Bigod, which was ordered to 'hear all complaints of
trespasses, whoever had committed them' (Doc. 13). From 1278 the
commission of the justices in eyre regularly included such injunctions,
and the crown plea sections of the eyre rolls normally included 'rolls of
complaints'. 'Auditors of complaints' sat at Westminster for three years
after 1289 to deal with 'trespasses done by the King's ministers', and
on his accession in 1307, Edward II set up a commission of oyer and
terminer including the chief justices of both benches to receive complaints against Edward I's treasurer, Walter Langton, Bishop of Lichfield. Parliament was a final resort of complainants, and its rolls were filled
with bills couched in French, just like those presented to the justices in
eyre and to the special commissions of 1289 and 1307 (Docs. 14, 22).[6]

Edward I's linked inquiries into royal rights, baronial franchises and
official abuses, piled burdens on the eyre which it could not carry. By
1290, when the king compromised with the barons in the matter of
their franchises, the eyre was visibly failing, just as Wales, Scotland and
France were presenting Edward with problems which were to pre-
occupy him down to his death in 1307. Sessions of the eyre in Lancashire
were taking three weeks in mid-century, but one lasted (with interrup-

[3] G. J. Turner, *Brevia Placitata* (Selden Society, London, 1947), pp. xliv
and xlvii.
[4] R. L. Henry, *Contracts in the Local Courts of Mediaeval England* (London,
1926); W. C. Bolland, *Select Bills in Eyre* (Selden Society, London, 1914).
[5] H. G. Richardson and G. O. Sayles (eds.), *Select Cases of Procedure without
Writ* (Selden Society, London, 1941); F. M. Powicke, *The Thirteenth Century*
(Oxford, 1953), p. 143; cf. above, p. 63.
[6] E. F. Jacob, *Studies in the Period of Baronial Reform and Rebellion* (Oxford,
1925), p. 70; Helen M. Cam, 'Studies in the Hundred Rolls', *Oxford Studies in
Legal and Social History* (1921), p. 136; T. F. Tout and Hilda Johnstone (eds.),
State Trials of the Reign of Edward I, 1289–93 (Camden Society, London,
1906); G. J. Hand in *Proceedings of the Royal Irish Academy* (1961–3), on complaints of trespass in Ireland; Alice Beardwood (ed.), *Records of the trial of
Walter Langeton, 1307–1310* (Camden Society, London, 1969).

tions) for two years in 1284–6, and by 1296 people in the county were petitioning for 'special justices' because the eyre came so rarely. Between them, the king and the mass of poorer litigants had killed the eyre which had been created for the needs of a small class of richer gentry.[7]

By 'special justices' the men of Lancashire meant justices of assize and gaol delivery who were not bound to listen to every complaining voice like the justices 'for all pleas' (*ad omnia placita* – a popular name for the eyre) and could fulfil their precise and limited commissions much more expeditiously. After 1270 the increase in the numbers of gaol-delivery commissions accelerated sharply.[8] In the 1290s there was a reorganization: circuits were laid down for gaol delivery, assize and *nisi prius* hearings to be held in combination, though changes continued to be rung on the types of justices used. Royal judges were too busy, local gentry liable to corruption. In the course of the fourteenth century, the justices of the peace were generally accorded the power to deliver their local gaols (Doc. 23), but the assize judges, bench justices who also had *nisi prius* and gaol-delivery powers, remained as a centralizing force in the administration of justice. In the fifteenth century, there were usually three justices of assize, a judge, a serjeant-at-law and a local man, who went on circuit twice yearly in the vacations following Hilary and Trinity terms (i.e. in February and late July or August).

There was an attempt in fact to make the assizes into something approaching an eyre, but one which should visit each county much more frequently. This still could not cope with the flood of *querelae*. In 1298, Edward I was compelled to issue an emergency commission to a professional lawyer and a local knight on each of a number of circuits, 'to hear and determine [oyer and terminer] all manner of grievances done to his people in his name' on account of the war. They were to hear cases 'as well through their offices' (that is, by taking presentments) 'as at the suit of anyone' (by *querela*).[9] In the hearings before the country-wide oyer and terminer commissions of 1305 and later to deal with the armed gangsters ('trailbastons') of a wartime society, the intertwining of jury presentment and the individual's *querela* shows clearly.[10] During the great crisis of justice and order at the turn of the thirteenth century,

---

[7] Helen M. Cam, 'The Quo Warranto proceedings under Edward I', *History* (1926); Donald W. Sutherland, *Quo Warranto Proceedings in the Reign of Edward I* (Oxford, 1963), pp. 185–7; E. Miller, *The Abbey and Bishopric of Ely* (Cambridge, 1951), pp. 216–17; J. Parker, *A Calendar of the Lancashire Assize Rolls* (Lancs. and Cheshire Record Soc., 1904–5), pp. x and xv–xix.

[8] R. B. Pugh, *Imprisonment in Medieval England* (Cambridge, 1968).

[9] W. S. Thomson, *A Lincolnshire Assize Roll for 1298* (Lincoln Record Soc., 1944).

[10] For the original Trailbaston inquiries, see Powicke, *Thirteenth Century*, pp. 345–6; for a commission, G. O. Sayles (ed.), *Select Cases in the Court of King's Bench* (Selden Society, London, 1936–71), vol. iv, pp. 132–3.

the commission 'to hear and determine' looked like providing a whole new judicial system and certainly encouraged new procedures for the prosecution of criminals.

Commissions of oyer and terminer had always thrived on complaints of trespass. Investigations into local disturbances often took the form of commissions of inquiry into trespasses against particular complainants, which revealed so many trespassers that powers of oyer and terminer had to be added to those of inquiry rather than the accused be left over for a later visit of justices.[11] Amongst trespass writs in the *Register*, there are a number of commissions like the one ordering the sheriff of Hampshire to empanel juries to present the abuses of the Bishop of Winchester and his bailiffs, in preparation for the arrival of justices 'to hear the complaints of all and everyone wishing to complain on our behalf or their own [*pro nobis vel pro seipsis*] and determine them at our suit or anyone else's [*tam ad sectam nostram quam aliorum quorumcumque*]'.[12]

The trailbaston proceedings show this same distinction (derived ultimately from the appeal of felony) between the king's suit and the suit of the individual complainant, and simultaneously reveal the dependence of the king's prosecution, and so the maintenance of public order, on the initiative of the private accuser. This is a crucial fact in the history of medieval England – and not of England alone. In thirteenth-century Spain, the *Pesquisa* or inquisition into local disorder, instituted on the complaint of bishop or individual victim, was increasingly used; and in France royal inquiries were set to elicit complaints of such offences as raiding neighbours' territory and victimizing the poor with force and arms.[13] The extension of justice, like the action of trespass itself, was still founded on the idea of the king's peace, though in cases of riotous injury the interests of the king and of the injured persons were equally balanced and it was expedient for the public authority to encourage the private interest in order to bring wrongdoing to light.

Many of those arraigned before the justices of trailbaston and gaol delivery (Doc. 23) were taken 'at the suit of' a private person who was expected to appear and prosecute the case, on behalf of the king as well as himself (*pro domino Rege quam pro seipso*). Indictment in the proper sense, in use before the justices of the peace by the mid-fourteenth century, consisted in the confirmation of the private complaint by the grand jury: 'Richard complains to the king's justices . . . the jurors say

[11] F. W. Maitland (ed.), *Bracton's Note Book* (London, 1887), case no. 1520; *Calendar of Inquisitions Miscellaneous* (London, 1916–), vol. I, nos. 103, 122, 195, 197, 2056, etc.

[12] *Registrum Brevium Originalium* (London, 1531), fol. 125v; cf. MS. Bodley 941, fol. 122v (14th century).

[13] Evelyn S. Procter on the Pesquisa, *English Historical Review*, Supplement (1966); A. Esmein, *Histoire de la Procédure Criminelle en France* (Paris, 1882), pp. 59, 82.

the bill is true'.[14] Only through the presentation of private bills of complaint to the grand jury could the huge number of specific crimes previously dealt with (if at all) in the sheriff's tourn, have found their way before the king's justices.

The acuteness of the crisis of order at the end of Edward I's reign is shown by the mobilization of the court of King's Bench itself to cope with it. There was already a special 'king's roll' or 'crown roll' kept in King's Bench to record appeals of homicide, robbery and rape and other serious criminal pleas where the defendants had to answer 'at the king's suit' even though the appellants were non-suited. By 1300 the appeal of felony was sometimes written down in the form of a bill, and after 1318 bills alleging crimes flooded into King's Bench, for in that year the justices of King's Bench began regularly to deliver gaols wherever they might be with the king.[15]

Yet in some ways these emergency measures simply made matters worse since special commissions of oyer and terminer, relying on private complaint but restricted to the violent repression of crime, were easily used as declarations of war by particular groups in the community against other groups. This was obviously the case in the Wars of the Roses in the fifteenth century, and the long lists of commissions in the patent rolls suggest that it was already so in the troubled third decade of the fourteenth (Doc. 21). Edward I's aggression in Wales and Scotland under the guise of extending his 'peace', had brought the atmosphere of war into English society also and planted it there for two centuries. A political song of the time hailed the capture in Scotland of 'William Wallace, master-crook' as an achievement of the trailbaston measures,[16] while in England gang-leaders flourished amongst the bands of returning soldiers. The new judicial weapons were indiscriminate: many innocent people were maliciously indicted and imprisoned (Doc. 25, 1351–3) or were driven into the woods with the guilty. The singer of the Trailbaston Song, an old soldier who has served his ungrateful lord, King Edward I, 'in Flanders, in Scotland, in Gascony his own land', resolves to 'keep within the woods', for 'there is no deceit there nor any bad law, in the forest of Belregard, where the jay flies and the nightingale always sings without ceasing'; and if he gets his hands on justices Spigurnel and Belflour, he will 'teach them the game of Trailbaston . . . break their backs and rumps, their arms and their legs . . . cut out their tongues and their mouths into the bargain . . .'.[17]

[14] B. H. Putnam (ed.), *Proceedings before the Justices of the Peace in the 14th and 15th Centuries* (Harvard University Press, 1938), pp. xcixff; cf. Sir Thomas Smith, *De Republica Anglorum*, ed. L. Alston (Cambridge, 1906), p. 87.

[15] Sayles, *Cases in King's Bench*, vol. IV, introduction.

[16] T. Wright, *Political Songs* (Camden Society, London, 1839), pp. 320–2.

[17] I. S. T. Aspin (ed.), *Anglo-Norman Political Songs* (Anglo-Norman Text Society, Oxford, 1953), pp. 73–6.

Society as a whole 'largely ceased to place its trust in royal justice: its agents, the royal justices, were treated with undisguised contempt and even physical violence'. Soon after Christmas 1331, while justices of trailbaston were sitting throughout England, Richard Willoughby, justice of King's Bench, was ambushed on his way to Grantham by the Folville gang, taken off to a gathering of the criminal brotherhood (*quendam socialem comitivam*) in a nearby wood and forced to pay 1300 marks to save his head. The 'society' of the Folville brothers, as the records call it, was typical of the period, when people were compelled to look for security in 'local bands and private associations'. This was a conflict not between poor and rich so much as between 'outs' and 'ins', between the rogues in the woods and the rogues in authority. The Folvilles were gentry, the eldest of the brothers a 'respectable' J.P., and the Trailbaston Song is in French, the gentry's language. Since the judicial system was being twisted into a weapon in local struggles for power, men literally 'took the law into their own hands'. In 1336, one 'Lionel, king of the rout of raveners' issued a writ at his 'castle of the North Wind' ordering Richard of Snowshill to 'do right' to the Abbey of St Mary's, York, in the matter of a vicarage: Snowshill was bidden to show the writ to the king of England and tell him to leave off his 'false confederacies' on pain of £1000 damages. The Trailbaston commission of 1332 mentioned criminals who demanded money by letters 'in the royal style'. There was a vogue for stories like the pseudo-Chaucerian 'tale of Gamelyn' in which the 'criminal' is rescued by heroic comrades at the foot of the gallows and the justice tried and hanged in his place. When the murderers of John of Holtby, who had been 'too busy about the king's business', were indicted before the King's Bench at Ipswich in 1344, the whole town, 'the greater as well as the middle and lesser folk . . . brought to the aforesaid felons . . . presents such as food and drink and gold and silver and sang so many songs of rejoicing in their honour there that it was as if God had come down from Heaven'.[18]

Around 1330 there were anxious discussions in Parliament and elsewhere of the prevalent disorder, and it is significant that the judges then looked back to a golden age in the thirteenth century, when the eyre had visited the whole realm every seven years 'by which the peace of the land was well kept and right done to rich and poor'. The golden age had never existed, but it is true that the disappearance of the eyre was a revolution in government, more important perhaps than those turning-

[18] G. O. Sayles, *King's Bench in Law and History*, p. 13; J. R. Lumby (ed.), *Chronicon Henrici de Knighton* (Rolls Series, London, 1889–95), vol. i, pp. 460–1; E. L. G. Stones on the Folville gang, *TRHS* (1957); J. G. Bellamy on the Coterel gang, *EHR* (1964); Sayles, *Cases in King's Bench*, vol. III, 93, VI, 37; B. H. Putnam, *The Place in Legal History of Sir William Shareshull* (Cambridge, 1950), pp. 63, 68 and 147; for the tale of Gamelyn, *The Complete Works of Geoffrey Chaucer* (Oxford, 1897), and E. F. Shannon, *Speculum* (1951).

points in the growth of the central bureaucracy which English historians have studied exhaustively and, one may think, too exclusively, ever since Tout's great work on medieval administration. One of the perennial problems of government is geographical: how are the king's wishes to be transmitted to the localities without losing impetus on the way, and how is the king to oversee the enforcement of his orders from a distance? There is no reason to doubt the opinion of Chief Justice Scrope in 1329 that the eyre had been this vital link between 'headquarters' and the local administration, its primary purpose to see that those who possessed jurisdiction over the king's people exercised their franchises properly so that 'son pople seit mene adreit': his people be well governed.[19]

NEW JUSTICES IN THE COUNTIES

Seignorial justice – judicial power attributed to landlords as such – had been greatly reduced in significance by the resourcefulness of the courts of the supreme royal landlord. Everywhere – even in the 'palatinate' of Durham – the lords lost the battle for jurisdiction over the really important civil pleas. But what they lost as landlords the gentry recovered as the king's agents. The scale of Angevin government, especially in time of war, could not be maintained by a small group of all-purpose ministers in the *curia regis*, and as the thirteenth century advanced the king was forced to delegate more and more authority to the local gentry. The *quo warranto* proceedings emphasized that all government stemmed from the king just when and probably because the gentry were acquiring powers of government at the greatest rate. To the extent that 'feudalism' means the exercise of government by landlords, the later Middle Ages is the most feudal in English history, and it is comprehensible that Scrope should have talked in 1329 of the eyre's function as the inspection of 'franchise', which was 'jurisdiction over the king's people'. For it was in these years that the power of the gentry was receiving an enormous fillip from appointment to new offices such as the office of J.P. which were quickly assimilated (in the gentry's minds) to the other rights flowing from land-ownership.[20]

Of course, the gentry had always been indispensable as the enforcers of the procedures on which the common law rested and the peace which it aimed to preserve, for 'unlike France, England had a centralized government before she had a bureaucracy'.[21] To the sheriff, still for

[19] Helen M. Cam, *EHR* (1924); G. D. G. Hall, *EHR* (1959); R. V. Rogers, *Bulletin of the John Rylands Library* (1951–2).

[20] M. T. Clanchy, *TRHS* (1967); Jean Scammell, *EHR* (1967).

[21] J. R. Strayer, quoted in J. P. Dawson, *A History of Lay Judges* (Cambridge, Mass., 1960), p. 137.

Lambarde in the sixteenth century 'the ordinary conservator of the peace', had been added the coroners, described by Britton in the thirteenth century as 'the principal guardians of the king's peace'. But the intricacies of procedures imposed by the king's judges so enmeshed sheriff and coroner that they could not be effective peace-keepers. A separate 'chief constable' was therefore appointed for each county during the threat of attacks on the English coast which followed the loss of Normandy to the French in 1204; and he was to appoint constables for hundreds and townships. These under-constables of 1205, who never entirely disappeared, were sometimes termed 'keepers of the peace' (*custodes pacis*), but the name was first generally applied in the years 1263–5 to the rival sets of captains (*capitanei et custodes pacis*) appointed throughout the shires by the king and his baronial opponents. The *custos pacis* became established, ominously enough, as the partisan military leader in a civil war; and with him probably began the 'arraying' or conscripting of infantry soldiers from the men of the shire on which were based the armies which fought late medieval wars. Lambarde in the sixteenth century showed great historical judgment and echoed the commission to the constables of 1205 when he wrote of the *custos pacis* that he was 'not ordinarily appointed, but in times of great trouble only, much like as the Lieutenants of shires are now in our days [1581]. And he had charge to defend the coasts and country, both from foreign and inward enemies, and might command the sheriff and all the shire to aid and assist him.'[22]

After 1265, the office developed in two directions and eventually split. The defence of the coasts and country against foreign enemies led to the wardenships of the Scottish and Welsh marches, the military lieutenancies of the later Middle Ages and the Tudor lords-lieutenant of counties (which were something like a revival of the thirteenth-century *custodes pacis* at a time when the J.P.s for each county had reached double figures). Meanwhile defence against inward enemies was turned into regular policing duties by the Statute of Winchester of 1285, and on these crystallized the judicial functions of the keepers, making them justices of the peace. The most important requirements of the Statute of Winchester were the equipment of every man with 'harness for to keep the peace' (even the poorest having 'bows and arrows out of the forest') and the twice-yearly inspection of these arms.[23] Through the 'view of arms' the *custos pacis* had control of the local militia, which he might use for the Crown's purposes or for his own.

A striking feature of English social history from the fourteenth right into the seventeenth century is the combined use of civil and criminal

---

[22] Alan Harding, 'The origins and early history of the keeper of the peace', *TRHS* (1960); W. Lambarde, *Eirenarcha* (London, 1610).

[23] W. Stubbs, *Select Charters*, 9th edn (Oxford, 1913), pp. 466–9.

law by members of the gentry class, in order to gain local advantage. Though it is possible in a legal textbook to keep the various branches of the law in neat compartments, it is impossible for the historian to do so. The technique was to accuse your opponent of forcible entry upon the land in dispute, in breach of the king's peace (later you would do this in the Star Chamber); and if you were a J.P. you could actually arraign him for it (Doc. 25, 1403–4, 1474–5; doc. 28). 'Though Downing could get no justice to come thither', runs the account of one dispute, 'yet Eden would have justices shortly that should set Downing and all his from the parsonage.' As late as 1838, the possession of Stanfield Hall in Norfolk was contested by the same methods. The owner, Isaac Jermy, was away from home when a Mr Larner 'appeared at Stanfield Hall with a band of eighty men, cheering and waving their hats, in which most of them were wearing laurel leaves'. Larner's men cleared out Jermy's servants and barricaded themselves in the house, but then Jermy returned with two police constables and as a magistrate was able 'to read the Riot Act outside his own front door and then outside the back door. . . . About 5.45 p.m. a detachment of the Fourth Dragoon Guards arrived from Norwich, surrounded the Hall, and ostentatiously loaded their weapons. The invaders were given five minutes to surrender.'[24]

As much as anything, it was this use of the commission of the peace as a weapon in local politics which created the notorious lack of respect for the law in late medieval England (Doc. 27). Very often a royal inquiry revealed that justices were themselves to blame for the disturbance of their sessions, which their armed retainers and overbearing behaviour had provoked. It is perhaps not fanciful to regard the fate of Chief Justice Tresilian, accused by the Lords Appellant and hanged at Tyburn for 'treason' in 1388, and the other vindictive state trials of the time, as the application of local methods to national politics. Certainly, Tresilian himself is one of the judges we can catch in the act of cajoling indictments and verdicts from juries, on behalf of the king indeed, but in the same partisan way that the gentry drummed up indictments and used packed juries against each other.[25]

Probably because it sensed the consequences, the government admitted local gentlemen to the status of justices with reluctance. Edward

[24] R. Jeffs, 'The Poynings–Percy dispute', *BIHR* (1961); W. T. MacCaffrey, 'Talbot and Stanhope', *BIHR* (1960); N. J. O'Conor, *Godes Peace and the Queenes* (Oxford, 1934), pp. 51–79; O. Chadwick, *Victorian Miniature* (London, 1960), pp. 106–7; for statutes of Forcible Entry, see A. W. B. Simpson, *An Introduction to the History of the Land Law* (Oxford, 1961), p. 39, and *Law Quarterly Review* (1957), p. 125.

[25] Putnam, *Proceedings before the Justices of the Peace*, pp. cxi–cxii; *Calendar of Close Rolls, 1339–41*, p. 631; *Calendar of Patent Rolls, 1436–41*, p. 89; J. G. Bellamy, *The Law of Treason* (Cambridge, 1970), pp. 139–40 and 167.

II (1307–27) was the first king to issue frequent commissions to *custodes pacis*, and it is significant that his reign marks the beginning of almost two centuries of intermittent anarchy. In 1307 and 1308, keepers were empowered to arrest people on suspicion; and by the crucial Kent Commission of 1316 they were given gaol delivery (that is, judicial) powers over those they had themselves arrested (Doc. 23). These justices therefore hanged felons of all sorts, but they also dealt with complaints of assault, theft and even rape in which the plaintiffs feared to add the terrible 'words of felony' and had to be content to see their enemies imprisoned and fined. When the J.P.s were excluded after 1332 from giving damages to plaintiffs, these offences were seen as a lesser class of crimes, called indictable trespasses until sixteenth-century lawyers found for them the name of 'misdemeanour', leaving 'trespass' to refer to the civil action for damages. The usefulness of the concept of indictable trespass is reflected in the great increase of temporary imprisonment and of royal revenue from judicial fines in the early years of the fourteenth century.[26]

The commons in parliament – not surprisingly, since they were the gentry and leading burgesses who enjoyed the commission of the peace – repeatedly petitioned on behalf of the keepers: the advocacy of local justices may have been the first conscious policy the commons had. Perhaps also because they were the men on whom the king relied to fight the 'Hundred Years War' with France, the keepers slowly prevailed over the prejudices against them in high places. A statute of 1361 (34 Edw. III c. 1) made them justices, by authorizing them, without the need for a supplementary commission of gaol delivery, to try the criminals accused of 'all manner of felonies and trespasses'. Seven years later they were made responsible for the enforcement of the wage regulations inspired by the shortage of labour after the Black Death. This is an early indication of the special part the J.P.s were to have in the regulation of the country's economic life, in conjunction with the government's device of making statutory offences of undesirable economic practices such as forestalling (the interception and buying-up of goods before they got to market, in order to sell them 'at a more high and dear price in prejudice and hurt of the common wealth and people'). The almost unlimited scope of the J.P.s for the regulation of morals also began to be discovered; and it became more hazardous for the eaves-dropper to listen under windows at night to learn the secrets of his neighbours and mock at them for payment (Doc. 25, 1361–4, 1372, 1403–4, 1474–5).[27]

[26] Harding, *TRHS* (1960), p. 104; F. Palgrave (ed.), *Parliamentary Writs and Writs of Military Summons* (London, 1827–34), vol. i, pp. 398–400; Pugh, *Imprisonment in Medieval England*, pp. 32ff.
[27] This paragraph is based on the work of B. H. Putnam in various books and

Though the real core of their duties was always the suppression of riots by enforcing statutes against forcible entry and binding over actual or potential peace-breakers to keep the peace in future (Doc. 25, 1403–4), the justices had an important place in the growth of the concept of crime. There were now two classes of crime to be handled by them, felonies and trespasses, and in some cases it seems to have been up to the plaintiff what he called the injury done to him. 'A fuller and more rational classification of criminal acts' was needed, and the J.P.s, with their vast experience of criminal administration and often M.P.s themselves, were best placed to obtain the necessary statutory definitions. In fact, these definitions sometimes originated with the indicting juries, which gave lurid, but increasingly stereotyped, descriptions of what they regarded as serious offences which should not be pardoned. The allegation of feloniousness was often supported by the statement that the deed was premeditated or done by night (Doc. 25, 1393–6, 1410–14). The first qualification became fixed in the definition of murder and the second played its part in the differentiation of burglary from mere housebreaking.[28]

On the J.P. was focused a new system of criminal justice. Right into the fifteenth century King's Bench, in poor imitation of the eyre, lumbered round the countryside to deal with indictments before the *custodes pacis* where an exceptional level of disorder, as in the Welsh marches after Glendower's rebellion at the beginning of the fifteenth century, seemed to require it. The J.P.s were instructed to leave difficult cases to the judges of the bench, or to the justices of assize and gaol delivery. At each of their twice-yearly visits, the justices of gaol delivery might find thirty to forty prisoners in the county prison, of whom about half might have been indicted before J.P.s (most of the rest would have been arrested on suspicion, a few indicted before coroners). As Sir Thomas Smith describes gaol delivery in the sixteenth century, 'the justices of the peace, according to their estate and degree', sat next on each side to the two judges sent down from Westminster, and when a prisoner was brought in the judges could ask which of the justices had sent him to prison. The king's judges were themselves justices of the peace: the commission of gaol delivery was automatically added to that of assize, the commission of the peace to both of them. For instance, John Cokayn, a Derbyshire man and justice of Common Pleas from 1406, was on the commission of the peace for the eight counties of the midlands assize circuit, the six of the eastern circuit and the four of the northern circuit.[29]

articles which are cited in her *Proceedings before the Justices of the Peace*; the definition of forestalling is John Rastell's in *Les Termes de la Ley* (London, 1567).
   [28] See the commentary by Professor Plucknett in Putnam, *Proceedings before the Justices of the Peace.*
   [29] Elizabeth G. Kimball, *The Shropshire Peace Roll, 1400–1414* (Shrewsbury,

Not only justice but local society also was reintegrated in the commission of the peace and manifested in the general sessions held quarterly at Hilary, Easter, Midsummer and Michaelmas. Though the local gentry provided the 'working justices', lawyers were included in it to ensure more expert justice and 'some of the high nobility . . . for honour's sake', so that by Sir Thomas Smith's time the numbers of J.P.s had 'come commonly to thirty or forty in every shire, either by increase of riches, learning or activity in policy and government'. The commission of the peace was by then less of a divisive influence in local society because all the gentry of the county were coming to be included in it, almost as though by hereditary right. The authority of the ruling class in the boroughs also fed on the new type of jurisdiction, just as it had grown in earlier times on the jurisdiction of the hundred. In London, for instance, appeals of felony and compurgation were replaced by plaints and indictments of trespass and trial by jury by the end of the thirteenth century, and commissions of the peace began to be issued to the mayor and the sheriffs. The addition of the commission of the peace to the existing authority of the ruling groups was an important part of the tightening of social control which is characteristic of the life of the English boroughs in the later Middle Ages.[30]

The gentry were secure in their position as the natural governors of the countryside, and the rich merchants as the natural rulers of the towns. It was the magnates with pretensions to 'bear the rule' over wide tracts of the country whose power was insecurely based on their skill in building up followings amongst the J.P.s, recruiting them into their retinues and councils (Doc. 27). Where there were two magnates in a county whose resources were equally balanced, the commission was inflated as each strove to get his clients on, and the politics of that county were likely to be stormy. In 1330, Edmund, Earl of Kent, ended a letter to the chancellor: 'God keep you . . . and will you cause to be made keepers of the peace in Sussex Monseignur Rauf de Camoys and Monseignur Nicholas Gentil for love of us'. The malign aspect of the 'bastard feudalism' to which the disturbance of late medieval England has been attributed was not the monetary nature of the bond between magnate and client (though this was certainly much more unstable, because more easily created and broken, than the tie of land in old-style feudalism): it was rather that what the retainer placed at his lord's

1959); Putnam, *Proceedings before the Justices of the Peace*, pp. 6 and 105–7; Pugh, *Imprisonment in Medieval England*, pp. 203 and 366–9; Smith, *De Republica Anglorum*, p. 96.

[30] Smith, *De Republica Anglorum*, p. 85; Putnam, *Proceedings before the Justices of the Peace*, pp. 3 and 106–7; A. H. Thomas (ed.), *Calendars of Plea and Memoranda Rolls of the City of London* (London, 1926–32), vol. I, pp. xi–xxxiii, 22–3, 128 and 271; M. Beresford, *New Towns of the Middle Ages* (London, 1967), p. 218.

disposal was not the strength of his sword-arm but the authority of his public office. Of the ninety men retained by Lord Hastings between 1461 and 1483, thirty-three were at some time J.P.s and about twenty sheriffs. The Tudor Privy Council damped down the violence of these regional power struggles by recognizing a victor in each county in the person who was appointed lord-lieutenant. The lieutenants took over both the military functions of the magnate supervisors of arraying who were appointed from time to time in the fourteenth and fifteenth centuries and the leadership of the commission of the peace of the *custos rotulorum*; and their authority in a newly integrated shire hierarchy was expressed in their right to recommend new J.P.s, and in their appointment of deputy-lieutenants for the half a dozen or so administrative divisions which emerged in each county towards the end of the sixteenth century for the holding of 'petty sessions' of the justices.[31]

Local justice was fitted neatly to the social structure, and only occasional commissions of oyer and terminer composed of the king's councillors were left outside the system, as dramatic and uncontrollable assertions of royal power for the suppression of treason and rebellion.

NEW AND OLD COURTS AT THE CENTRE

The disorder of late medieval England to which the J.P.s contributed demanded new measures from the government. The flood of complaints which helped to create the commission of the peace itself moved on to the king, carrying with it stories of overbearing justices, sessions broken up in confusion, the overmighty's *maintenance* of legal actions simply as a way of scoring off rivals, and their *embracery*, or manipulation of juries and witnesses, when the cases came to trial (cf. Doc. 25, 1403–4). The Paston Letters are full of the campaigns waged against each other by the gentry by means of riotous entry; countered, if the local justices were ineffective, by special assizes to decide the civil disputes and commissions of oyer and terminer to deal with 'the trespasses, extortions, embraceries, offences and misprisions'; and answered again, if the loser's stories are to be believed, by '400 horse', under whose persuasion the sheriff empanelled partial juries and the judges altered their judgments (Doc. 28).[32]

[31] B. Wilkinson, 'The Chancery', in *The English Government at Work*, ed. J. F. Willard and W. A. Morris (Cambridge, Mass., 1940), vol. i, p. 204; W. H. Dunham, *Lord Hastings' Indentured Retainers* (New Haven, 1955), pp. 37–9; G. Scott Thomson, *Lords Lieutenants in the Sixteenth Century* (London, 1923).

[32] For maintenance etc. and statutes against these offences, see Sayles, *Cases in King's Bench*, vol. III, pp. livff; S. B. Chrimes and A. L. Brown (eds.), *Select Documents of English Constitutional History, 1307–1485* (London, 1961), pp. 40, 43–4 and 157–8; C. Stephenson and F. G. Marcham (eds.), *Sources of English Constitutional History* (New York, 1937), pp. 243–4.

For remedies, people naturally looked to parliament, which was at the peak of its importance as a high court because of the king's – and then the king's critics' – use of it for state trials. Nicholas de Segrave, a leading English baron, was sentenced by the king on the advice of the peers in the parliament of 1305 for deserting the royal army in time of war; in 1376, 'William, Lord Latimer, was impeached and accused by clamour of the commons' in parliament; and in 1388, five 'lords appellant', a duke and four earls, marched arm in arm into Westminster Hall to 'appeal' five of the king's ministers of treason before the 'merciless' parliament. The procedure used by parliament varied and was more or less summary, but it was always an adaptation of common-law procedure (appeal was used in 1388 because it was a private suit and the right of any citizen, and did not require the concurrence of a reluctant king). After 1400, treason was usually dealt with by commissions of oyer and terminer composed of royal councillors, but parliament kept some of its half-judicial, half-legislative powers, enshrined in the great Treasons Act of 1352, to declare that this most terrible of crimes had been committed, and to apply the terrible punishments which went with it. Acts of attainder 'convicting' those named therein of treason were necessary to legalize the forfeiture of the estates of those defeated in open rebellion against the crown.[33]

On occasion, parliament answered petitions for remedies against the prevailing disorder by applying the concept of treason, or at least the deterrent of attainder, to such crimes as the killing of judges, and to stealers of the sacrament and repeatedly criminous clerks. At the same time as they worked to restrict the definition of treason as committed by their own class, the aristocracy in parliament extended the concept to cover peasant rebellion, conspiracy and arson. The inclusion in the Statute of Riots of 1453 of the penalties of attainder represented the taking of 'the law of parliament' into the common law.[34]

In these ways, parliament was already the ultimate guardian of the common law of England that Coke and his friends proclaimed it to be in the early seventeenth century. Not only on the definition of treason, but also on the framing of judicial commissions, Edward III seemed to concede that ultimate authority lay with the community and was expressed through parliament. But parliament's function was increasingly a legislative one; and to deal judicially with the mass of particular cases coming to it, the king's council had to look to resources within itself. Its most valuable asset was the expertise in framing writs and devising solutions possessed by the chancellor, the most important figure in the government after the disappearance of the justiciar. Edward I began to transfer the burden of the initial sorting of petitions to the chancellor

[33] Bellamy, *Law of Treason.*
[34] *Ibid.* pp. 62, 78, 104–5, 125, 133, 180 and 188–91.

and his staff. Though Fleta speaks of the king having 'his court in his chancery', the chancellor was at this stage very much the servant of the king for expediting the procedures of council and parliament (Doc. 22). A good example of the way that commissions of oyer and terminer, council, parliament and chancellor worked together to answer petitions against the overmighty is provided by the 'impeachment' of the Abbot of Abingdon by the townsmen of Abingdon in 1368 for extorting dues and usurping royal privileges. (Impeachment seems to have meant not only 'the clamour of the commons' in parliament but any communal 'impetitioning' or accusation.) Begun by bills to commissioners of oyer and terminer, the case 'came before the king's council and was remitted for examination of difficult points to officials who reported to the chancellor'; at length an answer came back from parliament, restoring the abbot to full possession of the town and referring the aggrieved townsmen back to 'the common law'. There are two other features of this case which are characteristic of proceedings by bill: 'the indeterminate way in which it hovered between criminal and civil jurisdiction, and the identification throughout of royal interests with private wrongs'.[35]

'By the reign of Richard II many petitioners were addressing their complaints directly to the chancellor and he was summoning parties to appear before him by subpoena.' These complaints were against the violence, maintenance and corruption of justice perpetrated by the overmighty, particularly the great franchise-holders, and petitioners were asking for the normal remedies of damages and sureties of the peace, or, like John Paston in 1450, for commissions of special assize or oyer and terminer (Doc. 28). To quote Miss Avery once again,

'the chief advantage of the court of chancery over the ordinary courts in these "common law" cases was not so much that it offered substantial remedies which were unavailable at common law, but that it possessed superior machinery for bringing offenders into court, for examining parties and for enforcing its judgments. The subpoena was not limited by restrictions of venue and privilege; it could be used to summon parties for offences committed at sea and could penetrate the great franchises. . . . Once in court, the parties and witnesses were examined verbally, which was a much more effective means of discovering the truth than the rigid proceedings at common law.

[35] Elsa de Haas and G. D. G. Hall (eds.), *Early Registers of Writs* (Selden Society, London, 1970), pp. cxxvi–cxxvii; Wilkinson, 'The Chancery'; Margaret E. Avery, 'The history of the equitable jurisdiction of chancery before 1460', *BIHR* (1969), p. 141; Sayles, *Cases in King's Bench*, vol. v, pp. lxviiff; J. S. Leadam and J. F. Baldwin (eds.), *Cases before the King's Council* (Selden Society, London, 1918), pp. 5–8; Gabrielle Lambrick, 'The impeachment of the Abbot of Abingdon in 1368', *EHR* (1967), pp. 250, 257, 275.

Local inquiries might be made by a special commission to chancery clerks or local gentry appointed under the writ *dedimus potestatem*.'[36]

By injunctions the chancellor would stay a trial at common law while deeds were discovered and witnesses examined; and 'quiet' or protect a tenant from interference till his common-law case was decided, preventing his immediate ejection if the case went against him. Chancery's characteristic jurisdiction consisted more in this procedural control than in court hearings (Doc. 29); and although by the fifteenth century chancery enjoyed the immense asset of a clerical staff 150 strong, the chancellor was for long its only judge. Indeed, the administrative nature of the chancellor's work means that the emergence of a separate *court* of chancery was slow and that it is difficult to date. Since equity was simply a way of working the common law, there was never any special training for chancery lawyers, who were only ordinary barristers practising in chancery.

Nevertheless, a Court of Chancery can be said to have appeared by 1450, because the common-law side of chancery's work (where the papers were in English) had by then much declined before the Latin side, which comprised substantial problems unrecognized by the common-law courts. Between 1420 and 1450 the annual number of petitions coming before the chancellor quadrupled, the long chancellorship of John Stafford, Bishop of Bath and Wells and later Archbishop of Canterbury, the first 'Lord Chancellor', probably providing the continuous encouragement necessary to establish a new area of justice. In 90 per cent of the cases heard in the later years of Henry VI's reign, the sub-poenas went out to summon defendants and witnesses in disputes over *uses*. A use was created when a man enfeoffed a group of friends with property to be held by them for the use (*ad opus*) of the real beneficiary of the arrangement (called the *cestui que use*). This device was a crucial development in the land law, for it allowed a feudal tenant to enfeoff away all his property before death, thus avoiding the feudal incidents of relief and wardship for his heir, and at the same time preserve the normal succession of the land by settling the use on to his heir; and if he chose to bestow the use on someone else, he effectively achieved the devising of land by will which feudal law forbade. The danger was that the *feoffees to use* (the trustees, as we should say) might treat the property as their own and, 'contrary to all good conscience', refuse to recognize the heir's standing or 'estate' in it, in which case the heir had 'no remedy by the common law'. But the chancellor, who was, till the sixteenth century, almost without exception a high ecclesiastic, was concerned with breaches of faith, and he had his procedural weapons to turn on the faithless trustees – though now in support of his own principles of equity (Doc. 30).[37]

[36] Avery, *BIHR* (1969), p. 141.

[37] *Ibid.*; A. D. Hargreaves, 'Equity and the latin side of Chancery', *Law*

The chancellor went on to modify common-law judgments enforcing contracts without regard to the fraud or unintended evil which would result, or the ruinous penalties they contained; and also to enforce contracts not recognized at common law (Doc. 29). He could order the specific performance of a contract (the common-law courts only gave damages for non-performance), adjudicate on the validity of a will (here poaching upon ecclesiastical preserves) and protect the interests of a married woman. Through commissions to groups of gentry or merchants, he provided for arbitration in many disputes which do not reach a court of law even today, often mercantile disputes delegated to him by the Council, which was concerned with them because they involved treaty rights and international questions.

Very early on there was some resentment amongst common-law judges at the chancellor's powers. Parliament and judges were agreed that a man should not lose his freehold as a result of the chancellor's unusual methods. As a way of initiating actions, the sub-poenas which 'flew so thick abroad' had the great advantage over writs that they were valid everywhere (not only in particular counties which had to be specified) and did not commit plaintiffs to narrow lines of attack which they might not have fully understood when they started on them. But of course it was sometimes unfair to a defendant to be summoned by a missive, rather too easily procured, which did not set out what it was he would have to deny. The decline in the number of 'common-law' cases in chancery in Henry IV's reign was probably due to the opposition of the Commons in parliament, and in 1437 petitioners in chancery were required by statute to find pledges to pay damages if their complaints proved to be untrue or matters for the common law courts. There was no jury-trial in chancery and the chancellor was the judge of fact as well as law. The Court of Chancery was particularly effective in wheedling out the truth by verbal examination of parties and witnesses, but in 1482 the judges were still objecting to the calling of witnesses to prove a case against the common-law heir of a trustee: 'if a descent can be disproved by two witnesses in chancery it follows that one may disprove twenty descents, which is against reason and conscience. . . . It is a lesser evil to cause him, who allows his feoffee to die, still seised of his land, to lose his land, than by testimonies in chancery to cause many persons to lose their inheritances.' In the rise of the Court of Chancery, English law harvested for a second time the fruits of procedural experiment, but the common lawyers found some of its methods strange and disquieting (Doc. 29). The common law and equity remained different things.[38]

Quarterly Review (1952); J. M. W. Bean, *The Decline of English Feudalism* (Manchester, 1968).

[38] W. C. Bolland, *Chief Justice William Bereford* (Cambridge, 1924); W.

Too much of a gap must not be assumed between chancery's earlier concern with local violence and its later preoccupation with the technicalities of land settlements. Both local violence and the development of uses and mortgages were by-products of struggles for land and consequent power within an increasingly unbridled aristocracy. The Court of Chancery arose in answer to the demands of the aristocracy at a time when the Crown was weak and the barons in the king's Council strong (uses deprived and were intended to deprive the king of much of his feudal revenue). It was 'a tribunal for landowners who wished to escape the restrictions imposed by common law upon their freedom to deal with their lands as they wished',[39] and also another field on which they could conduct their endless battles.

The Courts of Chivalry and Admiralty likewise answered the needs of the propertied class, this time the professional soldiers and leading merchants whose wealth and power were made in the Hundred Years War; and they also were 'conciliar courts', performing functions delegated by the Council. The Court of Chivalry was held by the Constable and Marshal of England, to whom was delegated the hearing of disputes which arose from 'the business side of medieval warfare' (disputes about the contracts between captains and troopers by which medieval expeditionary forces were mainly assembled, and about the ransoming of prisoners) and which were outside the jurisdiction of the ordinary courts because they concerned events outside the realm or because the parties were aliens. An interesting anticipation of the Court of Chivalry on its 'commercial side' was the court which the Steward and Marshal of the Household held within the Verge, reckoned to extend twelve miles on each side of the king's person. This court had the same comprehensive jurisdiction as the justices in eyre, but it probably came into existence during Edward I's tour of his French dominions in 1286–9 and was needed primarily to register and enforce recognisances of debts to the foreign merchants, often Italians, who provided much of the finances as well as the supplies for the wars between England and France. It seems to have been unpopular with Englishmen because it acted on mere complaint and was untrammelled by the dilatory procedures of common law, and statutory limitations were placed on it in 1300.[40]

The Constable and Marshal of England, who were responsible for the 'logistics' of the king's armies as the Steward and Marshal of the

Lambarde, *Archeion*, ed. C. H. McIlwain and P. L. Ward (Cambridge, Mass., 1957), pp. 51–70; Avery, *loc. cit.* pp. 142–3; A. K. R. Kiralfy, *Source Book of English Law* (London, 1957), pp. 260–1.
[39] R. Virgoe, *BIHR* (1970); Avery, *loc. cit.* p. 143.
[40] Sayles, *Cases in King's Bench*, vol. III, pp. lxxxiii–lxxxviii, vol. VI, p. 136; Hubert Hall (ed.), *Select Cases on the Law Merchant* (Selden Society, London, 1929, 1932), vols. II–III, vol. II, p. 6, vol. III, pp. xlvii and lix.

Household were responsible for those of the royal court, are found holding a court in 1348, nine years after the outbreak of the Hundred Years War, when they ordered the arrest of a French prisoner-of-war who had betrayed the trust of his captors and so deprived them of their legitimate ransom. The most sensational ransom case began at the battle of Najera in 1367 when two squires in the Black Prince's army, Robert Hauley and John Shakell, captured a Spanish nobleman, the Count of Denia, whom they released on his surrender of his eldest son as pledge for payment of the ransom. Some years later, the ransom still unpaid, the king's Council demanded the hostage for use as a diplomatic bargaining-counter, and imprisoned the squires in the tower when they resisted. In 1378 they escaped to sanctuary in Westminster Abbey, where Hauley and a cleric were sensationally murdered on the altar steps by the Council's agents. Hauley's rights in the ransom passed to a London fishmonger, John Hoton, and from 1390 to 1432 Hoton and his executors sued Shakell and his heirs in the Court of Chivalry, at first for the long-suffering hostage and then for the letters of marque against Aragonese shipping which Shakell obtained in default of the ransom, 'entitling him to 21,050 francs, 6,145 marks and 100,000 florins'. Such matters of hard cash as these were the main concern of the court at its beginning, rather than the claims and counter-claims to arms in the heraldic sense with which it later became preoccupied, or the dramatic appeals of treason which bulk large in histories of it; and 'chivalry' in its title simply meant 'the knightly class'.[41]

Appeals of treason naturally came to the court if they concerned events outside the geographical scope of the common law (for centuries, appeal in the Court of Chivalry was to be the only means of prosecuting even ordinary crimes in the Channel Isles or Isle of Man): the first recorded was Sir John Annesley's accusation against Thomas Caterton in 1380 that he had treacherously sold the castle of St Sauveur to the French. The vogue for appeals of treason at this time led to the refurbishing of the ritual of trial by battle on lines perhaps suggested by French chivalry. The court was also an obvious place to bring charges of open rebellion within the realm, and in 1405 the rebels against Henry IV were convicted on the king's record 'according to the laws and usages of arms of the Court of Chivalry in England'. The punishments for treason inflicted by the court included degradation from honours – the traitor's loss of his coat of arms and peculiar signs of infamy at his execution.[42]

[41] A. Rogers, 'Hoton versus Shakell: a ransom case in the Court of Chivalry', *Nottingham Mediaeval Studies* (1962 and 1963).

[42] G. D. Squibb, *The High Court of Chivalry* (Oxford, 1959); M. H. Keen, *TRHS* (1962); Bellamy, *Law of Treason*, pp. 159–62; G. Neilson, *Trial by Combat* (Glasgow, 1890), pp. 167ff and 188–90.

Though the Lord High Admiral was holding a court by 1357, the development of admiralty jurisdiction was held back by parliament's inveterate suspicion of the conciliar courts. Yet the courts kept by the admirals and vice-admirals in the various parts of the coast were badly needed to settle commercial cases according to the sea-laws and other conventions upon which the Western European trading area depended (Doc. 26). The borough and fair courts of Piepowder gave inadequate protection to merchants of international standing, and the common-law courts tended to be disdainful of the 'Law Merchant'.[43]

Still the Council could not shift the ultimate responsibility for maintaining order and justice on to these specialized courts – indeed, the very specialization of Chancery, Chivalry and Admiralty forced many petitioners back to the Council, or (like 'the poor and simple inhabitants in the town of Swaffham' in 1451: Doc. 28) back to parliament which could act effectively only through the Council. Besides coping with petitions, the Council examined those accused of high crimes and misdemeanours and supervised the drawing of the indictments against them by the Crown's lawyers. In 1388, the Council became involved in the examination of heretics with the aim of forcing recantations from them, perhaps because Thomas Arundel, then chancellor, was also Archbishop of York. It was the Council that persuaded Roger Bolingbroke, 'a great astronomer', to confess that in 1441 he had tried to kill Henry VI by sorcery, on the orders of Eleanor Cobham, Duchess of Gloucester. Examination by the Council developed as more weight was given by the courts to evidence and less to 'the clamour of the people'. Confessions, even ones extracted by torture, were a step towards a more rational procedure.[44]

Though it had such power in pre-trial proceedings and even on occasion declared to the judges that the alleged crime was treasonable, the Council could not sentence a man to lose life, limb or freehold as a common-law court could: that is why it became accustomed to send the accused for trial before a 'common-law' commission of oyer and terminer – made up of its own members. But it could impose enormous fines. The Earl of Devonshire was examined by the Council in 1392 on charges that he had protected unruly servants and abused Devonshire J.P.s, telling one of them 'that he knew all the roads by which he must come and go, and that he should not escape'. The earl admitted his guilt, and the Council sent him to prison 'until he paid to our lord the king fine and ransom' at the king's pleasure. Then it remitted the imprisonment and put the earl on probation: if he again failed to

[43] Kiralfy, *Source Book*, pp. 353–4.
[44] Bellamy, *Law of Treason*, pp. 108, 117, 151–5 and 214; H. G. Richardson, 'Heresy and the Lay Power under Richard II', *EHR* (1936); Margaret Aston, *Thomas Arundel* (Oxford, 1967).

'sustain ... the laws of our said lord the king ... as well as his ministers in guarding the laws', the king would take cognisance of his recent trespasses 'as though they were trespasses and malfeasances committed and perpetrated by him anew'. As the chancery was excluded from common-law cases and became preoccupied with uses, the Council had to resume the entire burden of suppressing local disorder. Thus, on 10 February, 1439, 'at Westminster in the Star Chamber', we find the Council, consisting of the Duke of Gloucester, the chancellor (the Bishop of Bath), the Bishop of St Davids, the Earls of Salisbury and Northumberland, the Treasurer of England (Lord Cromwell), the Keeper of the Privy Seal and the Keeper of the Wardrobe, examining witnesses about a riot at Bedford, where the sessions were alleged to have been disturbed by Lord Fanhope and a force of sixty men 'with thick doublets and swords and bucklers'.[45]

By the end of the fifteenth century, 'the Council in Star Chamber' was acquiring a settled jurisdiction in cases of riot. It is important to understand that this jurisdiction was once again built upon the bills of private individuals, and bills often addressed in the early days to the chancellor, who dominated the Council when it met in the Star Chamber of the Palace of Westminster for the transaction of judicial business. Star Chamber heard cases of 'Maintenances, Oppressions, or other Outrages of any persons in the Country ... at the Suit of the Party', though it certainly treated the wrongs complained of as crimes. The story of trespass was repeated. In order to get a complaint heard by this effective new court, the plaintiff attached the label of riot as the plaintiff in trespass attached the label, 'with force and arms',[46] and the incredible accounts in Star Chamber bills of thousands of rioters armed to the teeth seem to develop straight from the elaborations of the phrase *cum vi et armis* in trespass cases (Doc. 25, 1474-5). One is almost led to think that the picture of local disorder in the sixteenth century is an illusion created by this formality of Star Chamber procedure – the legal fiction that a case in the court was one of riot. In fact, Star Chamber may have reduced local violence by providing yet another place for the fictional battles of litigation. The aristocracy assimilated the procedures of this court as it did those of the J.P.s and chancery to the tactics of its local struggles: forcible entry into disputed property was alleged in many cases. Star Chamber was a place for tying up your opponents, not to win your case but to avoid losing. The underlying issues were really civil ones of landownership, though the legal importance of the court lay in its willingness to develop new concepts of crime – in such areas as con-

[45] Leadam and Baldwin, *Cases before the King's Council*, pp. 77–81 and 104–7; Avery, *loc. cit.* p. 142.
[46] C. G. Bayne and W. H. Dunham (eds.), *Select Cases in the Council of Henry VII* (Selden Society, London, 1956), pp. 123–7.

spiracy, forgery, defamation, perjury – at a time when King's Bench was inactive.[47]

Most of these developments were to happen beyond 1500. But Star Chamber did not exhaust the judicial fruitfulness of the Council in the fifteenth century, under the stimulus of the stream of complaints. In 1483 there appears a second clerk of the Council with responsibility for the 'custody, registration and expedition of bills, requests and supplications of poor persons'. Councillors were told off for the actual hearing of poor men's cases: churchmen – particularly the almoner who distributed the king's alms – seem to have been regarded as appropriate. The poor men's court, the Court of Requests, and Star Chamber appeared at about the same time and were only slightly different aspects of the same institution, but Requests diverged to cover essentially private matters, treated as questions of equity and conscience, and so became more like a poor man's Chancery. The expeditiousness of the court soon attracted plaintiffs who were anything but poor. Since its judges were usually competent civil lawyers, a variety of mercantile cases came to it, and matrimonial disputes which would earlier have gone to a church court.[48]

Finally, there must be mentioned the regional councils appointed in the north and in the marches of Wales from Edward IV's reign onwards, in order to curb the power of the wardens of the Scottish and Welsh marches. The powers of the regional councils were not delegated by the king's Council, though they were supervised from Westminster: in fact, they included a permanent common-law jurisdiction of oyer and terminer which the Privy Council did not have. The development of the jurisdiction of these other councils was rather parallel to that of the king's Council, the same general responsibility for order leading to the same functions in equity. In regulations of 1484, the holding of quarterly sessions 'to hear, examine and order all bills of complaint' was placed before the suppression of riots amongst the duties of the Council in the north. Perhaps the frequency of ecclesiastical presidents also helped to give the regional councils their equitable jurisdiction.[49]

Pleading in the conciliar courts was conducted by the exchange of written statements and answers. First came the bill itself, setting out the plaintiff's case, often at great length. Then the parties would fire off alternately with any number of *protestations* and *contestations, supplications, replications* and *duplications*, a copy of each of them being given to the opposing party (Doc. 26); and there would be further bills com-

[47] S. E. Lehmberg, *Huntington Library Quarterly* (1961); T. G. Barnes, *American Journal of Legal History* (1961, 1962).

[48] I. S. Leadam (ed.), *Select Cases in the Court of Requests* (Selden Society, London, 1898); G. R. Elton, *The Tudor Constitution* (Cambridge, 1960).

[49] C. A. J. Skeel, *The Council in the Marches of Wales* (London, 1904); R. R. Reid, *The King's Council in the North* (London, 1921); Elton, *Tudor Constitution*, pp. 195ff.

plaining of the delaying tactics of the opposition. The other party might admit each of the written pleas, or the judge might have to pronounce on its validity. Commissions of experts might be appointed to decide on particular issues of pleading, or arbiters to settle the case altogether.[50]

The chancellor, and hence the Council and its delegated jurisdictions, were equipped and willing to examine written evidence, beginning naturally with the terms of charters. Many suits in the conciliar courts were in fact for possession of the written evidences – the chest of title deeds – on which ownership of the property rested. From the ancient practice in the king's courts of invoking the witnesses to charters, the appeal to witnesses and tallies in cases under the Law Merchant and the Council's interrogation of the participants in local affrays, there grew also the use of oral evidence and the cross-examination of witnesses. Here the old device of the special commission made another contribution in the form of the commission to gentlemen of the shire to interrogate witnesses locally, perhaps at some well-known hostelry. What the commissioners did was to administer to the witnesses an agreed list of questions, called an *interrogatory* (Doc. 26), often questions of very wide scope, such as: 'Did not Mr Coke often declare or discover that he had a greater kindness for the defendant than for any other person whatsoever? Was there not an entire friendship and familiarity between them? Declare what you know or believe'. Only in writing could the depositions of the witnesses have been returned to the Council or its delegated jurisdiction.[51]

The circumstances of the cases and the actual language of the parties comes through the miscellaneous papers of conciliar court pleading much better than they ever did through the uniform Latin notes of procedural steps in the misleadingly-named 'plea-rolls' of the common-law courts, which began with and never escaped from the stereotyped phrases of the original writ. The bills and pleas of poor men and of petitioners complaining of affrays were naturally in English, and so generally were the answers to interrogatories; and the bills of knights and squires in the Court of Chivalry and sometimes in chancery were in their language, which was French. Only the headings put in by the clerks in the records and the pleadings in the more technical cases in chancery were in Latin. The conciliar courts did not use formal enrolments, but retained the written pleadings and depositions in their original form, keeping books simply to register their *acts*, *orders* and *decrees* when the courts' judgments or *sentences* became too lengthy to be endorsed in full on the backs of the plaintiffs' bills (Docs. 26, 30).[52]

---

[50] Lambrick, *EHR* (1967), pp. 253ff; Rogers, *Nottingham Mediaeval Studies* (1962), pp. 77ff, 85 and 88.

[51] Rogers, *loc. cit.* p. 79; Kiralfy, *Source Book*, pp. 272–3.

[52] Hargreaves, *Law Quarterly Review* (1952); Rogers, *loc. cit.* (1962, 1963).

Paper pleading was not, however, an invention of the conciliar courts, nor an adoption by them of civilian methods, but something which developed naturally in all English courts in the later Middle Ages: merely a writing-down of the complexities which had grown up in oral pleadings. The records of the new courts simply make plain what the older pattern of records in the common law courts conceal. The bill, though reminiscent of the Roman *libellus*, was probably no more than the scribbled draft of the poor man's oral complaint. Soon the defendant would also need his answer ready in writing, as in a case of 1482 in Common Pleas: 'and he further says that he is not learned in the law and he drew out from his pocket a certain written bill in pauper's form in English in these words: "John Pecock in proper person saith that to the taking of this inquest the judge ought not [to] proceed . . ." He asks that the bill and the writing therein with what he said before be received as his plea . . .'. Even in the thirteenth century the clerks sometimes asked to have a written copy of a complicated oral plea. The record of the court had acquired such authority that pleading became directed to producing a particular result on the roll. The judges and clerks jealously guarded the rolls from vulgar eyes, but in order to keep business moving at all they were forced to permit the parties' attorneys to put in amendments to their pleas. For both judges and clerks necessity opened up unforeseen advantages. The former discovered that a good deal of business could be sent straight down to 'Hell', the clerks' office below Westminster Hall, for written pleadings to be copied immediately on to the roll. The latter found that they virtually controlled the judicial process and its profits (Doc. 24, 1347).[53]

The Courts of Common Law were not exempt from the spate of bills, and the adaptation which this forced upon them led, in the case of King's Bench, to the development of new criminal procedures. It was in 1318, when they travelled up to York and were made a permanent commission of gaol delivery wherever they might be, that the judges of King's Bench were fully exposed to the flood of petitioners. They began to hear the bills complaining of trespasses which had earlier been presented to the justices in eyre; and bills of criminal Appeal, which could by then be presented through attorneys from the very first stages in the county court. Five years later, the court was instructed to become a court of first instance for indictments – that is, to deal with all bills of accusation approved by presenting juries. The older forms of criminal procedure began to be dissolved away by the principle that a man was compelled to answer the king even though there was no writ or appeal. Even the submission of a bill to a jury for the formal indictment was

[53] Kiralfy, *Source Book*, pp. 50–1; Sayles, *Cases in King's Bench*, vol. II, pp. ci–cii; Margaret Hastings, *The Court of Common Pleas in the Fifteenth Century* (Ithaca, 1947), pp. 31, 37 and 40–1.

not absolutely necessary, and the king's judges began to act on mere *information* that an offence had been committed.[54]

If appellant or informer failed to pursue the case, the king had legal agents to prosecute the king's suit. The first official guardians of the king's interest in King's Bench had been the judges themselves, who were keeping a second set of plea-rolls already in the thirteenth century (the *Rex* rolls) as memoranda of cases which were being prosecuted for the king. Walter of Wimborne, judge of the King's Bench from 1276 to 1290, was remarkable for the way in which he combined that position with the duty of 'suing for the king'. All a judge could do, however, was to keep an eye on the king's interest, leaving the private plaintiff to prosecute the king's suit with his own. So by 1247, even before Wimborne's time, Lawrence del Brok was being retained by the king to act as his permanent attorney in King's Bench. Thenceforth the office was continuous, and the king's attorney had often to engage other attorneys to act in particular cases. His rolls, sometimes called the *Controlment Rolls*, included copies of indictments, lists of prisoners and confessions of approvers. He came to be known as 'the coroner of England', since he looked after the king's interests in the central court as the ordinary coroner did in his county.[55]

The written bill, since it could be presented by an attorney or taken over by the king's attorney, hastened the passing of the initiative in prosecution to the law officers of the Crown. Eventually, the king's attorney or the attorney-general (an official who appears in the fifteenth century with general responsibility for the king's suits in all the courts) would file a suit 'at the relation of' the informer, or put in a bill of information on his own account (Doc. 24, 1373).[56] The origins of this public prosecution are revealed by the fact that the king's attorney might claim the informer's statutory reward, as Simon of Kegworth did in 1362 when he secured a conviction in a plea of contempt by bill (Doc. 24, 1362); by the telltale words which continued in Elizabeth I's reign to describe the private informer as one who sues for the queen as much as for himself (*tam pro eadem domina Regina quam pro seipso exhibuit . . . quandam informacionem*); and by the cases where the informer gives way, and the attorney-general 'now sues for the queen' (*pro eadem domina Regina modo in hac parte sequitur*).[57] Modern public prosecution stems less from Henry II's presenting juries than from the procedure by bill of trespass.

[54] Sayles, *Cases in King's Bench*, vol. III, pp. xliiiff, vol. IV, pp. lxviiff, vol. VI, p. 32; Bayne and Dunham, *Select Cases*, p. lii; T. F. T. Plucknett, *TRHS* (1936).
[55] Sayles, *Cases in King's Bench*, vol. I, pp. lv–lvi and cx–cxi, vol. V, pp. xxixff.
[56] J. Ll. J. Edwards, *The Law Officers of the Crown* (London, 1964), pp. 262–7.
[57] See for examples Public Record Office, KB 27/1303, membranes 7 and 60.

An indictment could be accepted as 'good in substance', although it was general and imprecise in its terms or even inaccurate in details. With this new emphasis on the offence rather than the procedure, 'indictment' came to mean a colourful written accusation from the rhetorical phrases of which were culled the new definitions of crime. An indictment purported to be the accusation of a presenting jury, but for a serious crime like treason it was always drawn up by the Crown's lawyers, so that there was a consistent development of the concept of treason which mirrors the government's policy towards dissent. But procedure by indictment was not much more rational than appeal: the indictment was read out to the prisoner in English when he was brought into court, but he was not allowed to have a copy of it, nor to retain counsel, give evidence or call witnesses, nor even to make a statement. He could merely plead guilty or not guilty, and challenge up to thirty-five of the trial jurors. The judges sometimes cajoled juries, but the easiest way to secure convictions was for them to act as prosecutors and browbeat or trick the prisoners into confessions.[58].

The multiplication of civil remedies and the conceptual development of private law in the later Middle Ages is reflected in the Register of Writs, which had grown from about sixty writs in the first half of the thirteenth century to about 890 in c. 1320 and 2,500 in the first printed Register of 1531. But the Register merely reflected the new ideas arising from the argumentation of counsel in the course of pleading (Docs. 20, 29) – often pleading in cases begun by bill. It is to the exchanges between counsel reported in the Year Books that one must go to appreciate, for instance, the momentous development of ideas of tort and contract within the context of actions of trespass. The Roll of Common Pleas for Easter term, 1466, records Henry Hull's action against Richard Orynge for trespass 'with force and arms, that is, with swords, bows and arrows', in which Hull alleged that Orynge broke his close 'and did by walking with his feet tread down and consume his grass . . . and [commit] other enormities etc., to his serious damage and against the King's Peace. . . .' Only the Year Book shows the importance of this famous case. Orynge had gone on to the plaintiff's land to pick up clippings from his own thorn hedge, but the judges awarded damages against him after listening to a remarkable discussion (full of vivid examples of straying beasts, accidental shootings and falling trees) about the difference between criminal liability, for which malice aforethought had to be proved, and civil liability by which even unintended damage had to be paid for.[59]

By soon after the beginning of the fourteenth century, there were

[58] Bellamy, *Law of Treason*, pp. 166–7.
[59] de Haas and Hall, *Early Registers of Writs*; Kiralfy, *Source Book*, p. 128.

more formal schools for lawyers than the courts themselves. These 'Inns of Court', the only 'universities' for the laity in medieval England, were soon taking mainly students who were aiming for the top of the profession, the ranks of the serjeants-at-law. Chaucer's serjeant was a real aristocrat,

> 'who paid his calls
> Wary and wise, for clients at St Paul's . . .
> He often had been Justice of Assize . . .
> His fame and learning and his high position
> Had won him many a robe and many a fee . . .
> Though there was none so busy as was he
> He was less busy than he seemed to be . . .
> He could dictate defences or draft deeds:
> No one could pinch a comma from his screeds . . .'

At first, the distinction between serjeant and ordinary attorney was merely one of the quality of work performed and the pay demanded: the serjeants were those who received regular retaining fees. When pleading became largely written, the serjeants' business seemed likely to be lost to the attorneys and clerks of the court who did the routine drafting of pleas. But the serjeants held on to the prerogative of signing special pleas, and moved to the new techniques of examining witnesses and presenting evidence. In Common Pleas they obtained a monopoly of the right to speak. Although their oath talked of loyalty to their clients (whom they traditionally consulted in the porch of St Paul's) and not of service to the court, the serjeants were appointed by royal writ and installed with greater splendour than the judges, whom they hardly exceeded in numbers.[60]

The small number of serjeants had to leave much routine business to the senior students at the Inns. Students remained 'apprentices' for twenty years or so, in which time they would have married, obtained wide legal practices and held public office. Only then might they become serjeants and betake themselves to one of the two serjeants' Inns, from which they and the judges would still often return to dine in their 'old college', their Inn of Court. It was from one of the activities of the Inn that the senior apprentices, the advocates who were not serjeants, took their name of *barristers* (properly 'utter' or 'outer' barristers). They sat on the form or 'bar', in those outermost places reserved for senior students called upon to argue at the moots or mock courts. The barristers' business was increased by the eagerness of litigants to take their problems to them when an expensive serjeant was

---

[60] Sir John Fortescue, *De Laudibus Legum Anglie*, ed. S. B. Chrimes (Cambridge, 1942), for a vivid fifteenth-century description of the Inns; Chaucer, *Canterbury Tales*, ed. N. Coghill (Harmondsworth, 1951), pp. 33–4; Sayles, *Cases in King's Bench*, vol. v, pp. xxixff.

not essential, but their greatest opportunities lay in the service of the Crown. After 1400 barristers gained a monopoly in King's Bench like that earlier achieved by the serjeants in Common Pleas and some were retained as 'king's counsel learned in the law' to assist the new officers of attorney-general and solicitor-general, which a few of them could themselves aspire to become since the king's serjeants disdained to do so.

The judges of the later Middle Ages were drawn from the ranks of the serjeants, more than half of them from the *king's serjeants*. These had first been appointed to act for the king in the eyre during Edward I's *quo warranto* campaign, and the office was firmly established in 1315 when Edward II retained four very distinguished serjeants, two of whom were raised to the bench of Common Pleas in 1320. King's serjeants operated in all the courts, including parliament, to which they were summoned along with the judges, and their opinion was asked on such matters as the Duke of York's claim to the throne in 1460. They were already half-way to being judges, with whom they served on special commissions into the counties, especially when the king's rights were involved, and the recorded judgments of the courts sound more and more like serjeants' arguments. So there came the momentous change by which the judges ceased to be drawn from the clerks of the court and a single legal career was established, leading an able student up through advocacy to the bench. It was because by the fifteenth century almost all the serjeants who lived long enough went on to the bench that the appointments of serjeants were carefully controlled and attended with such dignity. The consequences of the fusion of the judiciary with the legal profession were immense. Being a judge became more a matter of technical skill than of government or politics. The common experience of judge and advocate led to a co-operation which expedited cases. At the same time, judges who could remember trying the same tricks themselves were healthily sceptical of meretricious brilliance in pleading. Success depended on quick and keen thinking, not – at least till the Renaissance reached England – on showy oratory.[61]

The high public standing of the judges in the later Middle Ages is shown by the rewards open to them and the punishments they risked. The fact that King's Bench was completely laicized by 1341 meant that the judges could no longer be rewarded by ecclesiastical benefices, yet the salaries of the judges remained right into the fifteenth century at the scale established in 1278: sixty marks (£40) a year for the chief justices and forty for puisne justices. The king made do with as few judges as possible (only two or three at a time in King's Bench) and made their positions more attractive by a complicated system of supplementary payments, by gifts of robes and by the automatic knighting of those

[61] Hastings, *Court of Common Pleas*, pp. 78–9; Sayles, *Cases in King's Bench*, vol. VI, pp. xxvii–xxxiv.

raised to the bench. In 1327, William Herle, Chief Justice of Common Pleas, was granted a supplement to his salary of 240 marks a year. Some extra income was derived from vacation work on assizes and special commissions in the counties, but justices of assize got only £20 a year and J.P.s a maximum of £2.40, and in a time of political upheaval this work was much more hazardous than lucrative. If the late medieval judges were very rich men, it was on account of other and more irregular profits. They acted as trustees for magnates who feared to lose their lands by attainder, and were presumably paid for their services; they shared amongst themselves large sums in fees from parties, mainly for the sealing of judicial writs; and the Chief Justice of Common Pleas dispensed, for payment, valuable clerkships and offices in the courts. Above all, they received all manner of gifts from hopeful litigants.[62]

Such oiling of the machinery of justice was accepted as normal and inevitable in the Middle Ages and long after, and simply reflects the importance of the law and the judges in aristocratic society. Many of the cases of the reviling and rabbling of judges which occurred are likely to have been the products of particular political situations in which they had reluctantly become involved by commissions of oyer and terminer, rather than of a general 'disdain for the law'. In the fifteenth century, most judges tried to keep out of politics and did so successfully, with the result that they enjoyed a surprising continuity of tenure despite the troubled times and the fact that they sat only 'during the King's pleasure'. Even the 'Readeption' of Henry VI and the defeat and death of Richard III at Bosworth left the bench of Common Pleas undisturbed. For judges could not be made overnight out of successful politicians: years of experience of advocacy was essential. The chief mark of the later medieval judiciary was a growing professionalism, and the period of the Wars of the Roses was also the period of two of the greatest judges, Thomas Littleton, author of a famous book, *Tenures*, and John Fortescue, author of the works *On the Governance of England* and *In Praise of the Laws of England*.[63]

While the bar was taking over the bench, it drew apart from the clerks and attorneys, who formed a separate section of the legal profession with its own rules and standards. In 'Hell' and, for less formal business, in the church of the London parish where the chief justice resided, the clerks and attorneys of Common Pleas practised their own special mystery. A church like St Bartholomew's was a convenient place for 'the clerks with the rolls and writs of the Common Bench and the

---

[62] Sayles, *Cases in King's Bench*, vol. VI, pp. xviff; Hastings, *Court of Common Pleas*, pp. 82ff; James Gairdner (ed.), *Paston Letters* (London, 1900–1908), vol. i, pp. 36–7.

[63] Sayles, *Cases in King's Bench*, vol. VI, pp. xx and xxvii; Hastings, *Court of Common Pleas*, pp. 11–12, 14, 91–3, 96 and 233.

attorneys' to 'come together after the noon meal'. One should not under-estimate the extent to which the clerks and the attorneys from amongst whom the clerks were increasingly appointed gave the courts their traditions and stability. It was a clerk who thought up, and an attorney who wrote a letter in 1344, asserting that King's Bench would do no more 'to meet the demands of the king or of Philippa, the Queen of England, than of anyone else in the kingdom'.[64]

LAW COURTS, SOCIETY AND THE CONSTITUTION AT THE END OF THE MIDDLE AGES

The system of courts in later medieval England reflected English society and to a considerable extent gave that society its structure and tone. The 'adversary system' of the common law, whereby every case, civil or criminal, was a combat originally physical and then verbal between opposing parties, diffused the spirit of the game through English life. In the ordeal, the wager of law or of battle, there was an element of the gamble congenial, perhaps, to a military aristocracy. By 1500, however, the game of law was much more a competition of skills, more suited to a commercial society.[65]

Less speculatively, one can say that the courts played a part in the development of both the communities of England and the class-divisions of English society, and helped to relate them in an increasingly domi-nant national community. At the bottom of the social scale, the manor court sometimes became a truly democratic village assembly, where, for instance, the manor was leased to the peasants or the ownership of it was subdivided so that there was no 'lord of the manor'. Though seignorial jurisdiction declined, the seignorial courts were indispensable for the making of the 'ordinances of autumn' by which 'the community of the whole town' regulated the harvesting of the open fields. The rolls of the manor courts and baron courts of Battle in Sussex, the Earl of Hunting-don's court-leet or court-baron of Loughborough in Leicestershire, the 'Borough and manor' of St Mawes in Cornwall, and the court-leet of Manchester, to mention just a few, run on from century to century, some well past 1800, their language changing in the course of the seventeenth and early eighteenth centuries from Latin into English. 'View of frankpledge' was repeated with the regularity of the passing seasons; constables and street-masters were appointed; and by-laws were made against the grazing of scabbed horses in the fields, 'muck-hills' in the streets, the leading of horses and performances of pipers

---

[64] Sayles, *Cases in King's Bench*, vol. VI, p. 36.
[65] J. Huizinga, *Homo Ludens* (London, 1949), ch. 4: 'Play and Law'; Chaucer, *The Parlement of Foulys*, ed. D. S. Brewer (London, 1960), p. 86; Neilson, *Trial by Combat*.

and minstrels on the Sabbath day, tippling after 9 o'clock in winter and 10 in summer, and scolds who 'rail against their neighbours and take away their credit and good name'.[66]

The bulk of court business in the last centuries of the seignorial courts was the conveyancing of copyhold property by the vendor's *surrender* of the land to the lord of the manor and the *admission* of the purchaser. Copyhold property consisted originally of the tenancies-at-will of the villeinage, but in the later Middle Ages such property was given a legal protection hardly less strong than that accorded to freehold, and the copy of the entry in the manorial court roll recording the tenant's admission was regarded as his title-deed. On the surrender-and-admission procedure (and with the help of the magic phrase 'to the use of') were built up ways of selling, mortgaging, leaving by will and entailing copyhold land; and since this became widely dispersed amongst the yeomen and gentry, the old villein techniques of conveyancing remained essential to the life of the rural community.[67]

Just as the court-leet was the public expression of the village community, and saw to the appointment of its officers, so the shire court was the public expression of the county community and the place where coroners and knights of the shire in Parliament were elected, the king's sheriffs and escheators sworn in and public business transacted in the eye of the people. Judicially, the county court still dealt with a mass of small disputes between the inhabitants of the shire (Doc. 19), though the really influential days of the court, when it probably brought under the common law the whole field of tort and misdemeanour, had come to an end.

The decline of the shire court was more than counterbalanced by the rise of the justices of the peace, who enjoyed the same allround judicial and policing powers as the sheriffs had once had. In the later Middle Ages the stream of judicial authority this reversed itself once more, flowing back to the localities and to the landlord, who found himself again keeping a 'peace' – though this time it was in theory the king's and not, as in Anglo-Saxon times, his own. The magnates' councils, from which emerged one very important court in the Duke of Lancaster's Court of Duchy Chamber, along with the king's regional lieutenants, the wardens of the marches and the later councils in the marches, reflect, on a higher level still, the fact that the government of England in the later Middle Ages was a kind of federalism.[68]

[66] W. O. Ault, 'Village assemblies in medieval England' in *Album Helen Maud Cam* (Louvain, 1960); Miller, *Ely*, pp. 208–10; 'Penal Laws of Ashby de la Zouche', 1620: MS. in Huntington Library, San Marino, California.

[67] A. A. Dibben, *Title Deeds*, Historical Association Pamphlet (London, 1968), pp. 23–6; *Court Rolls of the Manor of Acomb*, ed. and tr. H. Richardson (Yorkshire Arch. Soc., Wakefield, 1969).

[68] J. R. Maddicott, *Thomas of Lancaster* (Oxford, 1970); Miller, *Ely*; R. Somerville on the Court of Duchy Chamber, *TRHS* (1941).

At the local level, if not at the national one, the Church courts helped to reinforce community. The courts of the archdeacon, the bishop's official and the bishop himself in his court of audience, kept the clergy of the diocese up to the mark, disciplining any who failed to serve his living with matins and vespers; neglected to visit the sick, the paralysed and pregnant women with communion; allowed the chancel and church-yard to become ruinous; or was a 'public fornicator' with his parishioners or a 'communis fabulator' destroying their devotion. They did their best to sort out the matrimonial disputes of the gentry of the diocese, which had great dynastic implications. If the Church courts were less beneficial than they might have been, it was because there were too many of them. There was conflict between them over jurisdiction, and appeals from one to another could take intolerably long.[69]

Commercial developments produced special types of community such as the Stannaries into which the tin-miners of Devon and Cornwall were organized. There was a Warden of the Stannaries, who supplied 'the place both of a judge for law and of a chancellor for conscience', and appointed four stewards to hold Stannary Courts in the four quarters of the Stannary area. There was right of appeal from the Warden 'to the Lords of the Council, and from their Honours to her Majesty's person'. The borough court is, of course, another example of a court adapted to the needs of a commercial community.[70]

Communities were marked out by the possession of courts; and litigation in the courts seems to have arisen from the interests of com-munities as much as of individuals. 'The men of Wiltshire were far from being alone when they established a common fund which was to be used for maintaining their law-suits, whether legal or illegal, and raised a large sum for that purpose.' Nor was the Chapter of Lichfield cathedral the only ecclesiastical institution to have a regular association with a criminal gang. The court records are full of bands of liveried retainers of the landlords, the 'conventicles' and 'illicit congregations' of peasants and outlaws, and the 'conspiracies' (Doc. 20) of groups of people of all classes to gain advantage over their neighbours.[71]

For there is an obvious class element to these communal struggles, which the courts tended to emphasize, since they meant power for their 'owners' as well as community for those who used them. The J.P.s represent the emergence of a gentry which was a ruling class as the

[69] Aston, *Thomas Arundel*, pp. 40, 64 and 68, and chs. 2, 3, 4 *passim*; Gair-dner, *Paston Letters*, vol. ii, p. 364 (spelling modernized).

[70] L. F. Salzman, 'Mines and Stannaries', in *English Government at Work*, vol. iii (ed. W. H. Dunham); Richard Carew of Antony, *The Survey of Cornwall*, ed. F. E. Halliday (London, 1953), p. 100.

[71] Sayles, *Cases in King's Bench*, vol. VI, p. xxvi; J. G. Bellamy on the Coterel gang, *EHR* (1964); B. H. Putnam, *Kent Keepers of the Peace* (Kent Arch. Soc., Records Branch, 1933), p. xii.

feudatories of the Conquest never were. The gentry were 'the people of the realm' who told the king in parliament of the multitude of vagabonds and malefactors infesting the countryside, and were given in response, in the Commission of the Peace, authority to keep in order a peasant mass which was seen as essentially unruly and dangerous. For Sir Thomas Smith, there 'was never in any commonwealth devised a more wise, a more dulce and gentle, nor a more certain way to rule the people, whereby they are kept always as it were in a bridle of good order . . .'. The sessions of the J.P.s replaced the manorial courts as a means of social control in proportion as the relationship of peasant to landlord changed from a legal subjection to a purely economic subjection. In the fourteenth century, when the population of England was drastically reduced, peasant labour became scarce and had to be bought with rising wages, and peasant holdings would only be taken up under the greater legal security of copyhold tenure. It became impossible to prevent peasants from moving off in search of better terms, and a landlord who tried to do so ran the risk of an indictment for false imprisonment (Doc. 25, 1351-3). Yet the landlords succeeded in maintaining their position, by obtaining the Statutes of Labourers and other economic legislation, which they enforced as justices of the peace.[72]

The right of trial by one's peers, soon identified with trial by jury, indicated a society where rank counted for much. It is noticeable that the right was most jealously guarded at the top of the social scale, where the right of members of the 'peerage' to be tried by the House of Lords was abolished only in 1948.[73] Against anyone but the king, the courts operated to the advantage of the magnates. In a system worked by the corruption of juries and the 'grace' of officials the rich had an overwhelming advantage. 'Law', said Langland, 'is so lordly, and loth to make end without presents.' The self-help from which legal procedures emerged was necessarily an unequal force, depending on social position, and the strong, whether in ancient Rome or medieval England, did not quickly submit to the equalizing principles of justice.[74]

The lawyers who made the courts work and evolved the concepts of

[72] On the formation of the gentry class in the twelfth and thirteenth centuries, see the articles by Edmund King and Sally Harvey in *Past and Present* (1970); Putnam, *Proceedings before the Justices of the Peace*, pp. 1-2; Smith, *De Republica Anglorum*, p. 89; R. H. Hilton, *The Decline of Serfdom in Medieval England* (Economic History Society pamphlet, London, 1969), pp. 36, 40.

[73] Holdsworth, *History of English Law*, vol. i, pp. 386ff; L. W. Vernon Harcourt, *His Grace the Steward and the Trial of Peers* (London, 1907), pp. 416ff, esp. p. 434.

[74] J. M. Kelly, *Roman Litigation* (Oxford, 1966); W. J. Jones, *The American Journal of Legal History* (1962).

law, constituted the first 'profession' in England; a profession which existed to guard the interests of the landed aristocracy and controlled virtually the only way into the aristocracy for able plebeians. In pre-Reformation England there were only about 400 lawyers practising at Westminster and 200–300 law students but 'London lawyers' also controlled the courts of the Marches and the Palatinates and some of the larger boroughs. Borough Recorderships sometimes brought them election as burgesses in parliament. Most of the lawyers educated at the Inns of Court, and especially the Inns of Chancery, had to be content with a career in 'the provinces', where they mingled with local practitioners, the yeomen-lawyers who kept manor courts and acted as general bailiffs, rent-gatherers, and scriveners for the landlords. At the other end of the scale, lawyers rose very high in the state, and preserved a rather old-fashioned judicial rather than administrative approach to government. Everyone of the twenty-two Speakers of the Commons from 1484 to 1559 was a lawyer. Successful lawyers were ideally placed to invest their earnings fruitfully in landed property and unite their dynasties with aristocratic ones. Unlike even the greatest merchants, they could become landlords themselves without giving up the occupation by which they had risen.[75]

The courts contributed to the formation in the later Middle Ages of a national community which transcended these local communities and social classes. In medieval conditions, greater dependence on the local gentry for order and justice was unavoidable if the government wished to control in greater detail a society which was growing more complex. The undesirable by-products of such delegation were eventually curbed by the new conciliar courts, though the picture of the justice of the peace as a dutiful agent of the Crown is illusory at any rate until the arrival of the Tudors. By 1500, a centrally directed system of justice had been re-established, and one which better satisfied society's more varied needs and government's more insistent demands.

The courts were the principal formal institutions in existence, and the judicial system may be described as a system of communications for English society. There was as yet little concept of appeal from the decision of a lower court to the authority of a higher one to link the courts together. Yet in the fourteenth century, when they ceased to attend the king's Council as a group, the judges did begin to meet in a room at Westminster called the Exchequer Chamber to discuss difficult cases, and naturally the decisions of this 'court' had authority in the courts where the judges who consented to them normally sat (Doc. 29). What is important is the way in which the cases came to Exchequer Chamber. They were directed there by the king's writ, usually after bills of complaint to Council or Parliament. King's Bench, in which the

[75] Eric Ives on the legal profession in *TRHS* (1968).

king might still sit in person,[76] corrected 'errors in the record' of borough courts, shire courts, sessions of justices of assize, gaol delivery and oyer and terminer, and the Court of Common Pleas. The errors of King's Bench were a matter for Parliament (Doc. 24, 1374). If a complainant could show that the record of his case revealed errors in the lower court's handling of the procedure or pleading, then an outlawry in the shire court might be declared void, or the Court of Common Pleas might be told to accept a plea or proof and give judgment in the light of it, or the error might be deemed so slight that the record was simply amended rather than the judgment quashed. Once again, what is important is the fact that such cases were brought to the king's notice by petition to Council or Parliament, and that directions for their final settlement were issued by the king's writ.[77]

A case which dragged on from 1338 to 1344 shows how the king and his council controlled the judicial system. Geoffrey of Stanton, the plaintiff in a case in Common Pleas against John and Amy of Stanton, presented a petition 'before us and our council in our parliament' that there should be a scrutiny of 'the transcript of the record and process of the said plea' which 'we caused to come before us in our chancery'. After 'the aforesaid business had been discussed with no little argument before our said council', the Court of Common Pleas was instructed to ignore the defendants' latest plea and proceed to judgment. But then John and Amy got an ordinary writ of error from chancery, 'stating that errors had intervened in the record and process' as they then stood in Common Pleas, and so the case went to King's Bench and the transcript of the entire suit was written into that court's rolls. Geoffrey invoked the rolls of parliament and was sure 'that the court here' would not 'wish to repudiate anything therein'. Yet the case was adjourned from term to term until Easter 1343, when there came a writ close from the king to inform the justices that John and Amy had taken the case back to parliament and that a conference of all the judges was considering it. At Trinity 1344, a further writ enclosed the petition of John and Amy to parliament, and another from Geoffrey insisting on the judgment which had been 'ordained and agreed in two full parliaments by great deliberation of all those wise in the law', and ordered King's Bench 'to view and examine the record and process which the said petitions mention and to proceed to final discussion of the matter'. At that point the case was decided by the default of John and Amy.[78]

Here we see justice being moved by petition and administrative order. If King's Bench was ineffective in bringing malefactors to book,

[76] C. H. Williams in *Law Quarterly Review* (1924).

[77] Sayles, *Cases in King's Bench*, vol. I, pp. 153ff, vol. IV, pp. 17–18, 100–2, 122 and 142.

[78] *Ibid.* VI, 1–11.

the king might order Star Chamber to lend the assistance of its more stringent processes. When error was alleged 'in the record and process' of the highest court, of parliament itself, the only remedy was for the king to intervene and order parliament to reconsider its own decision.[79]

Bills and writs which began as the language of judicial administration became the language of administration in general. (It must be remembered that judges assisted the king in many of the tasks of government.) In the late thirteenth and fourteenth centuries, the complaint which was always necessary to evoke a writ reaffirmed its priority in the legal system as the written bill. To the long journey of a complaint in the days of the 'executive writ' (from plaintiff to king to culprit), the returnable writ had added a further stage (from plaintiff to king to sheriff to justices) or two stages if one counts the judicial writ by which final judgment was enforced. The bill cut out the stages taken up by the writ's journey from royal chancery to sheriff and back to the appropriate court. Their greater thrust made bills enormously popular. There grew up 'a vast system of bills, a system with its own regulations and methods, an interconnected system in which actions by bill can be transferred or evoked from lower to higher courts, a system which involved parliament and does much to explain the purpose of that institution'. Bills allowed a fruitful confusion of private wrongs and royal interests which radically changed methods of prosecution, forced the creation of the conciliar courts and made possible a much more complex administration. Writs were the technical instruments of the law: bills, approved by presenting juries or 'avowed' by the Commons in parliament, became the medium of communication for the nation's politics and government. Of course, the flood of bills merely reflected the appearance of a literate laity, whose public self-expression could not be limited to the choice of the appropriate technical forms provided by a small group of chancery clerks, and this literate laity and the use of petitions was a European phenomenon.[80]

It was in ways like these, by the diffusion of the habit of litigation through the politically important section of society and changes in the pattern of litigation, rather than by actual judgments like those which established 'treason by words', that the courts affected the English constitution. Civil actions of trespass 'against the king's peace' and bills of trespass sued by the complainant 'as much for the king as for himself' emphasized the identity of interest between subject and sovereign. London and the prerogative of the king gained most from a bill-system which cut through the local power-structure, its key figure the writ-serving sheriff, and took complaints directly to the source of executive

---

[79] Williams, *Law Quarterly Review* (1924); Sayles, *Cases in King's Bench*, vol. V, p. 12.

[80] Sayles, *Cases in King's Bench*, vol. IV, p. lxxxv; C. R. Cheney, 'The Study of the Medieval Papal Chancery', *Edwards Lecture* (Glasgow University, 1966).

power in the king's council. Lambarde saw that it was petitioners that made the king's council 'a supreme Court of Prerogative, whereunto his Subjects in such their necessities may provoke, as to his own Royal person', and where 'he again knowing himself to be the Chief Justice and Lieutenant of God within his own Realm, thought himself bound to deliver judgment and Justice', resorting 'to the Kingly and absolute Power' to enforce it.[81]

Royal supremacy was advanced by other developments in the courts. When Bishop Despenser of Norwich insisted in 1383 on leading a fiasco of an expedition into Flanders without a secular lieutenant to exercise discipline over the troops, and prelates generally played at politics with the same unscrupulousness as the lay members of the noble families from which they came, they were naturally liable to attack by bill and in the last resort to impeachment before parliament for their treasons or 'misprisions', just like laymen. The stringent procedures of the conciliar courts did not distinguish between clerical and lay transgressors. The affirmation of Henry VIII that there was only one jurisdiction in England, and that was his, threw its shadow a long way before.[82]

But the subjection of the Church to the king stemmed more from a general sense of the superiority of the common law, the law of the national community, over the laws of sectional communities and of other countries. In the fourteenth century, John Wycliffe sought to prove the existence of an *ecclesia anglicana*, an instrinsic part of the Catholic Church but with its own particular and especially wholesome customs, from the fact that the king's courts had jurisdiction in cases involving ecclesiastical property and ensured better than Canon Law (so Wycliffe believed) that the Church in England used its wealth properly. Similarly, lawyers maintained that the eternal principles of law were nowhere better expressed than in the customs of England, as declared by the judges.[83]

All were agreed that the virtues of English law and its exact consonance with natural law were to be seen in the public and oral mode of trial by jury, 'strange to all nations that do use the civil Law of the Roman Emperors'. No other nation could enjoy jury-trial because no other had the men to make juries from. Only fertile England could produce the required numbers of respectable yeomen who were not entirely immersed in agricultural work and were 'more apt and disposed

[81] Bellamy, *Law of Treason*, p. 116; Lambarde, *Archeion*, pp. 51–70.
[82] Beardwood, *Records of the Trial of Walter Langeton*; Margaret Aston, on the impeachment of Bishop Despenser, *BIHR* (1965); Bellamy, *Law of Treason*, pp. 219–20.
[83] Edith C. Tatnall, 'John Wyclif and the *Ecclesia Anglicana*', *Journal of Ecclesiastical History* (1969).

to investigate causes which require searching examination than men who ... have contracted a rusticity of mind from familiarity with the soil'. So in England 'none lose their case or right through the dearth or lack of witnesses; here no unknown witnesses are produced – no unreliable hirelings, paupers, vagrants, nor any whose conditions and cunning is unknown'. Yet jury-trial was also strange to the conciliar courts, which did hear witnesses; and in this fact was stored up another of the great constitutional battles of the next two centuries. The most precious inheritance of Englishmen was jury-trial in the common-law courts, one of which proclaimed in 1470 that 'No other proof is effective in our law except trial by twelve men', but in his 'prerogative' courts the king was seen to dispense with juries. The common law of Englishmen and the royal prerogative were opposed, 'mighty Adversaries to encounter withall', and 'the Subject, which so desirously fled to the King and his Council for succour, did as hastily retire, and run back to the ordinary seat and Judge again.'[84]

[84] Fortescue, *De Laudibus Legum Anglie*, pp. 59–63, 69–71 and 75–7; *Year Book, 10 Edward IV and 49 Henry VI*, ed. N. Neilson (Selden Society, London, 1930), p. 97; Lambarde, *Archeion*, pp. 51–70.

DOCUMENTS

1. Letter Explaining to King Edward the Elder (899–924) the History of a Wiltshire Estate, translated from Anglo-Saxon by F. E. HARMER, *Select English Historical Documents of the Ninth and Tenth Centuries* (Cambridge, 1914), pp. 60–3.

Sir, I will inform thee what has taken place with regard to the estate of five hides at Fonthill, about which Aethelm Higa has a suit. When Helmstan committed the crime of stealing Aethelred's belt, Higa, together with other claimants, proceeded forthwith to make a claim against him, desiring to obtain the estate from him by litigation. Then Helmstan came to me and begged me to be his advocate, because I had stood sponsor to him before he committed that crime. Then I pleaded and interceded for him with King Alfred. Then, may God reward his soul! the king gave him leave to avail himself of the protection of the law against Aethelm, with regard to the estate, because of my advocacy and the correct account [which I had given of the history of the estate]. Then he commanded that an arbitration should be made between them, and I was one of the persons who were nominated for this purpose, together with Wihtbord and Aelfric, who was at that time keeper of the wardrobe, and Byrhthelm, and Wulfhun the Black[?] from Somerton, Strica, and Ubba and more men than I can name now. When both of them had stated their cases, we all decided that Helmstan might come forward with the title-deeds and claim the estate as his own, his claim to the possession of it being that Aetheldryth had made it over to Oswulf for a fair price, and that Aetheldryth had told Oswulf that it was fully in her power to sell it to him, because it had been her 'morning-gift' when she first came to Athulf. And Helmstan included all this in his oath. And when Oswulf had bought the land from Aetheldryth, King Alfred had given him his sign-manual that the sale should hold good, and so had Eadweard and Aethelnoth and Deormod and all those men whose signatures they then wished to have. Now when we were arbitrating between them at this time at Wardour, the deed was produced and read; then all the signatures were to be found there. Then all those of us who were at the arbitration decided that Helmstan should now be allowed to produce the oath.

But Aethelm did not wholly assent to this, until we went in to the king, and told him fully the decision to which we had come, and the reasons for it; and Aethelm himself was there standing with us. And the king stood washing his hands within the chamber at Wardour. When he had finished, he asked Aethelm why our decision did not seem to him just, adding that he could not imagine anything more just than that Helmstan should produce the oath if he could. Then I said that he wished to make the attempt, and prayed the king to appoint a day; and he did so. Then on the appointed day Helmstan produced the oath in full. And he had begged me to support him, saying that he would rather give me the land than that the oath should fail or . . . [hole in MS]. Then I said that I was willing to help him in a just cause (but never in an unjust one), on condition that he gave me the estate; and he engaged to do this.

Then, on the appointed day we rode [thither]; and Wihtbord rode with me, and Byrhthelm rode there with Aethelm. And we all heard him produce the oath in full. Then we all said that the suit was settled, when the [king's] decision had been carried out. And, Sir, when will any suit be settled, if it cannot be settled either with money or with an oath? And if every decision which King Alfred gave is to be set aside, when shall we be done with negotiating? Then as soon as the oath had been produced, Helmstan gave me the title-deed, as he had previously engaged to do. And I promised him that he might have the use of the land during his lifetime, if he was willing to keep himself out of disgrace.

Then a year and a half, or perhaps two years afterwards, Helmstan stole the stray[?] oxen at Fonthill, thereby utterly ruining himself, and drove them to Chicklade; and he was caught there. And the man who tracked him rescued the cattle that had been driven off[?]. As he fled, a bramble scratched him all over the face; and when he wished to deny the charge, this was brought forward as evidence against him. When Eanulf Penearding, who was reeve, intervened, he took from him all the property which he owned at Tisbury. When I asked him why he did this, he replied that Helmstan was a thief. And the property was confiscated to the king, because he was the king's man. And Ordlaf took his land; for since the land which Helmstan occupied was held on lease from him, he could not forfeit it. And then thou didst declare him an outlaw.

Then Helmstan made his way to thy father's body, and brought a signet to me, when I was at Chippenham with thee. Then I gave thee the signet. And thou didst give him back his home and rights, and the estates to which he has now returned[?]. But I took possession of my land, and then, with thy cognisance and that of thy council, gave it, namely five hides, to the bishop, in exchange for the estate of five hides at Lyddiard. And the bishop and the whole community gave me four hides [free of tithe]; but one was subject to tithe. Now, Sire, it is very necessary for me that both our recent proceedings and those of old should be ratified. If not, then I must and will be content with whatever voluntary gift is, in thy opinion, just.

Endorsed:

And Aethelm Higa withdrew from this suit, when the king was at Warminster[?], with the cognisance of Ordlaf and Osferth and Odda and Wihtbord and Aelfstan the Bald and Aethelnoth.

2. FROM King Ethelred's Code at Wantage (between 978 and 1008), translated from Anglo-Saxon by DOROTHY WHITELOCK in *English Historical Documents*, vol. i (Eyre and Spottiswoode (Publishers) Ltd, London, 1955), pp. 403–5.

These are the laws which King Ethelred and his councillors have decreed at Wantage, for the improvement of public security.

Namely, in order that his peace may remain as firm as it best was in the days of his ancestors, that peace which he gives with his own hand is not to be atoned for by compensation.

And the peace which the ealdorman and the king's reeve give in the meeting of the Five Boroughs, that is to be atoned for with twelve hundred [silver *ores*, of 16d each].

And the peace which is given in the meeting of one borough is to be atoned for with six hundreds; and that which is given in a wapentake, is to be atoned for with a hundred, if it is broken; and that which is given in an alehouse, is to be atoned for, if a man is killed, with six half-marks, and if no one is killed, with twelve ores . . .

And that a meeting is to be held in each wapentake, and the twelve leading thegns, and with them the reeve, are to come forward and swear on the relics which are put into their hands that they will accuse no innocent man nor conceal any guilty one.

And they are then to seize the men who have been frequently accused . . .

And if anyone is charged with feeding a man who has broken our lord's peace, he is to clear himself with three twelves; and the reeve is to nominate the compurgators.

And if he is discovered with him, they are both liable to the same penalty.

And a sentence where the thegns are unanimous is to be valid; if they disagree, what eight of them say is to be valid; and those who are outvoted there, are each to pay six half-marks . . .

3. The King sends a case to the shire court. Record of a lawsuit of 1014–16, translated from Anglo-Saxon by A. J. ROBERTSON, *Anglo-Saxon Charters* (Cambridge, 1939), pp. 137–9.

Here it is stated in this document how Wynflaed produced her witnesses at Woolmer before King Aethelred, namely Archbishop Sigeric and Bishop Ordbriht and Earl Aelfric and Aelfthryth, the king's mother, all of whom bore witness that Aelfric gave Wynflaed the estates at Hagbourne and at Bradfield in return for the estate at Datchet. Then the king sent straightway to Leofwine by the archbishop and those who had acted as witnesses along with him, and informed him of this, but he would not [agree], unless the matter were referred to a shire-meeting. This was done. The king sent his seal to the meeting at Cuckamsley by Abbot Aelfhere, and greeted all the councillors who were assembled there, namely Bishop Aethelsige and Bishop Aescwig and Abbot Aelfric and the whole shire, and prayed and commanded them to settle the case between Wynflaed and Leofwine as justly as they could; and Archbishop Sigeric sent his declaration to the meeting and Bishop Ordbriht his. Then Wynflaed was informed that she might prove her ownership of the estate, and she adduced proof of her ownership with the help of Aelfthryth, the king's mother, her supporters being first Abbot Wulfgar and Wulfstan the priest and Aefic, the Aethelings' seneschal, and Edwin and Eadhelm and Aelfhelm and Aelfwine and Aelfweard and Eadwold and Eadric and Aelfgar and the Abbess Eadgifu and the Abbess Leofrun and Aethelhild and Eadgifu of Lewknor and her sister and her daughter and Aelfgi[fu and her] daughter and Wulfwyn and Aethelgifu and Aelfwaru and Aelfgifu and Aethelflaed and many a good thegn and good woman, all of whom we cannot enumerate, so that the full number was produced, including both men and women. Then the councillors who were there declared that it would be better for the oath to be dispensed with rather than sworn, because thereafter friendship would be at an end [between them] and he [Leofwine] would be asked to return what he had seized and pay compensation and his wergild to the king. Then he dispensed with the oath, and handed over the estate uncontested to Bishop Aethelsige, [affirming] that henceforth he would make no further claim to it. Then Wynflaed was directed to produce all his father's gold and silver that she had. Then she did [as little] as she dared to protect her oath. Then he was still not satisfied with it, unless she should swear that all his property was there. She said that she could not [do so] for her part nor he for his. And the witnesses of this were Aelfgar, the king's reeve, and Brihtric and Leofric of Whitchurch and many good men in addition to them.

4. Cnut's Confirmation of the Liberties of Christ Church, Canterbury (1017–20), edited and translated from Anglo-Saxon by F. E.
HARMER, *Anglo-Saxon Writs* (Manchester, 1952), p. 182.

King Cnut sends friendly greetings to Archbishop Lyfing and Bishop
Godwine and Abbot Aelfmaer and Aethelwine the sheriff and Aethelric
and all my thegns, nobles and commoners. And I inform you that the
archbishop spoke to me about the freedom of Christ Church – that it
now has less *mund* than it once had. Then I gave him permission to
draw up a new charter of freedom in my name. Then he told me that he
had charters of freedom in plenty if only they were good for anything.
Then I myself took the charters of freedom and laid them on Christ's
own altar, with the cognisance of the archbishop and of Earl Thurkill
and of many good men who were with me – in the same terms as King
Aethelberht freed it and all my predecessors: that no man, be he
ecclesiastic or be he layman, shall ever be so presumptuous as to
diminish any of the things that stand in that charter of freedom. And if
any one do so, may his life here be shortened and his dwelling in the
abyss of hell, unless before his end he make reparation for it as strin-
gently as possible, as the archbishop shall direct him.

5. Writ-charters of King Cnut and King Edward (1020, 1052),
edited and translated from Anglo-Saxon by F. E. HARMER, *Anglo-Saxon Writs* (Manchester, 1952), pp. 160, 183–4.

King Cnut sends friendly greetings to all my bishops and my earls and
my reeves in every shire in which Archbishop Aethelnoth and the community at Christ Church have lands. And I inform you that I have
granted him that he be entitled to his sake and soke, and to grithbreach
and hamsocn and foresteall and infangenetheof and flymenafyrmth
over his own men within borough and without, and over Christ Church,
and over as many thegns as I have granted him to have. And I forbid
anyone to take anything therefrom except himself and his officers,
because I have given these rights to Christ for the eternal redemption of
my soul. And I forbid that anyone ever violate this, on [pain of losing]
my friendship.

King Edward sends friendly greetings to Bishop Aethelmaer and Earl
Aelfgar and all my thegns in Norfolk. And I inform you that my will is
that the land at Kirby and all things lawfully pertaining thereto shall
belong to the holy monastery at St Edmund's with sake and with soke
as fully and as completely as ever any man had it, and my mother
bequeathed it to that house. And I pray you all that you pronounce for
me a judgment concerning Semer, who has illegally occupied it, such as
you, in the sight of God, know to be my lawful right.

6. Record of a plea in the Court of William I (*c.* 1086) translated by
DAVID DOUGLAS and G. W. GREENAWAY in *English Historical
Documents*, vol. ii (Eyre and Spottiswoode (Publishers) Ltd,
London, 1953), pp. 453–4.

King William held a court at Laycock, a manor of William of Eu, and
there decided a plea concerning the claims which William of Briouze
had made respecting the possessions of the abbey of Holy Trinity
[Fécamp]. The trial lasted one Sunday from morning until evening,
and there were present with the king his sons and all his barons. There
it was decided and agreed, as to the wood of Hamode, that it should be
divided through the middle, both the wood and the land in which the
villeins had lived and which belongs to the wood; and by the king's
command a hedge was made through the middle of the wood, and our
part remained to us [i.e. the abbey of Fécamp] and William's to him.
As to St Cuthman's rights of burial, it was decreed that they should
remain inviolate; and by the king's command the bodies which had been
buried in William's church were exhumed by William's own men and
taken to St Cuthman's church for lawful burial. And Hubert the dean
restored the money which he had received for burials and wakes and for
tolling the bells, and for all dues for the dead; and he swore first through
the mouth of a relative that he had not taken more. As to the land at
'Udica' which William had claimed from Holy Trinity for his park, it
was adjudged that the park should be destroyed; and it was destroyed.
As to the warren which he had made on the land of Holy Trinity, it was
adjudged that it should be destroyed; and it was destroyed. As to the
toll which he took at his bridge from the men of Holy Trinity, it was
adjudged that it ought not to be paid, because it was never paid in the
time of King Edward; and by the king's command what had there been
taken in toll was returned, the toll collector swearing that he had not
taken more. As to the ships which go up [the river] to St Cuthman's
harbour, it was adjudged that they should be quit for 2 pence for each
ascent and descent [of the river], unless they should make another
market at William's castle. As to the road which William had made on
the land of Holy Trinity, it was adjudged that it should be destroyed;
and it was destroyed. As to the ditch which William had made to bring
water to his castle, it was adjudged that it should be filled up; and it was
filled up; and the land remained the abbot's. As to the marsh, it was
decreed that it should be the abbot's as far as the hill and the salt pits;
and it was so. As to the eighteen gardens it was adjudged that these
should belong to Holy Trinity. As to the weekly toll, it was adjudged
that the whole should belong to the saint but that William should have
half on Saturday. All these things remained free and quit to the church

at Fécamp; and in respect of them William placed his pledge in the king's hand, he being in the king's mercy.

These barons saw the conclusion of this business:

The sons of the king: William and Henry.

The archbishop: Lanfranc and Thomas.

The bishops: William of Durham; Walkelin of Winchester; Remigius of Lincoln; Geoffrey of Coutances; Robert of Chester; Robert of Hereford; Osmund of Salisbury; Maurice of London.

The earls: Robert [count] of Mortain; Alan the Red; Roger of Montgomery.

The barons: Richard, the son of Count Gilbert; Baldwin, his brother; Roger Bigot; Henry of Ferrières; Bernard of Neufmarché; William of Eu; Hugh of Port-en-Bessin; Richard 'Goiz'; Eudo the steward; Robert the dispenser; Robert son of Tetbald; William of Perci; Robert of Rhuddlan; Nigel of Thorpe; Roger of Courcelles; Alfred of Lincoln; William of Falaise; Henry of Beaumont.

The abbots: Serlo of Gloucester; Thurstan of Glastonbury.

The monks of Holy Trinity: William and Rahere and Bernard, son of Ospac.

The laymen: William 'Malcunduit'; Godfrey, his brother; Sotriz; Leviet; Richard 'de Bodes'; Geroldin.

7. Writs and cases recorded in the chronicle of Abingdon abbey, translated from *Chronicon Monasterii de Abingdon*, edited by J. STEVENSON (Rolls Series, London, 1858), vol. ii, pp. 84, 92, 117–18, 119–20, 180–1. (Cf. *Regesta Regum Anglo-Normannorum*, vol. II, and Van Caenegem, *Royal Writs*.)

(1101) Henry, King of England, to Hugh de Bocland and William, Sheriff of Oxford, greeting. Order the men of your shires on my behalf, that, as they love me, they tell the whole truth concerning three virgates of land Rualon of Avranches claims. If the land belongs to the manor of Stanton which I gave to Rualon, he shall have it; but if not, the abbey of Abingdon shall have it. Witness Roger the chancellor . . .

(1107 ?) Henry, King of England, to Nigel d'Oilli and William, Sheriff of Oxford, greeting. I order you to do full right to the Abbot of Abingdon concerning his sluice which the men of Stanton destroyed; and I wish to hear no further complaint of lack of justice in this matter, under penalty of £10. Witness Ranulf the Chancellor, at Westminster.

(1109–1110) In the full shire court sitting at Sutton in the tenth year of the reign of King Henry, chiefly to settle this matter, the Lord Abbot Faritius and the monks of Abingdon made good their right to the land of Culham, as being entirely for the use of the church of Abingdon, free from all customary obligations and the rights of all men; and particularly they proved the injustices of the exactions made from that land by the men of the manor of Sutton, who took turves from that land for the king's mill and fishery. Just as his predecessor, Abbot Ethelhelm, when the elder William was king and Froger the sheriff, secured the freedom of the said village of Culham from such exactions, so Abbot Faritius did at the said day and time, in the presence of Sheriff Hugh (a good and wise man who was sheriff not only over Berkshire but over seven other shires as well, so renowned he was and dear to the king) and of a multitude of people from three different shires. After this proof, not daring to seize in the public eye what they had taken before, they sought to get it in secret. Messengers took news of this to the abbot, who passed it on to the sheriff who then ruled Berkshire, Hugh de Bocland, and on his orders right was done concerning this injustice to the church and abbey, by judgment of the hundred of Sutton attached to the said royal vill of Sutton.

(1100–1135) From the time of the Lord Abbot Orderic it has been the customary right of this church that from each boat of the city of Oxford passing along the Thames as it flows southwards by the abbey of Abingdon, there is rendered to the cellarer each year between the Purification and Easter a hundred herrings or an equivalent sum of money, the boatman bringing them without argument. If someone was found to have withheld this custom, it was lawful for the cellarer to stop the boat from passing until right was done. In the time of the Lord Abbot Faritius, the Oxford boatmen took it into their heads to wrest this custom from the church, but the abbot quickly suppressed their temerity by legal process: he made his allegation to King Henry, who sent a writ to his justices and sheriffs of Berkshire and Oxfordshire ordering right and justice to be done so that the church should no longer be deprived of this custom. So, in the eleventh year of that king's rule, when Thomas de St John and Richard de Monte were sheriffs of Oxfordshire, a plea concerning this matter was held in the city of Oxford at the house of Harding the priest, and it was adjudged by the common decision of the chief men there that the church of Abingdon justly claimed this thing and that it ought to be rendered every year by the ships of the whole city. Next year, Ralph the cellarer complained before a gathering of the leading men of Oxford that he had not yet had the adjudged customary payment from each of the boatmen amongst them, and it was commanded by those called together there that the boats should render the debt to the cellarer at the church. All those who were at that court are witnesses that this was the decision, and these were the people present at the proof: Richard de Monte, the sheriff at the time, Walter the archdeacon and many others.

(1139–1154) Stephen, King of England, to the Bishop of Salisbury and all the king's justices, sheriffs, barons, servants and faithful men, both French and English, in Berkshire, greeting. Know that I have granted to God and the church of the Blessed Mary of Abingdon, and Ingulf the abbot, and the monks serving God along with him in that church, the right to hold a market in the town of Abingdon, which they are to enjoy as well and as freely as that church and its abbots ever did, and in particular as Abbot Vincent did when King Henry granted him the abbey. An it is my wish and command that all men going to, remaining at and returning from that market shall fully enjoy my firm peace, so that they shall not be unjustly troubled, upon penalty of £10. Witness, William of Ypres, William de Chesney, Richard de Lucy and Richard de Camville, at Oxford.

(1139–1154) Stephen, King of England [etc.] I command that the Abbot and monks of Abingdon shall hold and have their lands, men and possessions as well, peacefully, honourably, freely and quietly as they did on the day King Henry was alive and dead, and on the day I was first crowned; and that they shall not be sued for them except when I come into that part of the country, because I do not wish them to have to plead except in my presence . . .

8. FROM The Assize of Northampton (1176), translated by DAVID
DOUGLAS and G. W. GREENAWAY in *English Historical Documents*,
vol. ii (Eyre and Spottiswoode (Publishers) Ltd, London, 1953)
pp. 411–13.

These are the assizes made at Clarendon and afterwards revised at
Northampton.

If anyone has been accused before the justices of the lord king of
murder or theft or robbery or of harbouring men who do such things,
or of forgery or arson by the oath of twelve knights of the hundred or,
if knights be not present, by the oath of twelve free and lawful men
and by the oath of four men from each vill of the hundred, let him go
to the ordeal of water, and if he fails, let him lose one foot. And at
Northampton it was added for the sake of stern justice that he shall
likewise lose his right hand with his foot, and shall abjure the realm and
within forty days be banished from the kingdom. And if he shall be
cleared of guilt at the water, let him provide sureties and remain in the
kingdom, unless he has been accused of murder or some other base
felony by the common report of the county and of the lawful knights of
the country; moreover, if he has been accused in the aforesaid manner,
although he may have come safely through the ordeal of water, nevertheless let him depart from the realm within forty days, and let him take his
chattels with him, saving the rights of his lords, and let him abjure the
realm at the mercy of the lord king. Moreover, this assize shall remain
in force from the time the assize was made at Clarendon continuously
up to the present time and from now on, so long as it shall please the
lord king, in cases of murder and treason and arson and in all the aforesaid articles, except in cases of petty thefts and robberies, which have
been committed in time of war, as of horses and oxen and lesser things . . .

Item, if any freeholder has died, let his heirs remain possessed of such
'seisin' as their father had of his fief on the day of his death; and let them
have his chattels from which they may execute the dead man's will. And
afterwards let them seek out his lord and pay him a 'relief' and the other
things which they ought to pay him from the fief. And if the heir be
under age, let the lord of the fief receive his homage and keep him in
ward so long as he ought. Let the other lords, if there are several,
likewise receive his homage, and let him render them what is due. And
let the widow of the deceased have her dowry and that portion of his
chattels which belongs to her. And should the lord of the fief deny the
heirs of the deceased 'seisin' of the said deceased which they claim,
let the justices of the lord king thereupon cause an inquisition to be
made by twelve lawful men as to what 'seisin' the deceased held there
on the day of his death. And according to the result of the inquest, let

restitution be made to his heirs. And if anyone shall do anything contrary to this and shall be convicted of it, let him remain in the king's mercy.

Item, let the justices of the lord king cause an inquisition to be made concerning dispossessions carried out contrary to the assize, since the lord king's coming into England immediately following upon the peace made between him and the king, his son.

Item, let the justices receive oaths of fealty to the lord king between the Octave of Easter and the final term, the Octave of Pentecost, from all who wish to remain in the kingdom, namely from the earls, barons, knights and freeholders, and even villeins. And whoever shall refuse to take an oath of fealty may be arrested as an enemy of the lord king. The justices shall also order that all who have not yet paid homage or allegiance to the lord king shall come at a time appointed for them and pay homage and allegiance to the king as their liege lord . . .

Item, let the justices see to it that the castles which have been destroyed are utterly demolished, and those which are due for destruction are razed to the ground. And if they do not do this, the lord king will have the judgment of his *curia* upon them, as on men who have held his commands in contempt . . .

Item, let the justices cause search to be made according to the custom of the land for those who have fled from the kingdom; and unless the fugitives be willing to return within the appointed time and stand trial in the king's court, let them henceforth be outlawed; and let the justices report the names of the outlaws at Easter and at Michaelmas to the Exchequer, and from thence let their names be sent to the lord king.

9. FROM *The treatise on the laws and customs of the realm of England commonly called Glanvill,* edited and translated by G. D. G. HALL (London, 1965), pp. 148–50, 151–3.

The various kinds of recognition

So far the questions which most often arise in pleas about right have been dealt with. There remain for discussion those which are concerned with seisin only. By virtue of a constitution of the realm called an assize these questions are for the most part settled by recognition, and therefore the various kinds of recognition must now be considered.

One kind of recognition is called mort d'ancestor. Another concerns the last presentation of parsons to churches; another, whether a tenement is ecclesiastical or lay fee; another, whether a man was seised of a free tenement on the day he died as of fee or as of gage; another, whether a man is under age or of full age; another, whether a man died seised of a free tenement as of fee or as of wardship; another, whether a man presented the last parson to a church by virtue of his fee which he had in his demesne, or by virtue of the wardship of someone. And if similar questions arise as they frequently do when both parties are present in court, then recognitions are used to settle the dispute, whether with consent of the parties or by award of the court. There is also the recognition called novel disseisin.

When anyone dies seised of a free tenement, if he was seised in his demesne as of fee, then his heir can lawfully claim the seisin which his ancestor had, and if he is of full age he shall have the following writ:

The writ of mort d'ancestor

The king to the sheriff, greeting. If G. son of O. gives you security for prosecuting his claim, then summon by good summoners twelve free and lawful men from the neighbourhood of such-and-such a vill to be before me or my justices on a certain day, ready to declare on oath whether O. the father of the aforesaid G. was seised in his demesne as of his fee of one virgate of land in that vill on the day he died, whether he died after my first coronation, and whether the said G. is his next heir. And meanwhile let them view the land; and you are to see that their names are endorsed on this writ. And summon by good summoners R., who holds that land, to be there then to hear the recognition. And have there the summoners and this writ. Witness, etc. . .

The procedure leading to the assize

When the sheriff has received the writ of mort d'ancestor and security for prosecuting the claim has been given in the county court, then the procedure leading to the assize is as follows. First, in accordance with the terms of the writ, twelve free and lawful men from the neighbour-hood are to be elected in the presence of both demandant and tenant, or even in the absence of the tenant provided he has been summoned at least once to attend the election. He must be summoned once to come and hear who are elected to make the recognition, and he can if he wishes reject some of them for reasonable cause so that they are excluded from the recognition. If, however, he has not come when the first summons is properly attested in court, then he shall be waited for no longer, and in his absence the twelve jurors shall be elected and sent by the sheriff to view the land or other tenement of which seisin is claimed. Here again the tenant shall have one summons only. The sheriff shall see that the names of the elected twelve are endorsed on the writ.

Then the sheriff shall arrange for the tenant to be summoned to be before the king or his justices on the day stated in the writ of the king or his justices, to hear the recognition. If the demandant is of full age, the tenant can essoin himself on the first and second return days but not on the third day, for then the recognition shall be taken whether the tenant comes or not, because no more than two essoins are allowed in any recognition which concerns only seisin. Indeed, in the recognition of novel disseisin no essoin is allowed. On the third return day, then, as stated above, the assize shall be taken whether the tenant has come or not. And if the jurors declare in favour of the demandant, seisin shall be adjudged to him and the sheriff ordered by the following writ to have him put in seisin:

The writ for delivering seisin after the recognition
The king to the sheriff, greeting. Know that N. has proved in my court, by a recognition concerning the death of a certain ancestor of his, his right against R. to the seisin of so much land in such-and-such a vill. And therefore I command you to have him put in seisin without delay. Witness, etc . . .

10. Criminal Cases of the Early Thirteenth Century recorded in the
Rolls of the Justices with the King, at Westminster, and on Eyre
in Lincolnshire, Northamptonshire and Bedfordshire, from *Select
Pleas of the Crown*, edited and translated by F. W. MAITLAND
(Selden Society, London, 1887), pp. 21–3, 40, 106–8.

The jurors [of the Hundred of Cleley] say that Hugh, son of Walter
Priest, was outlawed for the death of Roger Rombald at the suit of
Robert Rombald and afterwards returned under the [protection of the]
king's writ, and afterwards was outlawed for the same death on the
appeal of Geoffrey, Thurstan's son. The county therefore is asked by
what warrant they outlawed the same man twice for the same death,
and says that of a truth in King Richard's time the said Hugh was
outlawed at the suit of one Lucy, sister of the said Roger, so that for a
long time afterwards he hid himself; and at length he came into the
county [court] and produced letters of Sir Geoffrey Fitz peter in the
form following: 'G. Fitz peter etc. to the sheriff of Northamptonshire,
greeting, Know thou that the king hath pardoned to Hugh, son of the
priest of Grafton, his flight and the outlawry adjudged to him for the
death of a certain slain man, and hath signified to us by his letters that
we be aiding to the said Hugh in re-establishing the peace between him
and the kinsfolk of the slain; wherefore we command thee that thou be
aiding to the said Hugh in making the peace aforesaid, and do us to wit
by thy letters under seal what thou hast done in this matter, since we are
bound to signify the same to the king. In witness etc. by the king's
writ from beyond the seas.' And the said letters being read in full
county [court] the county told the said Hugh that he must find pledges
that he would be in the king's peace, and he went away to find pledges,
and afterwards did not appear. But the kinsfolk of the slain, having
heard that Hugh had returned after his outlawry, came to the next
county [court] and Robert Rombald produced Geoffrey, Thurstan's
son, who said that if he saw the said Hugh he would sue against him the
death of the said Roger, who was [his kinsman]. And the county showed
him how Hugh had brought the justiciar's letters pardoning him the
flight and outlawry, and that he was to find pledges to stand to the
king's peace, but had not returned. Whereupon the king's serjeant was
ordered to seek Hugh and bring him to a later county [court]. And at a
later county [court] Geoffrey offered himself against Hugh, and Hugh
did not appear; whereupon the king's serjeant being questioned said
that he had not found him, and the county advised [Geoffrey] to come
to another county [court], because if in the meantime Hugh could be
found, he would be brought to the county court. Then at the third
county [court] the said Geoffrey offered himself, and it was testified
by the serjeant that Hugh had not yet been found, wherefore the county

said that as Hugh would not appear to the king's peace, he must bear the wolf's head as he had done before.

To judgment against the coroners and the twelve jurors.

Our lord the king has commanded the justices of the bench that the duels which have been waged before them between Ranulf of Launcells and Hugh of Stoddon, and between William of Burnsland and Richard of Dunham, [in appeals] of robbery, be put before the king himself, for he wishes to see them.

Richard, John's son, appeals Geoffrey of Shireford, for that on Saturday, the eve of Holy Cross, as [Richard] lay in his house at Sowe in a sickness, which was adjudged to him [as an essoin] in an action, by four knights of the county sent to him by judgment of the county [court], Geoffrey with his force came and intruded into his house against him, and wickedly and in felony and premeditated assault, assaulted, and beat, and ill-treated him; and when Emma his wife heard the tumult, she came from her garden and found Geoffrey with his force thus beating her lord, and at once went out and raised hue and cry; hearing which, Geoffrey went out, and in felony wounded Emma his [Richard's] wife in the head as she was endeavouring to aid and succour him, and in robbery took from him a half-mark of his money; and that this he did wickedly and in felony and in the king's peace, he offers to deraign by his body as the court shall consider.

And Geoffrey comes and defends the peace etc. and the felony and robbery and all of it etc., but desires to speak the truth. He says that in truth Richard was adjudged sick by the judgment of the county by the four knights, as Richard says, and because it was told to [Geoffrey] that Richard was daily leaving his house and going to his plough and his other business, he, by his friends' counsel, came to the fields, and found Richard among his crops in the fields, and raised the cry against him and would have captured him, but the Prior of Coventry's men of that township took Richard from him, and then Emma came up and raised the cry, and one Alexander the chaplain who was there gave her a push so that she fell upon a stone and thus got the wound etc. Therefore let [Geoffrey] be in custody. And being asked whether he will say more, he says that he defends the wound and the felony and the robbery of the half-mark and all of it as the court shall consider.

And because the county and coroners testify that the suit is duly made, and Geoffrey does not confess the wound nor the robbery, it is considered that there be battle between them, and let Geoffrey give gage for defence, and Richard for proof . . .

A day is given them at Lichfield, on Tuesday the morrow of St Luke the Evangelist, and then let them come armed.

On that day the duel is fought and Richard is vanquished, and so let Geoffrey be quit thereof, and Richard is in custody.

11. FROM Thirteenth-Century Manor Court, Honour Court and Private Hundred Court rolls, and rolls of the Abbot of Ramsey's court in the Fair of St Ives, edited and translated by F. W. MAITLAND in *Select Pleas in Manorial Courts* (Selden Society, London, 1888), pp. 11-12, 21, 54-7, 60-2, 82-3, 88-9, 123-4, 140-5, 178ff.

WEEDON BECK [Northants., a manor of the Abbey of Bec in Normandy]. VIGIL OF ST MICHAEL.

Richard le Boys of Aldeston has sworn fealty for the land which was his father's and has found pledges for 4s as his relief, to wit, William Clerk of the same place, Godfrey Elder and Roger Smith.

Elias Deynte in full court resigned his land and William Deynte his son was put in seisin of it and swore fealty and found the same pledges for 5s as his relief. Afterwards he paid.

The whole township gives for the abbot's tallage 6 marks.

The township presents that they suspect Robert Dochy and William Tale because they made fine [an agreement] with the knights [who formed the jury] before the justices [in eyre] when they were accused of larceny . . .

William Green and Guy Lawman have gallons [the measures by which they sold beer] which are too small.

John Mercer will give three chickens yearly at Martinmas for having the lord's patronage and he is received into a tithing.

WRETHAM [Norfolk, also a manor of Bec]. FRIDAY AFTER THE FEAST OF ST MICHAEL.

Gilbert Richard's son gives 5s for licence to marry a wife. Pledge, Seaman. Term [for payment], the Purification.

The following women have been violated and therefore must pay the leyerwite, Botild Alfred's daughter [fine, 6d] . . . Agnes Seaman's daughter [fine 12d, pledge the said Seaman] . . .

HEMINGFORD [Hunts., a manor of the Abbot of Ramsey]. ON THE DAY OF ST HUGH IN THE TWELFTH YEAR OF ABBOT WILLIAM.

Names of the jurors: Reginald at Moor, Nicholas Farmer, Nigel Palmer, Nicholas of Elsworth, John Gunild's son, Jordan Trappe, Thomas Amabel, Henry Roger's son, Simon of Beneland, Adam Peter's son, William Ward, Henry at Well.

They give for chevage [a fine for being allowed to represent their tithings] 13s 4d . . .

From Henry Geoffrey's son 6d, for which Simon Geoffrey's son is pledge, that he may have the [judgment] of the court as to two roods of land which Henry Roger's son and Agatha the widow hold. And the jurors come and say that they never saw any ancestor of the said Henry holding those two roods these fifty years past. Therefore let the said Henry recover nothing by his claim and let [Henry Roger's son] and Agatha hold [the land in peace] etc.

Simon Roger's son and Reginald Peter's son the aletasters say that Katherine Ingol has broken the assize of beer, therefore be she in mercy, 12d . . . [Eight other women are fined for the same offence.] From Alice Cot, nothing, for she kept [the assize] and only brewed once. From Beatrice Mutun for constantly breaking the assize, nothing, for she is the man [sic] of Sir Reginald de Grey . . .

And they [the jurors] say that the Vicar of St. Ives has lopped two willows between his holding and Thomas Smith's wrongfully, for the said willows grow upon the abbot's land and the said boundary and the stream on which the willows grow belong to the abbot . . .

COURT OF KING'S RIPTON [Hunts., a manor of the Abbot of Ramsey, but enjoying the customs of one which had once belonged to the 'ancient demesne' of the king]. ON MONDAY NEXT BEFORE THE FEAST OF ST. PHILIP AND ST JAMES IN THE TWENTY-FIFTH YEAR OF KING EDWARD.

Bartholomew Ralph's son of King's Ripton demands against William William's son of King's Ripton and Roger his brother two acres of land with the appurtenances in King's Ripton and against Henry son of Simon Reeve one acre of land with the appurtenances in the same vill as his right by a writ of right close according to the custom of the manor etc.; and he says that one Sweyn Harvey's son, ancestor of the said Bartholomew, whose heir he is, was seised of the said tenements in his demesne as of fee and of right in the time of peace in the time of King Henry, father of the king that now is, by taking thence esplees to the value etc.; and from the said Sweyn the right descended etc. to one Robert as his son and heir, and from the said Robert the right descended etc. to one Agnes as his daughter and heir, and from the said Agnes to the said Bartholomew the now demandant as her son and heir; and that such is his right he offers etc. according to the custom of the manor etc. . .

[The defendants deny Bartholomew's account of the descent of the property] and they put themselves on a jury of the country, in lieu of the grand assize of our lord the king, according to the custom of the manor, as to whether they have right in the said tenements by the feoffment which William of Alconbury according to the custom of the manor made to the said William and Roger [the now tenants], which William of Alconbury was enfeoffed thereof . . . by . . . [the defendants recount a different transmission of the property by a series of 'enfeoffments'.]

The jurors . . . say upon their oath that the said William and Roger have greater right in the said two acres of land as they hold them than the said Bartholomew as he demands them . . .

COURT OF BROUGHTON [the Abbot of Ramsey's honour-court]. ON TUESDAY NEXT AFTER THE CLOSE OF EASTER IN THE SAME YEAR.

Roger Eyre complains of Elias of Stratford for that in the peace of the lord abbot he took and drove off four oxen of his wrongfully and detained them on Wednesday next before Michaelmas, and Roger would not have sustained this damage and shame for a half-mark, and he produces suit. And Elias defends tort and force etc. and says that he is not bound to answer, for that Roger in his count does not say in what year the said Wednesday was, nor of what price the oxen were, nor where he [Elias] drove them off. And for that the said Roger has insufficiently accused the said Elias, therefore by judgment of the court Elias goes without day and Roger is in mercy. Pledge, Roger of the Burn, and let him find other pledges at Cranfield . . .

COURT OF BROUGHTON ON WHIT TUESDAY IN THE SAME YEAR BEFORE THE LORD ABBOT, MASTER G. OF WHEPSTEAD, S. OF HOUGHTON, GEOFFREY RODLAND, ROBERT OF FOUGERES, THOMAS OF BEINVILLE, SEWAL OF HANINGFIELD AND OTHERS.

All the knights and freeholders of the court of Broughton have chosen Sir Berengar le Moyne . . . Sir J. of Kent, Silvester L'Enveyse and Ralph of Tyville to do for this occasion in the Welsh war the service of four knights due to the king on behalf of the Abbot of Ramsey and the commonalty of this court . . . And the whole court says that each of the said four knights after he has been placed in a squadron ought to receive every day for the forty days during which he is in the king's service four shillings, that sum being at present the fair rate owing to the dearness of the times. And the whole court at present assesses two shillings on every hide for the expenses of the said four knights . . .

PLEAS IN THE COURTS OF THE HUNDRED OF WHORWELSDOWN AND THE MANOR OF ASHTON [Wilts., a hundred and manor of the Abbess of Romsey].
ADJOURNED HUNDRED COURT FOR HOKEDAY HELD ON FRIDAY BEFORE THE FEAST OF ST BARNABAS IN THE FORTH-SIXTH YEAR OF KING HENRY III.
. . . Richard Hordy tithingman of Southwick comes and says that the house of Lucy Hogeman was broken on Tuesday next after the feast of St John before the Latin Gate and thence were carried off a coverlet and a linen garment and a sheet and a towel, bread and corn. On being asked whether he suspects anyone, he says No. And on the night of Thursday in Whitsunweek a beehive was stolen from Ducie widow of Richard

Miller. And he made mention that the house of Hugh Bokel was burnt and he [Hugh] inside it . . .

COURT OF THE FAIR [of St Ives, belonging to the Abbot of Ramsey]. ON THE NEXT WEDNESDAY, TO WIT, THE FEAST OF ST PHILIP AND ST JAMES IN THE SAME YEAR.

Adam Waderove complains of Geoffrey of Oxford, for that he unjustly detains and deforces him of 3s 1d and therefore unjustly, because whereas the said Geoffrey came on Monday last in the Fair of St Ives opposite the house of Roger Alexander's son and bought of the said Adam 5 fleeces of wool for 3s 2d the said Geoffrey only paid him 1d and thus has gone off with the said 3s 1d and with the said 5 fleeces and still detains them and is in seisin of them to his [Adam's] damage and dishonour 6s 8d; and he produces suit.

The said Geoffrey was present and defended the words of court and the damage and dishonour of Adam [to the amount of] 6s 8d. but made a certain confession, namely he said that he could not deny that he bought the said wool for 3s 2d and was in seisin of it as Adam alleged against him, but he said that Adam sold him the wool by weight as being $8\frac{1}{2}$ lb of wool and he [Geoffrey] found in it a deficiency of 1 lb, and that he, Geoffrey, was always ready and willing to pay the said Adam the said money provided that Adam would allow him out of it the value of the 1 lb. of wool which was deficient from the said weight of $8\frac{1}{2}$ lb; he offered to prove [this] sufficiently, if the court should award [him the proof]. A day is given him to make his proof to-morrow three-handed.

COURT OF THE FAIR ON THE NEXT THURSDAY IN THE SAID YEAR.

Geoffrey of Oxford came and sufficiently proved three-handed that . . . [the facts were as he had stated them]. Therefore by judgment of the court the said Geoffrey may deduct from the said 3s 1d the value of 1 lb of wool, and shall pay to the said Adam the whole of the residue, to wit 2s $8\frac{1}{2}$d . . . And let the said Adam be in mercy for his false claim; fine 6d . . .

12. FROM The Shropshire Eyre Roll of 1256, translated from Roll JI 1/734 in the Public Record Office. (The numbers refer to membranes, 'd' indicating that the case is on the dorse or back of the membrane.)

Civil Pleas

(m. 1) An assize comes to give a verdict as to whether William de la Grene, chaplain, and his brother, Nicholas, unjustly disseised William of Hampton of his free tenement in Alveley since the king's first crossing of the sea into Brittany. He complains that they disseised him of four acres of arable. William and the others say that William of Hampton complains unjustly, because he showed only three acres to the view. Further, William the chaplain says that a certain Henry son of William of Alveley gave him a good and peaceful seisin of those three acres, and William of Hampton never had seisin. William of Hampton admits that Henry son of William once made a charter of feoffment to William de la Grene for the land, but says that William never had seisin through the charter. For Henry son of William had demised the land to a certain Henry of Perry for the term of twenty years, a long time before the charter was made: he made the charter to William within that term and without conveying seisin. Afterwards, Henry of Perry died before the end of the twenty years and in his last will he left the remainder of the term [to his wife]. And a certain Henry of Morfe later married her and had seisin of the land. In the course of time came William of Hampton and prevailed upon Henry son of William of Alveley to enfeoff him with the land and make him a charter according to which he should pay rent to Henry of Morfe for the remainder of Henry's term. And William of Hampton prevailed upon Henry of Morfe to remit to him the remainder of his term, so that both through Henry son of William as feoffor and through Henry of Morfe as farmer William of Hampton had good and peaceful seisin of the land till William de la Grene and the others disseised him. As to the truth of this he appeals to the assize. The jurors swear that it is true. So William of Hampton shall recover seisin by view of the recognitors, and William de la Grene and the others are in mercy. Damages, half a mark.

(m. 4d) Did Roger son of William of Myddle . . . Hugh son of Alice, William Provost . . . John son of John . . . Roger Forester . . . Reginald Costard . . . and William Pynot [23 names altogether] disseise Reginald of Sleap of common pasture pertaining to his free tenement in Bomere ? He complains that they have disseised him of common in heathland about two hundred acres in extent, where he used to common his beasts of every sort all the year round. Roger and the others have not come, but their bailiff, William of Prees, answers for them and says that they are all the men of John l'Estrange and claim nothing in Reginald's alleged tenement and common except at the will of the said John: William calls the assize to witness to this. One of the recognitors, William of Bicton, has not come and is in mercy. Verdict: Roger and the others have no claim except at the will of John l'Estrange. So they are quit, and Reginald takes nothing and is in mercy.

(m. 5) An assize comes to give a verdict as to whether Coleman of Ludlow, uncle of Coleman of Ludlow, was seised of a messuage and 44 acres of land in Sheet and half a virgate in Whettleton and a messuage and two acres in Stokesay on the day he died etc. and whether Coleman is his next heir. Adam of Stokesay holds a messuage and two acres of the land, William Coterel five acres . . . Gillian, who was Coleman's wife, seven acres . . . the Master of the Hospital of St John at Ludlow ten acres and a half . . . [The land is now split into eleven parcels.] . . . Gillian who was Coleman's wife says that Coleman [the nephew and plaintiff, called 'le Blund' as well as of Ludlow] has brought the assize against her unjustly, for she holds the land in dower, as that assigned to her by Coleman uncle of Coleman le Blund, who would be bound to warrant her if someone else sued her for it. Coleman le Blund cannot deny this, so Gillian is quit, and Coleman takes nothing by the assize and is in mercy. William and all the others say that Coleman has brought the assize unjustly, for Coleman his uncle did not die seised of their tenements: a long time before his death he granted them to William and the others. They put themselves on the assize. Verdict: Coleman the uncle did die seised, and Coleman le Blund is the next heir, so he recovers seisin, and William and the others are in mercy.

(m. 9) Attorneys
The Abbot of Croxden appoints brother John, one of his monks, and brother John, one of his lay-brothers, as his attorneys in a plea concerning pasture-rights against John de Beleg and his wife Joan.

Civil Pleas
(m. 10) The same assize, with the same jurors, comes to give a verdict as to whether Odo of Hodnet made a ditch in Hopton to the nuisance of the same Robert's tenement in Hopton. Robert complains that whereas he used to have a drove-way for his cattle and right of way for the carting of his corn, the ditch deprives him of these rights. Odo says nothing to stop the assize. Verdict: no nuisance, because Robert was never accustomed to cart corn there, and no right of way is threatened by reason of the ditch. So Odo is quit, and Robert in mercy.

Foreign Pleas
(m. 20) Geoffrey Falconer put in an appearance on the fourth day to

answer Walter brother of William of Hyde, Robert son of Robert Short, Walter Mewy and Walter of Woodmanton as to why he and William of Hyde came with force and arms to Geoffrey's land in Beoley and carried off his plough without permission to William's home and beat and maltreated him against the peace etc. And the defendants have not come, and they defaulted on previous occasions so that the sheriff was ordered to distrain them through all their lands etc . . . and have their persons on this day. The sheriff returned that they are all staying in Herefordshire and have no land nor tenement in Gloucestershire by which they can be distrained. So the sheriff of Herefordshire is ordered to distrain them etc. and to have their bodies at Westminster one month from Easter. [In the margin against this case is a note that the case was adjourned to Shrewsbury from the Gloucestershire session of the eyre.]

Crown Pleas

(m. 21d) Presentment that Roger of Welhope, a serjeant of Thomas Corbet, and his fellows took Richard of Norbury and imprisoned him at Cause; and Richard could not get free until he gave them 12 pence. So judgment on Roger.

Presentment that Yareford, a man of the abbot of Buildwas, was taken and imprisoned at Cause by Thomas Bindefeud and later freed, but the jurors do not know how.

A day was set for the appearance of Thomas Corbet on Monday.

(m. 22) Eynun of The Haye killed Walter Pinchun and fled and is suspected. So let him be exacted and outlawed. He had no chattels. The first finder is present and is not suspected. And the villages of Mawley and Cleobury did not pursue [the killer] and are in mercy.

A stranger and his wife were lodging at the house of Isolda of Cleobury and there killed Philip son of Isolda and fled and placed themselves in the church of Neen, admitted the deed and abjured the realm before the coroners. His chattels, 3 pence. Neen Savage, Neen Sollars and Hopton Wafers did not make pursuit and are in mercy. The twelve jurors did not present the finder and are in mercy.

(m. 22d) Hamund of Birches was arrested and imprisoned in the prison of Bridgnorth when R. of Grendon was sheriff, and obtained the king's writ of replevin for his release on bail, but he gave half a mark to R. the sheriff before he could obtain release. So judgment on the sheriff. Hamund puts himself on the country for good or ill. Verdict: not guilty of any misdeed. So he is quit.

A stranger whose name is unknown was found dead in a field by the village of Clive. The first finder has come and is not suspected. It is not known who killed him . . .

William son of Herbert was crushed by a wagon and died three days later. Judgment: misadventure. Value of the cart and oxen, 24 shillings and 6 pence. On this there was testimony that Hugh the chaplain of Momeresfeud took an ox from the deodand as heriot for the Abbot of Shrewsbury, because William made a will and enjoyed church law, leaving the ox to the church of Momeresfeud of which the Abbot of Shrewsbury is rector. Judgment on William.

(m. 24) Walter Blethin appeals Reginald son of Andrew of Holdgate that when he was in the king's peace in a certain wood belonging to Walter de Clifford called Bernstre on the Tuesday after the Assumption in the thirty-fourth year [of King Henry] Reginald came and assaulted, wounded and maltreated him against the peace etc. Reginald asks that it be awarded to him that when Walter appealed him before, he said that this was done in the thirty-fifth year and now he says the thirty-fourth. Since this is proved by the coroners' rolls, the appeal is considered null, and William shall be imprisoned. But for the sake of the king's peace let there be inquiry of the country as to the truth of the matter. The jurors say that the said Reginald is guilty of the said trespass. So he shall be imprisoned. Afterwards the said William Blethin came and made fine by half a mark by the pledge of Richard Tyrel. The said Reginald is poor.

(m. 24d) Unknown malefactors came to the house of Stephen of Boscobel and killed Stephen and tied up his whole family. They fled and it is not known who they were. Claverley, where this happened, did not make pursuit.

(m. 24d) Presentment that Walter son of Ivo of Petton and Walter son of William of Petton gave Robert of Preen, bailiff of the hundred of Munslow, a measure of wheat so that they should not be arrested . . . [The jurors list sums taken from six other people for the same reason.] . . . So judgment on Robert.

(m. 27d) Brun of Norton . . . [and 23 others] . . . suspected of thieving and receiving thieves, have come and put themselves upon the country for good or ill. And the jurors say on their oath that they are not guilty of any misdeed. So they are quit. Afterwards it was found that William of Calverhall indicted Richard the smith of Calverhall and his brothers Thomas and William out of hatred and spite. So he is in mercy.

(m. 28d) Simon of Preen appeals William son of Robert Bedell of Preen that when he was in the peace of the lord king on the twelfth day of Christmas in the thirty-ninth year [of King Henry] in the village of Plaish William came there and assaulted him with a sword of Cologne and gave him a wound in the back and another in the head and a third in the stomach with a lance. And that he did this wickedly and feloniously he offers etc. ['to prove on his body': i.e. by battle]. Simon also appeals William's brothers, Adam and Hugh, of beating him – that they wickedly beat and maltreated him with a stick. William comes and says that he is a clerk and ought not to answer here. At this, there comes the official of the Bishop of Hereford who claims him as a clerk. But that it may be known in what condition he is handed over, let there be inquiry of the country. And the jurors say that he is guilty of that deed, and as such he is handed over to the bishop. Adam and Hugh come and ask that it be awarded to them that Simon has been inconsistent in his appeal, and since this is confirmed by the coroners' rolls the appeal is adjudged null. And let the truth be inquired of the country. The jurors say that the said Adam and Hugh were aidors and abettors when the felony was done. So they are committed to gaol. Afterwards come Hugh and Adam and make fine with the king by half a mark by the pledge of Richard of Acton and Henry the carpenter of Preen. Afterwards it was found that Simon possesses nothing, and on the order of S. of Walton he is to be delivered to Sir James of Audley.

(m. 30) THE BOROUGH OF BRIDGNORTH IS REPRESENTED BY TWELVE JURORS.

(m. 30d) Richard Bugge, suspected of larceny and receiving thieves, comes and denies larceny and everything and puts himself upon the country for good or ill. The jurors say on oath that he is not guilty of any thieving or harbouring. Therefore he is quit. But they say that this was imputed to him by John Glidd. John is therefore amerced at half a mark by the pledge of the twelve jurors of Bridgnorth.

13. FROM Rolls of Complaint in the Eyre, translated in *Select Cases of Procedure without Writ under Henry III*, edited and translated by H. G. RICHARDSON and G. O. SAYLES (Selden Society, London, 1941), pp. 85, 105–106.

ASSIZES AND JURIES TAKEN AT BERMONDSEY IN SURREY BEFORE HUGH LE BIGOD, JUSTICIAR OF ENGLAND, ON THE MORROW OF ST EDMUND THE KING'S DAY IN THE FORTY-THIRD YEAR [of Henry III: 21 November 1258].

Wotton Hundred
The same jurors have presented that John of Gatesden, while he was sheriff, made his turn twice a year, whereas no sheriff before him was wont to make more than one a year, with the result that he took two pence a year from every man coming to the turns whereas before they were wont to give one penny only. And John of Gatesden comes and freely acknowledges that he had that payment levied, but he says that it was by the king's order. But he shows no warrant for it. Therefore let him be amerced. And let there be discussion with the king whether he wishes that turn to be continued or not and whether the pennies should be paid twice or not. And Buckland township complains that he levied four shillings from it for that turn, which they are still paying. And the whole hundred of Reigate lays a similar complaint against him ... The same jurors and the whole county have presented that the county court of Surrey, which was always accustomed to be held at Leatherhead, is held at Guildford, and this has caused very great loss to the whole county. Therefore let there be a discussion with the king. John of Fishfold complains that Roger the baker and Roger Vigers, the servants of the parson of Wotton church, wrongfully beat, wounded and maltreated him in breach of the peace etc. And they do not come. Therefore the sheriff is ordered to distrain them to be in court the next day. Afterwards it was testified that they are not to be found in the county. And John does not sue against them etc ...

Bampton Hundred
The men of Roger Doilly of Bampton present several articles against Roger, complaining that he is distraining them to perform services which they ought not and were not wont to do and is tallaging them so heavily that they are unable to support their tenure etc.

And Roger comes by his son, John, and says that he can certainly tallage them as he pleases and deal with them as his villeins, because they are not sokemen and have no other privileges which prevent his tallaging them as he pleases. And as to this he puts himself on the country.

And the aforesaid men come and freely acknowledge that they are his villeins and not socage tenants. Therefore it is awarded that they are to be in mercy for a false plaint, and Roger is to be acquitted thereof . . .

14. Bills to the Justices in Eyre, translated from French by W. C. BOLLAND in *Select Bills in Eyre* (Selden Society, London, 1914), pp. 20–1, 41.

William Piers of Brompton complaineth to the Justices of our lord the king that whereas he was going in the peace of God and in the peace of the king in the town of Ludlow on the Sunday next before the Feast of St Michael in the eighteenth year of the reign of King Edward that now is, whom God preserve, Roger Clayband, Reynold of Posenhall, Hugh Bruton, Adam of Cayton, William the son of John of Boreford, William the dyer, Harry of Chabenore, William the son of William the Galis, together with all the commonalty of the town of Ludlow, whose names are unknown save that of Lawrence of Ludlow, came and suddenly attacked him with swords, axes, knives and other sharp-edged arms, and wounded him in the head and stripped off his hose, whereby he lost consciousness; and they maimed his left arm and a finger of his right hand and left him for dead; and they dragged him to prison and there they kept him for two days and two nights in prison and put him in shackles, wrongfully and against the peace, to the damage of this William of a hundred pounds; whereof he prayeth remedy for God's sake. Pledges for prosecution: Adam Wall of Brompton; Roger the summoner of Brompton.
[Endorsements: further notes of pledges for the appearance of the defendants and ...] ... William the son of John is dead ... Failed to prosecute.
Summoned in Munslow on the Thursday fortnight after St Martin.

   Avice the wife of John of Coleshill prayeth the Justices of our lord the king and craveth of you for the sake of the queen's soul that you will have pity upon her and show favour unto her against Harry of Thickness; for the aforesaid Avice, in the sight of the good folk of Newcastle, deposited with the aforesaid Harry the charters of all her land that he might take care of them, and this Harry now wrongfully detaineth the aforesaid charters; and the aforesaid Avice is now ejected from her land because she hath not these charters. Therefore the aforesaid Avice prayeth for the love of God and for the queen's soul's sake that the truth may be inquired of.
[Endorsement:] Failed to prosecute.

15. FROM *Placita Corone*, edited and translated by J. M. KAYE (Selden Society, London, 1966), pp. 19–20, 22–4. This is a description of pleading in criminal cases.

If a man be impleaded for felony he may find here the crown laws, by means of which he may defend himself; and if he be convicted, what judgment he will suffer; and how one may abate an appeal and by what exceptions; and how he will be impleaded and what delays he will be able to cause before having to reply. And be it known that a man will never be hanged so long as he does not admit his guilt by his own mouth.

A thief was once indicted by the country and brought before Laurence de Brok, then sitting as justice in such a place. And the justice said:

'My good friend, you are indicted by the country of such a thing: how do you wish to acquit yourself of such a theft?'

And the other replied to him, like the man in our former example, that he would defend himself by his body. And the justice spoke in the same way as the former justice, and the thief stuck to battle; and the justice wondered how he could bring the thief to give another reply, and asked him: 'Are you a good and honest man?'

'Yes, indeed,' said he who had been answering as above, 'and I am ready to defend myself by my body against this accusation'.

And the justice continued: 'I say are you good and honest?' and the thief said: 'Yes, sir, I am', and the justice said: 'How do you wish to prove it?' and the thief said: 'By the country, to be sure'.

And the country came, and said he was a thief and had committed such a theft, for which he had been indicted, and several others: so he was hanged; and in such a way he was tricked . . .

A man taken for a killing done in self defence

'Sheriff, why has this man been taken?'

'Sir, for the death of a man whom he is supposed to have killed in self defence, as he says.'

'What is your name?'

'Sir, Thomas de N.'

'Thomas, what was the name of the man whom you killed in pre-meditated attack, feloniously as a felon?'

'Sir, if you please, I have never been a felon and never did mischief to living man, in premeditated attack; and so I have done nothing wrong against the man whose name you ask: who, feloniously as a felon and in premeditated attack tried to kill me on such a day, at such an hour, in such a year in my own house in such a township, for no fault on my part and solely on account of his own malice.'

'Tell us the circumstances.'

'Sir, I was unwilling to lend or hire to him a horse for the purpose of riding about his business in the district: for I feared that I should be deprived of my horse, or of any other thing which I might have lent or hired to him, for he was an unprincipled man, full of fraud and subtle tricks, untrustworthy and of ill fame. And because I refused him the loan of my horse he ran at me in my own house with a Welsh knife, horn handled, in his right hand and inflicted several wounds on my head, shoulders, feet, and elsewhere on my body wherever he could reach. I did not at first return his blows; but when I realized that he was set on killing me I started to defend myself: that is to say I wounded him in the right arm with a little pointed knife which I carried, making no further onslaught and acting in this way only to save my own life.'

'Did he die of such a wound?'

'In truth, sir, I do not know: but had he not received this wound he would have killed me, feloniously as a felon and in premeditated attack.'

'Who put you in this prison?'

'Sir, my neighbours: for they were afraid of being involved in this affair and suffering loss thereby.'

'What happened to the other?'

'Sir, he at once fled out of their grasp.'

'Thomas, you have greatly embroidered your tale and coloured your defence: for you are telling us only what you think will be to your advantage, and suppressing whatever you think may damage you, and I do not believe you have told the whole truth.'

'Sir, I have told the whole truth, and related the affair from the beginning to the end in every detail: and of this I trust myself to God and the country for both good and evil.'

And so let an inquest be held.

And the jury said the same as Thomas had related. So the justice then says:

'Thomas, these good people testify by their oaths to the truth of what you have said. So our judgment is that what you did to him, you did in self defence. But we cannot release you from this prison without the king's special order. However we will send a report of your case to the king's court and ensure that you receive his special grace.'

'Sir, I thank you.'

16. FROM *The Chronicle of Bury St Edmunds*, edited and translated by ANTONIA GRANSDEN (London, 1964), pp. 88, 89, 92–3, 93–4.

1287

... On the morrow of St Hilary's day [14 January] the aforementioned justices in eyre sat at Cattishall. In this eyre John de Creyk, Godfrey de Beaumont and Ralph de Berners sued us for our manors of Semer and Groton. When the case had been investigated we at length declared that we would defend our right by judicial combat, as we suspected that the surrounding district supported and was in league with our opponents. Accordingly a day one month after Easter was assigned for the parties to appear before the King's Bench and the case was adjourned until then. The abbot paid a certain champion called Roger Clerk, who came from the district of Lincoln, 20 marks in advance from his own money. After the duel Roger was to receive 30 marks more from him. The champion during the whole time of waiting stayed with us, accompanied by his trainer, although under challenge. Our justices, Henry de Guildford, Henry de Schineholt and Richard Wayland, the steward of the abbot's lands, sat in the town of Bury St Edmunds. ... On St Calixtus's day [14 October] our enemies were victorious and our champion slain in judicial combat in London. And so our manors of Semer and Groton were lost without any hope of recovery ...

1289

... The king landed with the queen in England at Dover on 12 August, four years after he had set sail from England. He stayed a while in Kent and then in Essex, and on St Lambert's day came to Bury St Edmunds on his way to Norfolk next day ... He solemnly kept the feast of the Translation of St Edward [13 October] at Westminster.

Thomas Wayland, the king's chief justice, was indicted before a lower royal court, on a charge of having harboured some of his own men who had murdered a man, and was convicted by a jury. He feared to put himself at the king's mercy and fled to the house of the Friars Minor at Bury St Edmunds. There by the king's order he was besieged for several days by men of the neighbourhood; when there was little hope left he assumed the friars' habit. On hearing this the king sent a knight from his familiar circle to make the guard even more secure in collaboration with the officials of the country. At length, after two months' siege and when nearly all the friars had dispersed in various directions, Thomas took off his friar's habit, put on secular clothes and came out, and was taken to the king and imprisoned in the Tower of London. ...

1290

A parliament was held at Westminster and sat from the feast of the

Circumcision until after St Valentine's day. There they discussed the wrongdoings of the different justices; and according to their different deserts the king and his council passed different sentences. Among them Thomas Wayland had all his property, both movable and otherwise, confiscated forever and was exiled without hope of returning. Many justices of the King's Bench and justices in eyre were imprisoned in the Tower. The most important of these were the justices of the King's Bench, John de Lovetot, William de Brunton, Roger de Leicester and Robert de Littlebury. Of the justices in eyre were Solomon de Rochester, Richard de Boyland, Thomas de Southend, Walter de Hopton and Richard de Preston. While the first mentioned obtained their freedom at the end of this parliament by paying a considerable money fine, those mentioned last remained in the Tower and the king went away. But they returned to their homes almost immediately with the king's consent, and indeed by his command, in the same way as the others. . . .

17. FROM a Roll of the Norwich Leets for the year 1290, translated by WILLIAM HUDSON in *Leet Jurisdiction in Norwich* (Selden Society, London, 1892), pp. 33–5.

LEET OF CONESFORD ON THE MONDAY NEXT AFTER THE FEAST OF ST VALENTINE IN THE 18TH YEAR
Parish of St Peter de Southgate – Parish of St Edward – Parish of St Etheldreda – Parish of St Clement – Parish of St Julian – Parish of St Michael de Conesford.
Ralph, son of Henry de Southgate, sworn; Silvester Siger, sworn; Henry Atterowe, sworn; Richard Hydhef made default; afterwards he came and was sworn – William King and Richard Everich, sworn; Richard Boatman and John Slabbard, sworn; Richard Undermel and William Inge, sworn; Alan de Bacton and Robert de Aldeby and Richard de Honington, sworn.

The jurors present on their oath that Roger the miller is not in tithing. . . . They say also that the wife of Richard Boatman sells beer by the single pot and three pots do not make one gallon of beer. . . . They say also that Thomas Everich and Richard Sheepseye catch fish in fresh water with nets which are not according to the assize . . . Seman de Blythburgh because he harboured his son, John, who was not in tithing. . . .

The jurors present that John the Redepriest wrongfully raised the hue on Henry the Clerk. Also they say that the same John is guilty of the murder of a male child begotten of his concubine (let him be arrested). . . . Also they say that Roger Wortes and his wife of habit raise the hue wrongfully upon their neighbours to the terror of all their neighbours and to the great scandal of the whole people . . . Also they say that Cecilia, the wife of John Lomb, has stolen from the parson of St Michael eight silver marks (arrest). . . . Also they say that Richard, son of Alice Bele, stole from Robert de Hadiscoe $18\frac{1}{2}$d by night on the morrow of St Peter in chains in the seventeenth year of the reign of the king now (arrest). . . . Also they say that John de Fransham, chaplain, has hindered the lord king of his toll, for they say that he buys his corn outside the town of Norwich and has it carried by night to his house, whereby the Bailiffs lose their toll. Also they say that the said John, the chaplain, is an excessive usurer. . . . Also they say that John le Man has appropriated to himself a common way by a shop which he has wrongfully made. . . .

18. Documents illustrating the work of the shire court, translated from some of those printed by W. A. Morris in *The Early English County Court* (University of California Publications in History, 1926), pp. 160–1, 173–6 (the numbering of the documents is Morris's).

34. Reading of a Deed, 1295
Here are the names of those present at a full shire court of Essex with many others whose names are not written down, when the deeds of the manor of Westlee were read and exhibited in French and in English on the Tuesday before Christmas in the year of Our Lord 1295 at Chelmsford: *viz.* Sir Walter le Baud knight . . . [17 other names] . . . and almost all the free tenants were there on account of the eleventh [a tax] granted to the lord king.

36. Reading of Charters and Letters of Protection, 1254
The sheriff of Westmorland is ordered to have read in full shire court the royal charters which the Abbot of Byland has obtained for the liberties granted to him, and his royal letters-patent of protection; and to see that the liberties contained in them are strictly observed as the charters and letters witness, and do not fail in any respect because of [anyone else's] persuasion or power. Witness . . .

37. Reading of the Great Charter, 1256
The sheriff of Yorkshire is ordered to have read in full shire court the king's great charter concerning the liberties granted to the community of England, and to see, on behalf of the king and of everyone else in the realm of England, that those liberties are in future strictly kept and inviolably observed in his bailiwick, article by article. So that the king shall not be forced to show severity towards him for shortcomings in this matter. Witness the king at Clarendon 23 May. Each sheriff in England has similar orders.

38. Administrative Proclamation, 1292
Whereas foreign merchants, and inhabitants of the king's realm also, daily bring into the realm from overseas Royal money which has been clipped and mixed with counterfeit money from various dies, doing business and making purchases with this money to no little damage of the king and the whole people of the king's realm and also in subversion of all the king's money; the king, wishing to apply a remedy in this matter lest a longer forbearance threaten a greater peril, orders the sheriff of Norfolk and Suffolk to cause to be strictly forbidden and publicly proclaimed in his full shire court and in each city and market town of his

shire, that no foreign, or indeed native, merchant nor anyone else shall henceforth bring into the king's realm the king's money which has been clipped or counterfeited from other dies, or use it in merchandising or business. If they do this, they shall forfeit the clipped or counterfeit money the first time they are caught. And if the same people are caught a second time for the same offence, they shall forfeit the money and also the other goods found with them. And a third time, their bodies and all their goods and chattels shall be forfeit to the king. Those who are not Merchants and have clipped or counterfeit king's money shall immediately perforate it and send it to the king's mint to be minted anew under the king's die, or it will be instantly forfeit to the king, whoever shall be found in possession of it. Witness Master W. March, treasurer of the king at Westminster 4 October in the nineteenth year by writ under the great seal. In the same way instructions are given to the sheriffs of the various shires.

19. FROM the Rolls of a Shire Court, translated from extracts printed by W. A. Morris, *The Early English County Court*, pp. 181–6.

EXTRACTS FROM THE ROLLS OF THE COUNTY COURT OF CORNWALL, HELD AT LOSTWITHIEL ON THE MONDAY BEFORE THE FEAST OF ST THOMAS AND ON MONDAY THE MORROW OF THE DECOLLATION OF ST JOHN THE BAPTIST, 7 EDWARD III [5 July and 30 August 1333].

Philip de Polsulsek who complains by attorney against Sybil who was the wife of William Caul in a plea of mesne appears by attorney. He complains that she unjustly failed to acquit him of the services which William de Botraux exacts from him for the free tenement which he [Philip] holds from the said Sybil in Polsulsek: he holds from her a messuage and a Cornish acre with appurtenances in the said village by fealty and a rent of 2s 6d at Michaelmas and suit of court every three weeks, so that Sybil is his mesne lord and ought to acquit him of the services [to William de Botraux as overlord]. The said William distrains him to make suit to his court at Trenethou by [seizing his] oxen and cows, to his damage of £100. Sybil asks what she has for such acquittance, and Philip says she is seised of his services and so etc. . . .

David de Boskenal complainant against Henry de Pengersok in a plea of trespass essoins himself on account of the king's service, after one default.

Hamelettus Wille de Bossucraon complains against Gerard son of Daniel de Sancto Maderno, John Gentil and William Gillot, who has defaulted three times, in a plea of debt. . . .

John Melior is in mercy for a false complaint against John de Kerchyn in a plea of debt, as the inquest found. . . .

Richard de Campo Arnulphi complains against Ralph Bloyon [and three others] in a plea of replevin. He complains that they unjustly seized a horse from the beasts of David Soben . . . [and another horse, thirteen mares and three foals from nine named and other unnamed free tenants of Richard] . . . whom he is bound to defend. They seized the beasts in the village of Merther in a place called Wyketysdon and drove them and impounded them at Triewal, and hold them there to his damage of £40. The said Ralph defends the seizure because he found the beasts in the village of Annuallibry eating his grass, and not in the village and place where he complains he did, and asks for the inquest to be held, and (says that) the others named in the complaint came to his assistance without doing any injury. The inquest is stopped because Ralph produces a royal protection lasting till next Michaelmas.

20. Report of a Case in the Court of Common Pleas, from a Year Book of 1309–10, edited and translated by F. W. MAITLAND, *Year Books of Edward II*, vol. iii (Selden Society, London, 1905), pp. 194–7.

William of Goldington brought his writ of conspiracy against John of Bassingburn and three others, and complains that wrongfully in the second year of the present king they conspired at Chelmsford that a statute merchant [i.e. an acknowledgment of a debt] had been made at Winchester in 25 [Edward I], in which statute was contained that Ralph le Gras was held and bound to Richard le Gras his brother in two thousand pounds, by virtue of which statute, without Richard's knowledge, a writ of execution was sued in this court to have the lands and tenements which were in the seisin of the said [Ralph] on the day of the conusance; and [Ralph] had leased two manors in C. to William of Goldington, and suit was made by John and others in the name of Richard, but without his knowledge, insomuch that those manors were delivered, [to the intent that] Richard should grant them to John for the time of the debt, so that William sued [in the King's Bench] until this statute was attainted as false: wrongfully and against the form of the statute [here, 'act of parliament': conspiracy was defined by an ordinance of 1305] for that case lately provided and to William's damage, one thousand pounds.

Scrope defended tort and force and all that is against the form of the statute and the damages of William etc. And [said he] we do not think that you should be answered to this count; for the writ supposes that John and the others in the second year of the now king conspired about a statute made in A.R. 25 of the late King, whereas every conspiracy and alliance ought to be precedent to what is conspired and devised; so we pray judgment.

Herle. Our plaint is that at C. in the second year of the now king you conspired [to allege] that a statute was made at W. in 25 Edward [I], which statute was not made, and this was proved before the king.

BEREFORD, C.J. to *Scrope.* Say something else.

Scrope. Once more we pray judgment of this writ, for it says that we conspired this statute for the profit of Richard, who is not named [as a party] in this writ. Judgment.

Herle. We have said that by your conspiracy and false alliance we are damaged to the amount of a thousand pounds. What say you to that?

Scrope. You say that this conspiracy was made against you and Ralph, and do not state the damage to Ralph, but only to yourself. Judgment.

Herle. We say that you conspired a statute made in favour of Richard, which was never made, and that thereby we received damage.

Scrope. To this writ you ought not to be answered, for at the beginning it makes us 'conspirators,' and in the final clause it makes us 'procurers'. Judgment of the variance.

BEREFORD, C.J. These seven years I never was put to study a writ so much as this; but there is nothing in what you say.

Herle. Our action is founded on three things. First, you conspired among yourselves at C. that a statute, which was never made, was made at W. Secondly, you machinated against us travail and expense. Thirdly, you procured a suit against us, whereby under judgment of this Court we were ousted from our manors.

Scrope. Judgments are not to be 'procured'; they proceed from law.

BEREFORD, C.J. If the judgment was not 'procured' by you, still you knew the suit upon which the judgment was made, and their complaint is of your false alliance.

Herle. By your false alliance etc., and thereupon you procured a suit to be made in this court, upon which a judgment was made, and this judgment has been annulled and found to be a deceit [arising from] your false conspiracy.

Scrope. Then you can have a writ of deceit. Judgment of this writ.

Herle. The deceit was found and attainted; but he complains that you and the others forethought this malice, whereby he was aggrieved.

BEREFORD, C.J. If you are of my counsel, and I pray your counsel to set going some business, although the thing be bad in itself, still, if you do not know the evil, you will have no punishment for giving your counsel. So say I in this case. His complaint is that you knew the evil, and you procured its being taken in hand.

Passeley. If you hold that this writ is founded on law, we will say something else.

BEREFORD, C.J. This writ is not founded on law [i.e. not on common law, because it was provided by statute], but is provided to punish falsehoods and wicked deeds, from which we all ought to fly.

BEREFORD, C.J. In the time of the late King Edward a writ issued from the Chancery to the Sheriff of Northumberland to summon Isabel, Countess of Albemarle to be at the next parliament to answer the king 'touching what should be objected against her'. The lady came to the parliament, and the king himself took his seat in the parliament. And then she was arraigned by a justice of full thirty articles. The lady, by her serjeant, prayed judgment of the writ, since the writ mentioned no certain article, and she was arraigned of divers articles. And there were two justices who were ready to uphold the writ. Then said Sir Ralph Hengham to one of them: 'Would you make such a judgment here as you made at the gaol delivery at C. when a receiver was hanged, and the principal [criminal] was afterwards acquitted before you yourself?' And to the other justice he said: 'A man outlawed was hanged before you at

N, and afterwards the king of his great grace granted that man's heritage
to his heir because such judgments were not according to the law of the
land.' And then Hengham said: 'The law wills that no one be taken by
surprise in the king's court. But, if you had your way, this lady would
answer in court for what she has not been warned to answer by writ.
Therefore she shall be warned by writ of the articles of which she is to
answer, and this is the law of the land.' Then arose the king, who was
very wise, and said: 'I have nothing to do with your disputations, but,
God's blood! you shall give me a good writ before you arise hence.' So
say I here. You challenge this writ because of this word 'they procured',
and that is a point in his action, for the which he hopes to deraign
damages against you, and, if that word were not in the writ, it seems to
me that his writ would not warrant his count. So say something else.

Scrope. We will imparl [consult together].

BEREFORD, C.J. Go, then, and imparl until tomorrow.

On the morrow W. of Goldington proffered himself against John of
Bassingburn.

BEREFORD, C.J. Call John of Bassingburn.

He was called, and came not.

Herle. You see how John went out to imparl, and now he has departed in
despite of the Court. So we pray judgment against him as undefended,
and we pray our damages etc.

BEREFORD, C.J. We take note of your challenge. Await your judgments
until tomorrow, and meanwhile we will talk of this matter with our
companions . . .

21. Some (Latin) Commissions of Oyer and Terminer of December 1327 and February 1328, as printed in the *Calendar of Patent Rolls, 1327–1330* (London, 1891), pp. 278–9, 292–3. The commissions appear in the same order as in the roll; the dates and places given are those at which the commissions were issued.

(22 December 1327, Gloucester) Commission of oyer and terminer to John de Stonore, Ralph de Bereford, Henry le Gulden and Robert de Hungerford, on complaint by John, bishop of Winchester, that John le Devenisshe . . . and others, prevented the exercise of the bishop's liberties and the collection of his tolls at his fair held on St Giles's Hill, outside Winchester. This fair was held for sixteen days from the eve of St Giles. About sunrise on that day the bishop's justices of the pavilion [justiciarii pavilionis] received from the mayor and bailiffs the keys of the south and west gates, to which they appointed guards, and also the woodbeam. After proclamation prohibiting sales within seven leagues except at the fair, the major and bailiffs delivered to the justices the keys and custody of the north and east gates, accompanied them to the pavilion on St Giles's Hill and then returned home. From that time the justices had the keeping of the city; the cognisance of pleas of trespass, debt and contract for seven leagues round; and the nomination of townsmen or strangers to act as mayor and bailiffs to execute their summons, distraints and attachments, wherein the aldermen were bound to assist in their aldermanries. No merchant could trade or open a stall, and no pedlar open his pack without paying a fine to the bishop. The justices selected victuallers, bakers, butchers and fishmongers, receiving from them an oath to supply good victuals, and in default to lose their victuals and be fined. They tested measures, balances and weights, burning false ones, and exacting fines. No person not in the Gild Merchant of the city could enter the city with goods after the Nativity of the Virgin without paying a fine. The justices also tasted the wine in the taverns of the city, throwing away bad wine, and exacting fines. The bishop's coroner acted during the fair. Cordwainers, cobblers and other craftsmen were forbidden to sell their wares except in the fair, on pain of forfeiture. The bishop received also the fines for breaking the assise of bread and ale, and exacted stated tolls at the gates for firewood, coal, corn, hay, straw and other goods. Goods sent collusively by merchants to citizens or others were forfeited.
By [authority of] the king himself.

(13 February 1328, York) Commission of oyer and terminer to William de Scotho, William de Cotes and Thomas de Faversham, on complaint by Stephen Lovet that John Monyn . . . and others, broke his close at

Ikham, co. Kent, imprisoned him, carried him to Dover, and imprisoned him there until he made a fine of 100s to them, and carried away his goods.
Because on complaint [*de querela*].

(6 February 1328, York) Commission of oyer and terminer to Simon de Hedersete, John Claver, and Walter de Filby, touching the persons who, together with Thomas Martyn . . . [and twelve others named] . . . carried away the goods of Queen Isabella at Great Yarmouth, Co. Norfolk, and assaulted Walter Stampart of Ipswich, her servant.
By the king himself.

(12 February 1328, York) Commission of oyer and terminer to John de Sancto Mauro, Robert de Gatesby and Peter son of Warin, on complaint by John de Kynardeseye, Michael de Meldon and Elias de Stapelton, executors of the testament of Thomas, Earl of Lancaster, that certain evildoers took away forty horses, a hundred oxen, twenty cows, two thousand sheep and a hundred swine, worth £1,000, and other goods under their custody as executors, at Hegham, Raundes, Ryssheden, Wadenho and Bukkeby, Co. Northampton.
By the council, because on complaint.

(20 February 1328, York) Further commission to the same, on the like complaint of taking away thirty horses, thirty colts, eighty oxen, forty cows, two thousand sheep and two hundred swine, worth £600, at Leycestre, Shelton, Dufford and Donyngton.
By the council, because on complaint.

22. Petitions in Parliament, 1334, translated from French as printed in *Rotuli Parliamentorum*, Record Commission (London 1776–7), vol. ii, pp. 84–5.

To our lord the king and to his council show these humble chaplains, the prior and convent of the Church of Saint John of Pontefract, that, whereas the said prior and convent had the advowson of the Church of Saint Sampson in York by the gift of King Stephen, confirmed from king to king and by the king who now is; the time came when the said prior and convent were wrongfully ejected by the Archdeacon of Richmond, who now stands in the court of the king before his justices. And there was an order by writ to summon an inquest from the city of York to inquire of the right of the said prior and convent and of the collation; which inquest is so suborned that it will not come to speak the truth. Wherefore the said prior and convent pray to our lord the king that he will of his Royal Grace grant to the said prior and convent that they may have this Advowson according to the purport of the gifts and confirmations granted aforetime.

Answer. Prosecute the inquest at the Common Law.

To our lord the king and his council show these humble chaplains, the prior and convent of the Church of Saint John of Pontefract, and pray that for the love of God and the maintenance of the state of the Holy Church he will have regard to and make provision for the chapel which was founded on the mountain where Monsieur Thomas the former Earl of Lancaster died [Lancaster was executed at Pontefract in 1322], it being sited partly at the convergence of two highways on the waste place between them and partly on the land of Robert de la More of Pontefract and the land of Adam Jurdan. This land the said Robert and Adam granted in the presence of our Lord the king at the original foundation of the said chapel, in honour of God and the said earl. And now the said Robert and Adam have sold the same land on which the chapel is sited to the Lord of Wake; for which reason the said Lord of Wake has taken possession of the said chapel and the Offerings coming to it, and has taken the keys, so that neither the said prior nor the convent can have the disposal of the offerings, as they were accustomed and ought to have because they are spiritual things within their jurisdiction and appurtenant to their Church, and because also this was ordained and commanded by our lord the king and his council aforetime.

Answer. Certain persons shall be assigned to inquire into the whole facts, and the inquest shall be returned into the chancery for the chancellor to do justice further in the matter. Meantime the prior shall have his offerings.

23. FROM the records of Kent Gaol Deliveries in 1317, translated from *Kent Keepers of the Peace*, edited by B. H. Putnam, (Kent Archaeological Society, Records Branch, 1933), pp. 80, 82, 88.

The delivery of the Gaol of Canterbury castle by Henry of Cobham junior, Roger Savage and John of Ifield, the lord king's justices assigned to the delivery of that gaol, on Wednesday . . . [20 July 1317]. . . .

William Saundre, indicted before the keepers of the peace of the felonious arson of the home of Christian ate Southlande. Charged with this, he says that he is not guilty and puts himself on the country. And the jurors say that William is not guilty of the said felony . . .

William Newecok of Rochester, taken on the appeal of the approver, Stephen ate Nelme, called Moonlight, who died at Canterbury, for the harbouring of the said Stephen, knowing him to be a thief, for the theft of five ells of white half-cloth and two hams from Robert French of Halling at Robert's home, and for having the cloth in his possession . . .

Robert Osbarn and his wife Avice, taken on the suit of John son of Benedict of Boctone, whose pledges were John Tenacre and John Dodesole, for the burglary of John's home and the theft from it of goods worth 10s in the hundred of Faversham. And because the said John has not prosecuted his complaint [querelam], the said pledges are judged to be in mercy and John is to be arrested. And Robert and Avice, charged with the felony on the king's suit, say that they are not guilty and put themselves on the country. And the jurors say that Robert and Avice are not guilty. . . .

24. FROM *Select Cases in the Court of King's Bench*, edited and translated G. O. SAYLES, vol. VI (Selden Society, London, 1965), pp. 54–5, 129–30, 168–9, 175.

(1347) John of Hackthorn, clerk, was attached here in court by bill to answer the king as well as John of Kegworth, clerk, of this, that whereas John of Kegworth was attorney for Griffin of Cauntytoun the younger, plaintiff, in the king's bench in a plea of trespass against Roger Bacheler, and by process continued thereon between them Roger was found guilty of the aforesaid trespass by the jury of the country on which Roger put himself regarding this before William of Thorp, the king's chief justice assigned to hold pleas before the king, at St Martin-le-Grand, London, by the king's writ of 'nisi prius', on Sunday after the Feast of the Purification of the Blessed Mary in the twenty-first year of the reign of the present king of England, the aforesaid John of Hackthorn on the Monday following, that is to say, after the aforesaid Feast of the Purification, in the King's Bench at Westminster falsely and wrongfully caused to be entered in the adjournment of a certain jury in connection with the aforesaid process between the aforesaid parties, that is to say, in the roll of Hilary term in the twentieth year of the reign of the present king on membrane 30 among the 'Common Pleas', these words, that is to say, 'Triffin de Tauntyton' for Griffin de Cauntyton', altering that letter 'G' in the proper name 'Griffin' into a 'T' and making a 'T' out of that letter 'C' in Cauntyton, in contempt and deceit of the king's court and the destruction and annulment of the aforesaid process and to the scandal of John of Kegworth, his loss and the manifest impairment of his estate, whereby he says that he is wronged and has suffered loss to the value of forty pounds. And he produces suit thereof etc. Pledges of prosecution: Griffin of Cauntyton and John Worthyn.

And John of Hackthorn denied the whole contempt, trespass, falsity, tort and deceit and whatever is in contempt or deceit of the king or his court etc. And he says that he is in no way guilty of the aforegoing charges against him etc. And as to this he puts himself on the country. And John of Kegworth likewise. Therefore let a jury thereon etc. come before the king at Westminster this very Friday in the Octave of the Purification of the Blessed Mary etc.

At that day the parties came before the king at Westminster. And a jury of clerks and attorneys of the aforesaid bench, namely, Thomas of Wilton, Adam of Lound', Thomas of Thorpe, Richard of Harston, John of Eton, William of Retford, John of Wilton, Robert of Whitehill, Richard of Newton, John Chamberlain, Simon of Stanion and Robert of Harborough, chosen, tried and sworn with the consent of the parties for this purpose, likewise came. They say on their oath that John of Hackthorn is guilty of the aforesaid falsity and deceit alleged against him. Therefore he is committed to prison in the custody of John of Holborn, the marshal etc. . . .

(1362) Richard of Barnby, butcher, one of the bailiffs of the city of York, was attached to answer the king on a plea of contempt by bill. And the king by Simon of Kegworth, who sues for him, complains thereof that, whereas it has been enacted for the common utility of the realm of England that no minister in cities or boroughs, who by reason of his office has to keep the assizes of wines and other victuals, may trade, wholesale or by retail, in wines or victuals whilst he is serving in such an office, the aforesaid Richard, who by reason of his office must keep such assizes in the aforesaid city, traded wholesale and retail in various victuals, that is to say, the flesh of oxen and all other meat bought wholesale, to the sum of two hundred pounds, in the aforesaid city in the thirty-fifth and thirty-sixth years of the reign of the present king, and he is still trading in contravention of the terms of the aforesaid statute, in contempt of the king of a thousand pounds. And he offers to prove this on the king's behalf etc.

And Richard comes in his own person and denies all contempt and everything etc. And he says that, whilst in office, he did not and does not trade in any flesh or other victuals, as Simon alleges against him on the king's behalf. And as to this he puts himself on the country. And Simon does likewise. Therefore let a jury thereon come before the king at York on Tuesday after the Octave of St John the Baptist, and who neither etc., to make recognition etc. Because as well etc.

At that day Simon who sues etc. as well as Richard came in their own persons before the king there. And the jury likewise came. And after being chosen, tried and sworn, they say on their oath that Richard, while he served in the aforesaid office, traded retail in meat bought wholesale, to the sum of ten pounds in contravention of the terms of the aforesaid statute, as is alleged against him. Therefore it is awarded that the king is to recover the said ten pounds from Richard and that Simon is to have the third penny thereof, that is to say five marks, for the aforesaid prosecution in accordance with the terms of the statute. And Richard, present in court, is committed to prison in the custody of the marshal etc. And thereupon Simon asks for a writ of 'fieri facias' etc. in order to obtain the aforesaid five marks, and it is granted to him etc. And thereupon Richard made fine with the king on his account, as shown by the rolls of fines of this same term etc. Therefore he is released.

Afterwards, that is to say, on Saturday after the Quinzaine of St John the Baptist in this same term, Richard came here in court and paid Simon the said five marks. Therefore let him be discharged thereof etc.

(1373) Memorandum that on Monday after Martinmas in this same term a certain William Cary, chaplain, who has himself styled prior of Horsley, came before the king at Westminster, brought by the marshal, and he was committed by the king's council to the marshal's custody. And thereupon Thomas of Shardlow, who sues for the king, proffered a certain bill on the king's behalf against William in these words:

To the justices of our lord the King's Bench shows Thomas of Shardlow, who sues for our lord the king, that, whereas a prohibition of our lord the king was delivered to one William Cary, chaplain, who has himself styled prior of Horsley, on Monday after the Feast of St Hilary in the forty-fifth year of our lord the king's reign, at Bruton in the presence of John of Merston, Peter of Acton and other worthy men, forbidding the said William to cross to parts overseas without leave of our lord the king or to attempt anything which would be in prejudice of our lord the king or of his laws, nevertheless since that time the said William crossed to the court of Rome without leave of the king and there made a complaint to the pope that the prior and convent of Bruton in the county of Somerset, John Benet, John Owlpen, John Stanley and others had despoiled and ousted him from the manor of Horsley in the county of Gloucester. . . .

(1374) Edward, by the grace of God, King of England and France and Lord of Ireland, to his beloved and faithful John of Cavendish, his chief justice, greeting. Adam of Wickmere, clerk, has besought us by his petition shown to us in our parliament convoked at Westminster on the Morrow of St Edmund the King last to this end: whereas he by the name of Adam of Wickmere, Warden of the college of scholars of Trinity Hall, Cambridge, had a long time ago prosecuted so effectively by our writ before our justices of the bench against the Prior of Binham by the name of William of Flamstead, Prior of Binham, and Thomas, the sub-prior of the said place, his fellow-monk, and others with respect to a trespass committed by them to the said Adam that the truth therein had been determined by an inquisition as resting with Adam, and now, on the ground that in the process on the said writ he is called 'fellow-canon' merely through the fault of the writer where in the original writ he is called 'fellow-monk', and in another part of the process 'Ralph' is put for 'Robert', although the process was properly and legally made as regards everything else, the prior is prosecuting effectively before us our writ of error to annul the judgement rendered in the aforesaid process in the said bench, we may be pleased to order the aforesaid record and process, so far as negligence by the writer is concerned, to be amended and corrected by advice of our council. Inasmuch as it is agreed in the aforesaid parliament that the aforesaid record and process should be remitted to the said justices of the bench, and the lords and magnates of the said parliament instructed you to send the said record and process there, and our beloved and faithful William of Finchdean, our chief justice of the bench, who was then in the said parliament, was likewise instructed to have the said record and process corrected and amended in accordance with the truth of the matter, we command you that you cause the record and process before the justices of the bench, with everything connected with them, to be sent back without delay to William of Finchdean, informing him on our behalf that he is to have the record and process amended and corrected in the aforesaid form in accordance with the terms of the aforesaid agreement. Witness myself at Westminster the twenty-sixth day of January in the forty-eighth year of our reign in England and the thirty-fifth year of our reign in France.

By virtue of this writ the whole record and process are sent back to William of Finchdean, and he is informed on the king's behalf that he is to have the aforesaid record corrected and amended in accordance with the force and effect of the aforesaid writ.

25. Illustrations of the work of the Justices of the Peace, translated from *Proceedings before the Justices of the Peace in the 14th and 15th Centuries*, edited by B. H. PUTNAM (Harvard University Press, 1938), pp. 12–18, 62–3, 102, 108–9, 140, 239–41, 348–9.

(1351–3: Devon proceedings) Also the jurors say that Maud Lercedeakne and Thomas de Souwy falsely caused Adam Chana to be indicted of the felonious stealing of eight oxen, each worth 10s from the goods and chattels of the same Maud on the Monday next after the feast of Saint Thomas the Apostle in the twenty-third year of the present king. [The indictment was made by] the tithing of Shokbrok at the hundred court of Crytton held there on the Monday next after Michaelmas in the twenty-fourth year of the present king, before Almaric fitz Waryn, formerly Sheriff of Devon. [In the margin:] Maud Lercedekne is quit; Thomas Souwy is quit.

Also they say that the said Maud and Thomas seized the said Adam Chana without cause or warrant at Newton St Cyres on the Saturday next after the feast of Saint George in the twenty-fifth year of the present king, and led him bound hand and foot to Shokebrok and put him in prison there and kept him in prison until he made an agreement with them to pay 26s 8d to them on the Tuesday at the feast of the Finding of the Holy Cross next following, which he did. [Margin:] Maud Lercedekne acquitted herself; Thomas Souwy acquitted himself. . . .

They also say that Simon Hody, on the Monday next after the feast of the Annunciation of the Blessed Mary in the twenty-fifth year of our reign, unjustly came to Blowesburgh iuxta Bradeworthy and there seized Thomas Trentaworthi and imprisoned him for two days, threatening him in life and limb, until he swore obedience to the said Simon as his villein, with force and arms and against the peace of the Lord King. [Margin:] Trespass, Simon Hody. . . .

(1361–4: Suffolk) They also say that Adam Meller of Watlesfeld, thatcher, in the thirty-fourth year took 3d a day in wages and board for roofing a house over a period of twenty days. . . .

They also make presentment that Thomas Baxter of the same place took by forestalling five quarters of wheat from John Laurence chaplain on the Saturday next after the feast of Saint John Baptist and six capons and twenty-four doves from William Reve on the same day in the thirty-sixth year of the reign of King Edward the Third, as they were going to Dunwich market, and that he is a common forestaller. . . .

They also make presentment that John Wlnard carpenter of Cratfild refuses to work at his craft in the township where he has his abode and has worked for the prioress of Flixston, taking 2d a day and food in winter; and he was sworn to keep the statutes of the king and altogether broke them. . . .

(1372, 1375–9: Norfolk) Robert Archer, staying in Fornesete, in search of high wages outside that township, leads out of it each autumn six or eight labourers, by which the people of the said township of Fornesete are greatly reduced and impoverished; and he takes for himself and his associates 6d a day and food, and does so against the prohibition of the constable of the township for this year. . . .

(1393–6: Nottinghamshire) Richard de Thomworth chaplain of Newark came to the home of John de Grene tailor of Newark on Wednesday in the week of Pentecost in the seventeenth year of the reign of King Richard the Second by night and feloniously raped Elizabeth the servant of the said John at Newark, and they say that the same Richard the chaplain is a common disturber of the peace against the lord king's statute. . . .

(*c.* 1403–4: The Justices' Charge to the Jurors, translated from French)

7. *Item* [you shall inquire] concerning those who assemble companies by agreement and ride forth on routs and riots and are sworn together that each will aid and maintain the other in their misdeeds and false dealings.

And concerning those who give robes or hoods, fees or other liveries by agreement to sustain their misdeeds.

And concerning those who bind themselves by oaths that each will support the other in their quarrels and actions, be they legal or illegal.

8. *Item* concerning those who ride forth and come, against the peace or with force and arms, before justice, sheriff or other minister of the king to disturb them in the performance of their offices. And of those who come forcibly against the king before justices of assizes and other ministers and intimidate the jurors so that they dare not tell the truth in the matters they are charged with.

9. *Item* concerning those who go or ride forcibly against the peace and make entries into lands, tenements or possessions and drive out people from their free tenements by such force and hold the same lands, tenements or possessions by force and waste the fruits of them. . . .

14. *Item* you shall inquire as to those who regrate and forestall victuals such as wines, corn, malt, oats, capons, hens and all other sorts of victuals whatsoever on the road before they reach the market, fair or mart, so that the victuals in the market, fair or mart are at a higher price than they would be if the victuals so regrated and forestalled came to the said market, fair or mart, to the harm of the people.

15. *Item* of all manner of victuallers who sell victuals by retail, such as butchers, fishermen and cooks, whether they sell victuals which are

mouldy and infected, deceiving the people, and whether they take *excessive gayne* [these words in English in the text]. . . .

22. *Item* you shall inquire if any man of whatever estate or condition, freeman or serf, who is strong of body and under the age of sixty years, lives neither by merchandise nor by the exercise of a craft, has no property from which he might live nor land of his own which he might occupy himself by tilling, serves no-one and will not serve anyone who requires his services for a reasonable wage according to the ordinance made on this matter. . . .

(1410–14: Leicestershire) The twelve jurors . : . present that Thomas Gardyner de Brantyngthorp, ploughman, on the Saturday in the second week of Lent in the first year of the reign of King Henry the Fifth since the conquest, killed and murdered Aluered Jacob at Brantyngthorp, feloniously by ambush and premeditated assault. . . .

(1474–5: Southants.) Inquiry on behalf of the Lord King whether Henry Alisaunder of the city of Winchester in the county of Southampton tailor, on the thirtieth day of October in the fifteenth year of the reign of King Edward the Fourth, came with force and arms, *viz.* swords, daggers and staves, to the said city of Winchester and there made an assault on William Stile servant of John Audeley, lord of Audeley [a justice], and struck the said William a heavy blow on the head with a stave and beat and wounded him, so that his life is despaired of, doing this unjustly and against the lord king's peace. [Endorsed:] A true bill and affirmed by John Kent and his fellows . . .

Inquiry for the Lord King whether Robert Morefeld of the soke of Winchester in the county of Southampton tailor is a common night-walker through windowed courtyards to listen to the counsels and secrets of his neighbours beneath their windows, and whether he is a common mocker of his neighbours for money during the night hours and a frequenter of taverns beyond the proper time, against the statute recently issued and the lord king's peace. [Endorsed:] A true bill and affirmed by John Yerdeley and his fellows. . . .

Inquiry for the Lord King whether, whereas by the law of England and the ordinance of King Richard the Second, progenitor of the present lord king, it was ordained and established that no one might make an entry into any lands or tenements where entry was not given by law, and that even if entry was permitted by the law into such lands and tenements no one, under penalties stated in that ordinance, might enter any lands or tenements by main force and in breach of the lord king's peace, nor hold or defend by main force and in breach of the lord king's peace lands and tenements to which the entry might have been peaceful; Robert Cave of the soke of Winchester in the county of Southampton smith, Richard Reder of Petersfield in that county mercer and Walter Reder of the same place mercer, with other unknown malefactors, on the twentieth day of August in the fifteenth year of the reign of King Edward the Fourth, with force and arms, *viz.* with bows, arrows, swords and daggers, entered by main force on the possessions of John Wellys at Petersfield consisting of a messuage with a courtyard and garden attached to it. . . .

26. FROM the Record of an Admiralty Court case of 1391, in *Select Pleas of the Court of Admiralty*, vol. i, edited and translated by R. G. MARSDEN (Selden Society, London, 1894), pp. 149–65.

Richard, by the grace of God, King of England and France and Lord of Ireland to his beloved and faithful John Holand, Earl of Huntingdon, lately our Admiral of England in the Western parts or to his lieutenant then and there Greeting: Being minded for certain reasons to be informed touching the tenor of the record and process of a plaint that lately [was pending] before you in the court of your Admiralty between John Sampson the younger of Plymouth plaintiff and John Curteys of Lostwithiel defendant touching a certain trespass upon the same John Sampson made (as is alleged) by the aforesaid John Curteys, We command you that without delay you send the tenor of the same record and process to us in our chancery clearly and openly [set forth] and this writ; Witness myself at Stamford the twenty-sixth day of May in the fifteenth year of our reign.

[The roll begins as follows:]

The tenor of the record and process of a certain plea in the court of the Admiralty of John, Earl of Huntingdon, Admiral of the Lord our King in the West, tried between John Sampson the younger of Plymouth plaintiff and John Curteys of Lostwithiel defendant ... In the court of Admiralty held before Nicholas Macclesfeld deputy and lieutenant general of John, Earl of Huntingdon, the aforesaid Admiral in the Western parts at Lostwithiel near to the flow of the sea on the twenty-eighth day of the month of March at the first hour and at the first tide in the fourteenth year of the reign of King Richard the Second, John Sampson of Plymouth ... by his sureties ... Cook and John Goldsmeth complaining of John Curteys of Lostwithiel in a certain [plaint delivered in the court] of Admiralty as follows in these words [the bill is in French]:

To the very honourable and very noble ... John [Earl of] Huntingdon Admiral of our Lord the King in the parts of the South and West or to his lieutenant ... John Sampson the younger of Plymouth [complains] of John Curteys of Lostwithiel, That whereas the said John Sampson on the Wednesday next after the feast of St Valentine in the thirteenth year of our lord the king had freighted a vessel of Brittany at Plymouth and likewise the said vessel had carried to Lostwithiel one bale of woollen cloth of the value of ten marks and one chest full of certain goods, that is to say, in the said chest were six score franks of gold, one silver girdle of the value of 40s, one long dagger garnished with silver of the value of four marks, one long skirt of silk and gold furred with squirrel fur of the value of £10, two doublets of silk and gold, nine pairs of new sheets of the value of nine marks, four pairs of stockings of scarlet, the which bale on the Sunday next following the aforesaid feast at Lostwithiel within high water mark without any process of law or legal or reasonable cause the said John Curteys took and carried away; [and] he broke open the said chest, and all the aforesaid goods contained therein he took out and carried away wrongfully and to the very great damage of the said John Sampson, without their being in any way delivered to the Admiral by the said John Curteys; for which he [Sampson] prays recompense, and that his bill is true in all points the said John Sampson is ready to prove if the court do so decree, making protest to amend this his bill and to add to and take away from it when-soever occasion arises.

And upon the aforesaid day the said John Curteys being cited and summoned by due citation made appearance and demanded a copy of the aforesaid bill and a day for answering the said John Sampson in the aforesaid cause; And then and at the same place he found bail for making answer in the aforesaid cause, John Kendale and John Quaynte; And thereupon a copy of the aforesaid bill was delivered to him and a day was given him to answer until the second hour and second tide of this day at the place aforesaid; And at the hour and tide aforesaid the afore-said parties being summoned came before the aforesaid lieutenant sitting as judge at the aforesaid place and made appearance; And the party of the said John Curteys handed to the Court his answer in writing, of which the tenor follows in these words. . . . [Curteys says, in French, that he seized the goods in execution of a judgment in the Admiralty Court against Sampson, and he vouches the record of the court.]
. . . And afterwards the said John Sampson prayed for a copy of the answer of the said John Curteys and for a day to make replication. And thereupon a copy was granted him and a day to make replication in the aforesaid suit was given him, until the twenty-ninth day of March then next following at the first hour and the first tide, at Fowey, near the flow of the sea. And when the said day was come the aforesaid parties being summoned appeared before the aforesaid lieutenant at the place above named; and the party of the said John Sampson put in before the court a certain replication expressed in writing, the tenor of which follows in these words [French]. . . .
[Sampson restates his case] . . . Making protest that he is ready to prove all the things aforesaid in all such points as lie on him [to prove], after that the court shall order him [to do so]; and also [protesting for leave] to amend his said replication and to add to it, take away from it, and make addition to it, as need may be.

And of this replication the party of the said John Curteys prayed a copy and a day to plead further in the aforesaid cause, if he should be so minded. And when the said hour and tide arrived, the aforesaid parties being summoned appeared before the aforesaid lieutenant; And the party of the said John Curteys then and there put in before the court a certain duplication expressed in writing, and the tenor of it follows in these words. . . .

[Curteys reasserts that he acted as an officer of the court, and is ready to prove it. Sampson hands in a triplication, and Curteys replies with a quadruplication.]

. . . And thereupon the party of the said John Sampson prayed that proof should be made of his aforesaid pleading. And because certain witnesses whom he intended to produce in that behalf were in distant parts, he prayed for a commission to the parts of Plymouth and Plympton. And thereupon at the same place it was decreed that the said John Sampson should prove his pleading by him above set forth; And a commission was granted to him to the parts of Plymouth and Plympton addressed to John Martyn the prior of Plympton and to Maurice Berde; And the tenor of the commission follows in these words. . . .

[In fact, there are two commissions, one to take the evidence of Sampson's witnesses, and another to take the evidence of Curteys's. Eventually . . .] the party of the said John Sampson came before the aforesaid Sub-Admiral with a transmission of [the attestations of] the witnesses produced and examined on his behalf enclosed and sealed under the seals of the said prior of Plympton, John Martyn, and Maurice Berd . . .

[The answers to the interrogatory are in Latin.]

. . . William Berd of Plymouth, the first witness, being of free condition and of the age of thirty years and upwards, as he says, having been sworn and carefully examined and questioned, says that on the Friday next after the feast of St Valentine the Martyr in the year last past, that is to say in the fourteenth year of the reign of King Richard the Second after the Conquest of England, he was present at Plymouth and saw that the aforesaid John Sampson did there freight a crayer of Brittany and at the same place and on the same day in the same year did lade on board the same crayer one bale of woollen cloth of the value of 10 marks of silver. . . . And the deponent also says that on the Sunday then next following he came to Lostwithiel for certain business of his own which he had to do there, and saw the said crayer had arrived there, and saw that then John Curteys of Lostwithiel [seized the said bale and chest with the aforesaid goods in it within the floodmark there in the said crayer and] without process of law or any reasonable cause caused them to be carried to his house. And the witness now deposing also says that he well knows that the said John Curteys on the same night following without process of law or any reasonable cause broke open the said chest and took out of it all the goods before specified and disposed of the same bale and goods according to his own pleasure, because

upon the morrow, to wit, upon the Monday next following, many trustworthy neighbours of the aforesaid John Curteys and the master and mariners of the aforesaid crayer told him that upon the same night the said John Curteys had broken open the said chest and had taken out of it all the goods aforesaid. And the public voice and report was and still is loud [to that effect], as the deponent says. And the deponent says that he had not been corrupted either by prayer or bribe. . . .
[Here follow the depositions of seven other witnesses, all to the same effect and almost in the same words. The process then continues:]

And then at the same place the party of the said John Curteys, being summoned [to appear] with the transmission of [the depositions of] his witnesses produced and examined on his behalf, appeared, and at the same time and place presented to the court a transmission of the [depositions of the] witnesses produced and examined on his behalf before the aforesaid Sub-Admiral. But this transmission the aforesaid Sub-Admiral has in his own possession; and the same Sub-Admiral is away in distant parts, and therefore is not able to deliver up the transmission of the said John Curteys without reasonable time [being given him]. And in witness of this record the seal of the aforesaid Admiral is appended. And this record is transmitted by the same Admiral by virtue of the enclosed writ. Given on the twentieth day of July in the sixteenth year of the reign of King Richard the Second.

27. The investigation by the King's Council in 1437 of the quarrels of Lord Grey and Lord Fanhope in Bedfordshire, printed in H. Nicolas, *Proceedings and Ordinances of the Privy Council* (Record Commission, London, 1834–37), vol. v, pp. 35–9. The English has been somewhat modernized. For a continuation of the story, see *Cases before the King's Council*, edited by I. S. Leadam and J. F. Baldwin (Selden Society, London, 1918), pp. 104–7.

The nineteenth day of June in the fifteenth year etc. in the Starred Chamber at Westminster, present my lords the Chancellor, Treasurer and Privy Seal, and the King's justices, King's serjeants and attorney. William Pek of Bedfordshire, late assigned with others by the king's commission, to enquire of felonies, insurrections, trespasses, deceits etc. as in the commission, [was] sworn upon a book before my said lords the justices for to say the truth of the things that he should be demanded of. First it was demanded of him how he and his other commissioners did their duty in executing the king's said commission, and if they sat not, why and for what cause; and if there was any gathering of people there that day, how and by whom; and shortly that he should inform my said lords of the truth, in deed and circumstances, of how they demeaned themselves by virtue of the king's said commission. To which demands the said William answered that by virtue of the king's said commission, that is on the Saturday, he delivered a precept unto the Sheriff of Bedfordshire for a sufficient panel to come before the said commissioners on the Tuesday next after that, at Silsoe in the said shire, to certify them of the points in the said commission. At which day the said William and John Ludshop, another of the same commissioners, came to the said Silsoe, where there was the Lord Fanhope, come to a place of his own. And as the said John and William stood in a place by the church where they purposed them to sit that day in sessions, there came Enderby with 100 or 120 men on foot with bows, some [ready] bent, arrows, plate-armour, some doublets of defence, and halberds and poleaxes and staves, and passed by them through the town [and] out of the same, and met with the Lord Grey coming towards it with fifty or sixty men as he supposed, arrayed as above, who all came to the town to the church there. At which time the said John and William wondered what the said Lord Grey did there and at the people who came with him, and the said Lord Grey on his arrival asked them what they did there; and they answered, to sit there by force of the king's commission directed to them and other persons, which they showed to him. And the said lord said that he would abide to see what was done there that day. At which time the aforesaid Enderby said unto the said John and William that the said commission was stolen out and laboured by night so as to indict the said Lord Grey's tenants, and that they that are now in the commission another time may be out of it. And then one Roger Squyer of Lord Grey's party said unto the said Pek that he marvelled that, being of Lord Fanhope's party, he should have given the said Lord Fanhope counsel to set the said sessions there, considering that it was the said Lord Grey's town. To whom the said Pek answered that it was the king's matter and none other's, and for him it was set there, and that the said Lord Fanhope had nothing to do with it; and one of the said Lord Grey's councillors desired of the said John and William that no sessions should be held there that day because of the multitude of people that was come there that day and was like to come. It was asked of the said Pek which it was and he answered that as he supposed it was Boughton. And thereupon came in Fitz with the parson of Shitlington and the parson of Barton, at whose coming Enderby said to the said John and William, Fitz is come, one of the justices of the peace in the quorum, and the said Lord Grey and he shall hold this day sessions here to inquire as well for the king as them. And thereupon the foresaid parsons laboured betwixt the foresaid lords to set them in rest and peace, entreating the said Lord Fanhope amongst other things to avoid the town with his following on the one side, Lord Grey agreeing to depart with his fellowship on the other, and that the sessions should be held. To which desire the said Lord Fanhope agreed, though after the agreement following the intercession of the parsons for the sake of the peace, seeing what multitude of people came to the Lord Grey, he sent to Ampthill for his armour and more men. And the said agreement being reported to the said Lord Grey and his council by the said parsons, the said Lord Grey's council answered that the said parsons had no authority of the Lord Grey to report to the Lord Fanhope as they did without the sessions being adjourned: for it was dishonourable to the Lord Grey to depart, and the sessions to be held where his tenants might be aggrieved. And the said commissioners, considering the peril that was like to have fallen that day if the said sessions had been held, and also that the said Lords Grey and Fanhope had come to an agreement by the labour of the said commissioners and parsons to stand by the award and arbitrament of certain persons concerning the marriage of a woman and certain goods etc., adjourned the said sessions to the end that a good end might be had therein and peace be kept.

28. FROM *The Paston Letters*, edited by JAMES GAIRDNER (London, 1900), vol. i, pp. 144–6, 150–3, 203–5, 207–8, 211–12, vol. ii, pp. 75–7, vol. iii, pp. 34–5. These extracts illustrate the use of judicial commissions and local courts in the struggles of the aristocracy for land and power. (Spelling modernized and English partly so.)

(1450) Unto the right reverend father in God and my right gracious Lord, the Cardinal Archbishop of York, Primate and Chancellor of England.

Beseecheth meekly John Paston that, whereas Robert Hungerford, Knight, Lord Moleyns, and Alianore, his wife, lately, with force and strength, and great multitude of riotous people, to the number of a thousand persons and more, gathered by the excitation and procuring of John Heydon against the king's peace, in riotous manner entered upon your said beseecher and others enfeoffed to his use in the manor of Gresham with the appurtenances in the shire of Norfolk; which riotous people broke, despoiled, and drew down the place of your said beseecher in the said town, and drove out his wife and servants there being, and rifled, took, and bore away all the goods and chattels that your said beseecher and his servants had there to the value of £200 and more; and the said manor, after the said riotous entry, kept with strong hand in manner of war, as well against your said beseecher and his feoffees, as against one of the king's justices of the peace in the said shire, that came thither to execute the statutes ordained and provided against such forcible entries and keeping of possessions with force, as appeareth by records of the said justice certified into the Chancery; and yet the said Lord Moleyns the same manor keepeth with force and strength against the form of the said statutes: May it please your reverend Fatherhood and gracious lordship, these premises considered, to grant unto your said beseecher for his feoffees by him to be named a special assize against the said Lord Moleyns, Alianore, and John Heydon, and others to be named by your said beseecher, and also an oyer and determyner against the said Lord Moleyns, John Heydon and others of the said riotous people in like form to be named, to enquire, hear and determine all trespasses, extortions, embraceries, offences and misprisions by them or any of them done, as well at the suit of our sovereign lord the king, as of your said beseecher and his said feoffees, and every of them, or of any other of the king's lieges: at reverence of God, and in way of charity.

John Paston to James Gresham

James Gresham, I pray you labour forth to have an answer of my bill

for my special assize, and the oyer and termyner, according to my said
bill that I delivered to my Lord Chancellor, letting him know that his
lordship conceived the grant of such a special matter might cause a
rumour in the country. Out of doubt, the country is not so disposed, for
it is desired against such persons as the country wishes to be punished;
and if they are not punished to reform what they have done amiss, it is
likely that the country will rise up against them. Men talk that a general
oyer and termyner is granted to the Duke of Norfolk, my Lord of
Ely, the Earl of Oxford, the Lord Scales, Sir John Fastolf, Sir Thomas
Fulthorp, and William Yelverton, and men are right glad thereof. Yet
that notwithstanding, labour you forth for me. For in a general oyer
and termyner a *supersedeas* [staying proceedings] may dash all, [but]
shall not in a special. And also if the justices come at my request, they
shall sit as long as I wish, [but] shall not by general [commission]. And
as for commissioners in my etc., Sir John Fastolf must be [a] plaintiff as
well as I myself, and so he may not be [a] commissioner; and as for all
the rest, I can think them indifferent enough in the matter, except my
Lord Scales, whose wife is aunt to the Lady Moleyns. . . .

William Wayte to John Paston
. . . Sir Borle Jonge and Josse labour sore for Heydon and Tuddenham
to Sir William Oldhall [a leading retainer of Richard, Duke of York,
the dominant figure in English politics at this time], and proffer more
than two thousand pounds to have his good lordship; and therefore
there is no other remedy but that Swaffham men be warned to meet
with my said Lord [the Duke of York] on Friday next coming, at
Pickenham on horseback in the most goodly wise, and put some bill
unto my Lord of Sir Thomas Tudenham, Heydon, and Prentys, and
cry out on them, and that all the women of the same town be there also,
and cry out on them [i.e. Tudenham *et al.*] also, and call them extor-
tioners, and pray my lord that he will do sharp executions upon them.
And my master counsels you that you should move the mayor and all
the aldermen with all their commoners to ride to meet my lord, and
that bills be made and put up to my lord, and let all the town cry out
on Heydon, Tudenham, Wyndham, and Prentys, and of all their false
maintainers, and tell my lord how much hurt they have done to the
city, and let that be done in the most lamentable wise; for Sir, unless my
lord hear some foul tales of them, and some hideous noise and cry, by
my faith they are otherwise likely to come to grace. . . .
. . . Sir, labour you to be knight of the shire. . . . Sir, all Swaffham, if they
are warned, will give you their voices. . . . Sir, labour you to the mayor
that John Dam or Will Jenney be burgess [M.P.] for the city of Norwich;
tell him that he may be it as well as Young is of Bristol, or the Recorder
is of London, and as the Recorder of Coventry is for the city of Coventry,

and it is so in many places in England. Also, Sir, think on Yarmouth that . . . some good man be burgess for Yarmouth. . . .

(1451) To the right wise, noble, and discreet Commons of this present Parliament.

Meekly beseech, bewail, and show the poor and simple inhabitants in the town of Swaffham, in the county of Norfolk, that whereas Sir Thomas Tudenham of Oxborough, knight, this sixteen years last past before the day of the Act of Resumption in the last Parliament before this, has occupied and governed the lordship and manor of Swaffham aforesaid, with the appurtenances, as steward and farmer of the same, in which occupation and governance, the said Sir Thomas, and others of his servants and adherents in a roll to this petition annexed named, have piteously and sinfully done and committed the trespasses, offences, wrongs, extortions, maintenances, embraceries, oppressions, and perjuries, in the said roll contained; and of diverse and many articles thereof, and of many other wrongs, and of that, that the said Sir Thomas is a common extortioner, the same Sir Thomas before the right noble, true, and plain lord, our good and gracious lord the Earl of Oxford, and others the King's commissioners of oyer and terminer within the same shire, the said Sir Thomas Tudenham, and others of his servants and adherents are indicted.

May it please your noble wisdoms to conceive that it hath been the common law of the land of long time that if a common thief were, in any country, so often indicted or detected of so many offences he should not, by the law of the land, be let [out] to bail or mainprise, but be kept in prison till he were put to answer of such crimes as he was so detected of. And also may it please your great wisdoms to conceive that all the judges of the king's bench, of long and late time sitting in their place, laudably have [been] used to commit to prison, without bail or mainprise, for a time, all persons that have been detected before them of any riot or great cruel offence against the peace, which offence might have been subversion of the law by any likeliness; and advertising the great mischifs that this noble realm has often stood in for the great extortions and oppressions that have been done in the same, and how great a subversion of the law and of the politic governance of the land such extortion is; and of your prudent and sage wisdoms may it like you to make requisition to the king our sovereign lord, and to the lords spiritual and temporal in this present Parliament assembled, that by the consideration that the said Sir Thomas would never appear, in his person, nor by his attorney, at no sessions of oyer and terminer held in the said county; it may please the king and lords aforesaid, to commit the said Sir Thomas Tudenham to prison, there to abide till unto the time that he to the said indictments has answered, and to the bills and complaints of the said inhabitants in form of law.

And moreover, whereas that the said Sir Thomas Tudenham has, among many other great wrongs, full sinfully caused a writ of assize of novel disseisin to be brought against John Aleyn and twenty-three others of the said town, in the name of the Abbot of Sawtry, and caused that assize to pass by perjury, as in the first article in the roll to this petition annexed it is more openly contained, may it please your great wisdoms, for the reverence of God by the consideration, that the jury of the said assize dared not, for dread of the horrible menaces of the said Sir Thomas, otherwise do but be forsworn in giving their verdict in the same assize, in which case the said inhabitants, for pity and remorse of their consciences, were loath to sue a writ of attaint, to pray the king and lords aforesaid to ordain, by authority of this present Parliament, that the said writ of assize, verdict, recovery, and the judgment thereof, with every other circumstance thereof, be void, revoked and annulled, for the love of God.

Debenham, Tymperley and White to John Paston
Master Paston, we commend us to you, letting you know that the sheriff is not so whole as he was, for now he will show but a part of his friend-ship . . . Also the sheriff informed us that he has writing from the king that he shall make such a panel [as] to acquit the Lord Moleyns . . . the sheriff will empanel gentlemen to acquit the lord, and jurors to acquit his men; and we suppose that is to be the motion and means of the other party . . .

Sir Thomas Howys to Sir John Fastolf
. . . But the more special cause of my writing at this time is to give you [a] relation of the untrue behaviour of this our [commission of oyer and] determyner, by the partiality of the judges of it; for when the counsel of the city of Norwich, of the town of Swaffham, yours, Master Inglose's, Paston's, and many other plaintiffs' had put in and declared, both by writing and by word, before the judges, the lawful exceptions in many wise, the judges by their wilfulness did not find it in their hearts to give as much as a nod nor a twinkling of their eyes toward (them), but took it to derision, God reform such partiality; and because Prisot thought that if the sessions of the oyer and terminer were held at Norwich as they used to be, he supposed it should not proceed so fast as Tudenham and Heydon and their fellows intended, [and] as it should in another place, they adjourned to Walsingham, where they have greatest rule, [for the sessions] to be held on Tuesday, the fourth day of May.

This knowing, my Master Yelverton, Denney and [the] others might well conceive how the governance of the oyer and terminer should proceed, for it was the most partial place of all the shire. . . . And the said Tudenham, Heydon, and other oppressors of their set came down thither, as I understand, with 400 horse and more; and considering how their well-willers were there assembled at their instance, it would have been right perilous and fearful for any of the plaintiffs to have been present, for there was not one of the plaintiffs nor complainants there, except your right faithful and trusty well-willer John Paston. . . .

(*1461*) *Thomas Playter to John Paston*

I should like your mastership to know that at the last sessions Erpingham hundred and other hundreds thereabouts were not warned [to attend], and the sheriff excused himself on the grounds that he could not know who was officer there. . . . Item, sir, at the last shire [court] was much people and ill-governed for they would not be ruled by nobody; they would almost have slain the undersheriff, for they told him writs of election were sent down and he kept them aside to beguile them . . .

(*1472*) *John Paston to Sir John Paston*

. . . Item, yesterday W. Gurney entered into Saxthorpe and there was he keeping of a court, and had the tenants attorned to him, but before court was all done, I came thither with a man with me and no more, and there, before him and all his fellowship . . . I charged the tenants that they should proceed no further in their court upon pain that might fall of it, and they stopped for a season. But they saw that I was not able to make my party good, and so they proceeded further; and I saw that, and set me down by the steward and blotted his book with my finger as he wrote so that all [the] tenants affirmed that the court was interrupted by me as in your right, and I required them to record that there was no peaceable court kept. . . .

29. FROM The Report of a Case in the Court of Common Pleas in 1459, translated in HEMMANT, *Select Cases in Exchequer Chamber* (Selden Society, London, 1933), pp. 147–52.

Debt was brought by J. Raynold of London against Mathew Philip, citizen and alderman of London, and J.C., citizen and alderman of London, and two others of London, at the quindene of Michaelmas, the thirty-seventh year of the king: at which day the defendants said by

Chokke [counsel for the defendants] that action did not lie; for, he said, formerly, to wit, on a certain day in the feast of Holy Trinity of the previous year, the aforesaid defendants made out a bill to the chancellor of England setting forth certain matter: how that one J. had bought from the said J.R. certain debts due to the aforesaid J.R. from divers men for the sum contained in the obligation; for which sum the said defendants, at the request of P. Arderne, Chief Baron, were liable, together with other obligations entered into by the said defendants to the said plaintiff for other merchandise, and because these debts were only chose in action which cannot be vested in the said J. because of this purchase, he cannot have any action to recover the said debts; but the duty of the said debts shall always remain with the said J.R. so that the said J. cannot have any *quid pro quo*. Thus the said obligation so made is void and of no value and they can have no remedy thereof at common law. Therefore they prayed him [the chancellor] that they might have a writ to the aforesaid J.R. [ordering him] under certain penalty to appear before the king in the Chancery to answer to this matter. Thereupon a writ of *sub poena* issued; on which day the parties put in an appearance. And because the matter was doubtful in law, the chancellor adjourned them to the Exchequer Chamber and there before himself and the justices of both benches the matter with other matters touching other obligations was rehearsed and much debated. And it was the opinion of all the justices that inasmuch as by the said contract no duty was vested in the said J., so the obligation made in consequence of this, ought in conscience to be restored to the said defendants or alternatively the plaintiff should make release to the said defendants; therefore it was awarded in the Chancery that the said J.R. now plaintiff should bring the said obligation into the Chancery, there to be cancelled and annulled, or else that he should make acquittance or release *ut supra*. J.R. refused to do this, thereupon he was adjudged to the Fleet prison for his contempt until he should do this, and he still remains there. This is the same obligation upon which the aforesaid award was made, and we cannot think that upon this obligation he ought to have action.

Billying [counsel for the plaintiff] demurs upon this. And so to judgment; and he had day until now. And *supersedeas* now comes from the Chancery rehearsing the whole matter and the judgment there, commanding them not to proceed; and now

Billying rehearses the whole matter and the *supersedeas* also, and says that it seems that they ought not to surcease because of this *supersedeas*; for he says that this court is the court of our lord the King and of as high authority as is the Court of Chancery. In which case you ought not to surcease because of their *supersedeas*, except for such thing as belongs to them by their privilege. For instance, if an officer of the Chancery is impleaded here in this court, in that case, if he shall buy a *supersedeas* because he is servant in that court, you shall then surcease because of their privilege, and this on account of a law long in force. And the reason for this is so that they shall have their privileges, for otherwise every clerk and servant of the Chancery might be impleaded here, so that no one would be in attendance there at the time of the court, and consequently no court would be held; which would be inconvenient: and for this reason the *supersedeas* shall be allowed in that case. But here the matter is not so: and the judgment is not thus 'that the obligation shall be void and null in law', but that he shall bring the obligation into court to be cancelled; and this proves clearly that the obligation is in force until it be cancelled. And even though the judgment had been so, yet is seems to me that it would not be binding unless it [is] proved before you that thus they should do, for their judgment is not of such force as a judgment here or in the King's Bench. For in these courts if an erroneous judgment be given, the party shall have writ of error to reverse the judgment, and this is the reason why it shall be a bar until it be reversed, for if the judgment be erroneous, it can be reversed and annulled. But of a judgment given in the Chancery one cannot have writ of error or any other means, to reverse the judgment; consequently, therefore, this judgment shall not bind him in another court; for it is against reason that an erroneous judgment shall bind him and he cannot have writ of error to reverse it: and this is the reason why, because he cannot have writ of error, he shall help himself by way of answer. . . .

Chokke. It seems the contrary and that the judgment is good. And the Court of Chancery is a court of record and as high a court as any that the king has, therefore its judgments shall be in force until they be reversed by error. And, Sir, the party shall have writ of error in Parliament of a judgment given in the Chancery in the same way as he shall have it of a judgment given in the King's Bench. And, Sir, the effect of this judgment is to annul this deed; just as in a writ of forger of false deeds when forgery is found, if at another time he wants to bring action on this deed, he shall be barred by this matter, and yet it is in another action. . . .

Prysot [Chief Justice of Common Pleas]. It remains to be seen in what matters the Chancery is a court of record so that one can have a writ of error, and in what matters [it is] not. Sir, in all pleas before them on patents, pleas of debt and the like between those of the court one shall have writ of error there; and a recovery there upon an obligation shall be good bar in another court; but in the use of writs of *sub poena*, it is not, except in these cases, a court of record, for then conscience only has to be examined, because we here in this court proceed to judgment in accordance with what has been alleged and proved, and we cannot go beyond that; and it is their business to examine the conscience, for when an act is good and always has been, their examination shall not make it bad, but their examination proves the act good and lawful in our law. And forasmuch as he cannot have remedy by our law, he sues there to have the obligation restored to him, and the effect of their power and their judgment is to restore the obligation to the party or to cause the defendant to make acquittance or release. And to execute this [judgment] the court can do nothing except order him to prison to be there until he is ready to do this; and thus this is all that the said court can do. And if the party would rather lie in prison than hand over the obligation, the other [party] is without remedy, and thus the Chancellor has no power to make the obligation void. . . .

30. Papers of a Case in Chancery in 1471, from *Select Cases in Chancery*, edited and translated by W. P. BAILDON (Selden Society, London, 1896), pp. 155–8. (The spelling of the bill has been modernized.)

To the right reverend father in God and my good and gracious lord, the Bishop of Bath and Wells, Chancellor of England.

Beseecheth your good lordship your humble orators, William Revelle and Maud his wife, Robert Blount and Ele his wife, the which Maud and Ele are cousins and heirs to one Alice Fleming, late deceased, that is to say, daughters to Nicholas Stanlake, son of Elizabeth Stanlake, daughter to John Thorpe, Father of John Thorpe, Father to the said Alice Fleming, that whereas Edward Gower, esquire, with others was and is enfeoffed in and of the manor of Thorpe with the appurtenances in the county of Surrey, in and of the manor of Henton Pippard with the appurtenances in the county of Wiltshire, and of the manor of Shawe with appurtenances in the County of Berkshire, by the said Alice to the use and behoof of the said Alice and her heirs; and after the death of the said Alice, your said beseechers in the right of their said wives, cousins and heirs to the said Alice, often times have required the said Edward to make estate to the said Maud and Ele, according to right and good conscience, The said Edward that to do utterly refused, and yet does so, contrary to all good conscience; of which wrong and injury your said suppliants have no remedy by the common law: May it please your good lordship these premises to consider, and to grant to your said suppliants a writ of *sub poena* to be addressed to the said Edward Gower to appear before you in the Chancery, at a certain day upon a pain by your lordship limited, there to be ruled in the premises as Faith and good conscience require; and your beseechers shall pray to God for the conservation of your said lordship.

    Pledges: William Edmond of London, yeoman,
             John Swepston of Rysley, yeoman.

[There follows Gower's answer, and then Revelle's replication. The judgment of the court is endorsed on the bill in Latin, of which the translation runs:]

Be it remembered that on the twelfth day of February, 11 Edward IV, 1472, this petition, exhibited before us in our Chancery in the tenth year of our reign by the within-written William Revelle and Maud his wife and Robert Blount and Ele his wife, cousins and heirs of Alice Fleming, against Edward Gower, esquire, and the answer and replication made and had thereto between the parties aforesaid having been read, heard and understood with mature deliberation in the said Chancery by the venerable father, the Bishop of Bath and Wells, our Chancellor, and by the Court of Chancery: It was considered and adjudged that, inasmuch as the said Edward hath sufficiently proved before us in the Chancery, that he purchased and bought the within-written manor of Hinton Pippard from the above-written Alice Thorpe [Fleming], to hold to himself, his heirs and assigns for ever, and satisfaction for the same manor was made by the aforesaid Edward to the said Alice, Therefore it was considered and adjudged by the aforesaid Chancellor and by the consideration of the Court aforesaid that the same Edward may have, continue, hold, enjoy, and possess the said manor of Hinton Pippard with the appurtenances, to himself, his heirs and assigns, for ever according to the consideration and judgment aforesaid; and that the same Edward be dismissed out of the Court aforesaid. And thereupon he is dismissed out of Court, quit and without day.

Index to Introduction and Documents

(In each item, a stroke (/) indicates where the references to the documents begin.)

Courts, conciliar (*cont.*)
181; Star Chamber, 48, 105ff, /
182; Requests, 107;
councils in the marches, 107,116,119;
court of Duchy Chamber, 116;
of Stannaries, 117;
court of exchequer chamber, 119, /
189
And see Judges; Rolls
Crimes, 15, 63, 64, 66, 82; treachery
and treason, 18, 23, 28, 82, 94,
98–9, 104, 111, 121; corruption of
justice, 22, 100, / 175; homicide
and murder, 28, 34, 55, 57, 66, 68,
90, 96, / 137, 149, 169, 176;
arson, 28, 34, 99, / 137; theft, 28,
55, 57, 66, 73, 95, / 137, 143, 150,
151, 157, 159, 169, 174; housebreaking, 28, 32, 96; robbery,
55, 66, 75, 90, / 137; harbouring
felons, 55, / 137, 151; rape, 67,
90, 95, / 175; assault, wounding,
false imprisonment, 33, 67, 73,
95, / 150; burglary, 96; conspiracy, 99, 107, 117, / 175; perjury,
107; forgery, 107, / 137. And see
Civil and criminal, Felony, Misdemeanours, Prosecution
Criminal societies, 91, 117, / 175
Crown pleas, 66, 72–74, 79, / 149–51
Custom of the manor, 32, 33, / 144

Damages, 15, 72, 95, / 145, 162–3, 170
David, Prince of Wales, execution of, 82
Despenser, Bishop, impeachment of,
122
Domesday Book, 17, 28, 36, 39, 59;
commissioners, 38, 40, 55
Duel. See Trial by battle

Ealdormen, 20, / 129
Edgar, King, 18, 19, 20
Edmund, King, 18
Edward the Elder, King, / 127
Edward the Confessor, King, 24, / 132
Edward I, King, 35, 73, 79, 81, 82, 87,
90, 99, 103, 113, / 157, 164–5
Edward II, King, 82, 87, 95, 113
Edward III, King, 99
Edward IV, King, 107
Error in the record of a lower court,
action on and jurisdiction in,
37, 77, 80, 120, / 172, 190
Ely, liberty of, 72

Equity. See Common Law; Courts,
conciliar courts, chancery
Essoins. See Procedure
Ethelred, King, 55, / 129, 130
Evidence, 26, 29, 48, 111. And see
Procedure
Exchequer, as an office, 50, 51, / 138.
And see Courts
Eyre, of 1166, 59; of 1176, 59; of 1194,
65, 74; of 1219, 67; of 1252, 63,
in Shropshire in 1256, 66, 67, /
147–51

Felony, and trespass, 96; felonies,
28, 57, 67, 70, 74, 95, / 155;
felons, 65, 72
Feudalism, 16, 30, 38, 55, 60, 92, 101
Final concords, 71, 72, 84; 'feet of
fines', 75, 84
Fines, 15, 33, 44, 54, 95, / 143, 150,
151, 158, 171. And see Profits of
justice
Finchdean, Chief Justice, / 173
Fleta, legal writer, 80, 100
Folk-moots, 14
Folville gang, 91
Forcible entry. See Misdemeanours
Forfeiture. See Penalties
Forms of action, 24, 58, 61, 63
Fortescue, Sir John, legal writer, 114,
122–3
Franchises, 34, 87, 92, 100, / 132, 160
Frankpledge, view of, 23, 35, 115
Freehold, 61, 102, 105; freeholders,
31, / 137, 145
Fugitives, 56, / 138, 149
Fulk FitzWarin, 69

Gamelyn, tale of, 91
Goal delivery. See Courts
Gaols. See Prisons
Gentry. See Knights
Glanvill, legal treatise, 51, 58, 61, 82, /
139
Glendower's rebellion, 96
Government, and the courts, Carolin-
gian, 29, Germanic, 29, English,
29, 80ff, 111, 116; through
gentry, 92; decline of the eyre as a
revolution in, 91
Grand assize. See Assizes
Grand jury. See Juries of presentment

Hengham, Chief Justice, 79, / 164